THE BHA
GITA
Comes Alive

Jeffrey Armstrong | Kavindra Rishi is the founder of Vedic Academy of Sciences and Arts (VASA), international speaker, jyotishi and poet.

Jeffrey is an award-winning poet and best-selling author of numerous books, including *Spiritual Teachings of the Avatar: Ancient Wisdom for a New World.* He has been featured in the CBC documentary Planet Yoga, the Leo Award-winning documentary *Take Back Your Power, Wings of Yoga*, and two documentaries on Ayurveda & Psychology for Mind Valley. He has degrees in Psychology, English Literature, and History and Comparative Religion, and he spent five years in an ashram as a *brahmachari* (monk).

Though born a Westerner he has dedicated most of his adult life to learning about, practicing, and teaching Vedic wisdom. At age 50, he left the corporate world and took a vow to only teach the Vedic knowledge as his dedication for the rest of his life. He has worked with prominent Indian organizations to help with the revival of Sanatana Dharma culture by teaching at Hindu youth camps, universities, and civic centers throughout India, America, and Europe. He is the vice-chairman of the Vedic Friends Association and is active with the British Board of Dharmic Scholars. He and his wife Sandi Graham live in beautiful British Columbia, Canada.

View the live Gita classes with Jeffrey Armstrong at http://www.bharat.gitacomesalive.com.

Praise For This Translation

The Bhagavad Gita is India's most translated book. It is also India's most mistranslated, subject to every possible misinterpretation. The Gita has too often been circumscribed by inappropriate terminologies, dichotomies, and theologies of western thought that cannot properly reflect the inner essence of the Gita's profound yogic and dharmic teaching relative to the universal Consciousness and transcendent Reality of Atman/Brahman. The result is that although we have many different versions of the Gita, few convey the real teachings of the Gita. Except for the rare edition by a great yogi, most translations are superficial, particularly academic versions that have little inner vision. The most meaningful Sanskrit terms are usually reduced to vague English equivalents in which all deeper insight is lost.

For those who know the deeper aspects of the tradition, there has long been a demand for a version of the Gita that corrects these distortions. Now, with this translation from Jeffrey Armstrong | Kavindra Rishi, who is a master poet in English but also one who deeply understands the connotations and subtle connections of the Sanskrit terms around which the Gita revolves, we finally have an extensive and profound Bhagavad Gita. Instead of just another shadow of the Gita being put out there in English, with *The Bhagavad Gita Comes Alive*, we can contact the true light, the inner Sun of the Gita, and discover a real perception of how the infinite and eternal flows through the text in a multidimensional microcosmic/macrocosmic manner as befits the planetary age.

So please, study this new Gita carefully, meditate upon it deeply, and you can discover the real Bhagavad Gita, Sri Krishna as the Yogavatara, and even your inmost Self in a way that is enduring and transformative to all that you do and are.

—Dr. David Frawley | Pandit Vamadeva Shastri
Padma Bhushan

For billions of Hindus, for over 7000 years, the Indic language editions of the Bhagavad Gita have been removing the suffering caused by the tangled knots of name and form, of duty and of identity. Today, with so much of the English-speaking world in mental turmoil, the appearance of this revolutionary English language edition is perfectly timed. Only a uniquely qualified scribe could have completed the task of creating an edition of the

Bhagavad Gita that is true to its original meaning and intent, whilst making the text not only 'translational' but still 'transformational.' Kavindraji is that scribe and he has achieved precisely that goal. With this version of the revered Gita, millions more will be nourished in their spiritual evolution, and Kavindraji will secure his place in the illustrious lineage of Maha Rishi Veda Vyasa.

—Pt Satish K. Sharma, MBCS FRSA
General Secretary–National Council of Hindu Temples (UK), President–Global Hindu Federation, Chair–British Board of Dharmic Scholars

By providing English-speaking seekers with the infinite wisdom of the Bhagavad Gita, Jeffrey Armstrong (Kavindra Rishi) has done a unique service in his translation of this "Song of the Spirit." Working for a decade to translate the Universal Scripture into elegant prose, Armstrong has carefully avoided inadequate English-equivalent words and kept the Sanskrit terms instead so as to not distort the original, deeper meaning. *The Bhagavad Gita Comes Alive!* eloquently speaks the thoughtful consideration he gave to each verse. This version of the text is a jewel reflecting the essence of the Gita, a product of Kavindra Rishi's profound understanding and appreciation of the beauty of Sanskrit and the richness of Hindu culture.

—Professor Ved P. Nanda, Padma Bhushan
Distinguished University Professor, Director, The Ved Nanda Center for Int'l & Comp. Law, University of Denver College of Law, Honourary Professor, Univ. of Delhi

Kavindra Rishi has produced a masterly translation of the great spiritual treatise Bhagavad Gita, carefully preserving its intended meaning by retaining many original Sanskrit terms that have no direct English equivalents. By unpacking the transcendental terminology of that ancient language into lucid prose, Kavindra enables the reader to unlock the profound messages delivered by Shri Krishna which are so often obscured by other versions. *The Bhagavad Gita Comes Alive* is a must read for all students of this ancient classic, and indeed for anyone wanting to better understand the supreme spiritual reality.

—Krishna Dharma
Vedic Scholar and Author of the world's best-selling English retellings of Mahabharata, Ramayana and Srimad Bhagavatam

The Bhagavad Gita Comes Alive: A Radical Translation by Jeffrey Armstrong represents a rare effort of devotion, knowledge, curiosity, and candor. Jeffrey | Kavindra Rishi brings this new perspective, not only because he is a master of the English language, but because he is so well-versed in the many concepts of the Bhagavad Gita. Armstrong has studied many versions that have been either ignorant or victims of misunderstanding. The Bhagavad Gita is a seminal piece of literature that provides humans a way to enter one's own inner self to explore, discover, and verify the existence all around. In addition, it is set in a battlefield that ultimately is the place to either perish or prevail, and thus there is no room for hesitation. This is important when one approaches the Gita—it presupposes the dedication to truth inside oneself. Many such concepts require the correct framework, extensive experience, and robust knowledge of the philosophy and language. Jeffrey Armstrong has proven that he has all of these qualities in his efforts to create this radical translation of the Bhagavad Gita and to bring it alive to the English-speaking world!

—Bal Ram Singh, PhD

President, Institute of Advanced Sciences, Professor and Director, Botulinum Research Center, Executive Mentor, School of Indic Studies, Institute of Advanced Sciences, Dartmouth University

Kavindraji has captured the timeless message of the Geeta. With words rooted in their true purport, in a way that a seeker of knowledge and pursuer of wisdom can easily understand and put into action, *The Bhagavad Gita Comes Alive* can elevate one's self closer to divinity.

—Dr. Abhijit Prabhakar Phadnis, PhD

With the intellectual churning of the internet, it is only recently that the western world has acquired the vocabulary, sophistication of thought, and ability to comprehend the timeless wisdom that is encapsulated in the Bhagwat Gita. Coming from an English literary background, having lived as a child of not one but three cultures, and undertaking profound spiritual practice, no one is better suited than Jeffrey Armstrong to give us this lifetime's work. *The Bhagavad Gita Comes Alive* is not just another translation of the Bhagwat Gita; it is the best English version there is.

—Rajesh Acharya,

B.Arch., MRAIC, COA, LEED AP, Architect

The Bhagavad Gita is a great practical, philosophical, and spiritual text for future generations. Mr. Jeffrey Armstrong's wonderful work and accurate translation of the dialogue between Krishna and Arjuna, in a simple and practical way, will guide not only the layman, but students and scholars of philosophy as well. I think everyone will love this book.

—Dr. Vasant Lad, BAM&S, MASc
Ayurvedic Physician, Author of *Ayurveda: Science of Self-Healing*, *Textbook of Ayurveda* series and more

Jeffrey Armstrong's version of the Bhagavad Gita begins the long overdue process of reviving and restoring key Sanskrit words to an English translation of the Gita. These key concepts carry an expanded and deeper meaning than the standard one-to-one and incorrect equivalent English synonyms currently used, such as religion for dharma, soul for atma, idol for murthi, and God for Ishvara. The world thanks Shri Jeffrey for rendering this immeasurable knowledge in such a beautiful way.

—Shrinarayan Chandak

The Bhagavad Gita is a message that is as ancient as time itself and comes from beyond our mundane perception. Kavindra Rishi's translation captures the essence of this classic text and provides the reader with a means to imbibe the message and deep insights quickly and efficiently, giving us a better understanding of who we are and our purpose for being here, which itself is a rare treasure.

—Stephen Knapp
Past President of the Vedic Friends Association, lecturer and author of nearly 50 books on India and its spiritual culture, including *Bhakti-yoga: The Easy Path of Devotional Yoga*

The Bhagavad Gita is the book for all times, but especially in present times as we deal with the crises of alienation and meaning in the Age of Machines. As an accomplished poet, Jeffrey Armstrong has brought forth all his skills to produce a wonderful translation that speaks directly to the reader.

—Subhash Kak, PhD
Regents Professor at Oklahoma State University
Author of *Mind and Self*, *The Circle of Memory*, *Matter and Mind*, and other books

The Bhagavad Gita has been translated in many languages, with hundreds of editions written by scholars from all over the world. The natural question is, do we need another interpretive edition? After reviewing this publication, the answer is a definitive yes! Rishi Armstrong has written a very creative interpretation, based on a deep understanding of Sanskrit words and how to express their meaning in common English language. For that reason, this translation will be of immense value to English-speaking readers with limited understanding of Sanskrit. It will also be of special interest to the large Indian diaspora in North America. As the title suggests, the message is innovative, inspirational, and insightful. As a global physician with a passion for a healthy society and an integrative holistic approach to health, I found the book very timely and well needed.

—Dr. Arun K. Garg, PhD, MD
Consultant Physician, Founding Chair, Canada India Network Society

The way Jeffrey taught the Gita has changed my life and how I speak the yogic path to English-speaking students, and it has deepened my understanding of this great wisdom. His teachings have given me significant tools to hold onto amidst today's worldly turbulence. Without doubt, this contemporary and eloquent translation of the Gita will bring comfort to people of all walks of life and provide a brilliant teaching tool for all yoga teachers and practitioners.

—Colleen Inman
Author *Zen Yoga: Theory, Postures and Remedies* and other books, E-RYT 500, Zen Yoga Master Teacher and co-owner

Kavindra Rishi has brought us the Gita in a long-awaited translation that allows the shlokas—filled with meaningful Sanskrit terms—to pour out, connecting the reader to the divine source. The clarity and simplicity that are expressed stay true to the divine message of Shree Krishna.

—H. Lucy Guest (Divya Prabha)
Co-founder Intl Chandramauli Charitable Trust, Sadhaka Pracharaka, Sanskrit research scholar

While writing my book *Discover the Arjuna in You* based on the Bhagavad Gita, I read numerous popular translations and commentaries of the Gita. I was surprised to see different translations and meanings of the same verse in each of them. In some cases, this could be because there is no proper English equivalent for some of the Sanskrit words, or because of the author's eagerness to reach out to a large English-speaking audience. As dear Jeffrey has mentioned, this could also be due in part to the enthusiastic English authors' incomplete understanding of the Sanskrit.

In Jeffrey's translation, he has retained many Sanskrit words and has resolved the contradiction in meaning in the shlokas, with the added responsibility of rightly explaining the meaning of Sanskrit words in the alien language—English—where these concepts and theories are not part of the culture.

Shri Kavindra has fulfilled this responsibility and achieved this very difficult task—the outcome of a lifetime of work. He has truly lived the Gita, working without the expectation of any result and living like a karma yogi. I am sure the near perfection he has achieved will please Krishna and he will become very dear to Him.

—Satish Modh, PhD
Author *Discover the Arjuna in You*, Director,
VESIM Business School, Mumbai

The uniqueness of *The Bhagavad Gita Comes Alive: A Radical Translation* by Jeffrey Armstrong | Kavindra Rishi lies in overcoming the inability to translate certain concepts in the Vedic tradition into the wholly different traditions of western culture—a process burdened by the discrepancies between the profundity of Sanskrit and the imprecision of the English language. Inspired by Kavindra's own yogic and meditative experience and study, the book creates a fusion of cultural horizons where the linguistic insights of the author and the perceptions of the English-speaking audience meet. Armstrong shows a consistent and uncanny mastery of the source material and an enviable talent for clarifying intricate conceptual puzzles, unfolding and refashioning the work into orderly wholes. Offering this and much more, I am confident Armstrong's translation of the Bhagavad Gita will receive appreciation and recognition from writers, academics, philosophers, students, and general readers worldwide.

—Professor Raghwendra Pratap Singh
Centre for Philosophy, Jawaharlal Nehru University

In this soaring, revelatory translation of the Bhagavad Gita, Jeffrey Armstrong presents the epic as if it were a sweet friend, inviting us to the ultimate love story—the story of love's struggle to exist in this contrary world and to triumph over death, decay, and doubt. This is a story of personal, collective, and global restoration; a reawakening of truth; a remembrance of who we are; a tale that, while eternal, comes just in time, precisely when we need it most.

—Laura Plumb
Vedic Counsellor, Director of VedaWise,
Author of *Ayurveda Cooking for Beginners*

THE BHAGAVAD GITA

Comes Alive

A Radical Translation by

Jeffrey Armstrong | Kavindra Rishi

RUPA

Published by
Rupa Publications India Pvt. Ltd 2022
7/16, Ansari Road, Daryaganj
New Delhi 110002

Sales centres:
Allahabad Bengaluru Chennai
Hyderabad Jaipur Kathmandu
Kolkata Mumbai

Cover Art: Shounak Tewarie, Digital Artist, Art is Well
Cover Design: Sandi Graham, Antonina Ananda
Editors: Andrea Goldsmith, Pete McCormack, Sue Chambers
Sanskrit Editor: Prahlad

www.bharat.gitacomesalive.com

ISBN: 978-93-5520-431-8

Second impression 2022

10 9 8 7 6 5 4 3 2

Printed in India

Dedication

This translation of the Bhagavad Gita is dedicated to Shrila Vyasa Deva who originally compiled the Bhagavad Gita, to Adi Shankaracharya who restored it, to Ramanuja Acharya who revived it, to Madhva Acharya who reawakened it, to Chaitanya Mahaprabhu who revealed it, to Bhaktivinode Thakur who envisioned it going out to the world, and to His Divine Grace A. C. Bhaktivedanta Swami who delivered it to the world. I bow with humility and endless appreciation to these and all great acharyas.

Jai Shri Krishna

Jeffrey Armstrong | Kavindra Rishi

Contents

Gold and Silver Chains

Arjuna and Krishna, who spoke together of old,
The precious chains made of silver and gold,

Cousins and friends, their sacred conversation,
Contains the truths on which to build a nation.

Raja vidya, the secrets of wielding power,
By protecting the innocent, where good men never cower,

Where the regent is accountable to they
Who live and speak the message of this way.

There is a Watcher seeing all we do,
There is a Centre around which everything grew,

And revolves in orbits pulled by gravity,
There is a code of conduct, a way to be,

A way to know what has not happened yet;
A thing to always remember and never forget.

There are three states of matter you must know,
When to sustain, when to recycle or grow,

There are five elements manifest every place,
Earth, water, fire, air, and space.

Evil is real, as certain as day and night
And though related, they must eternally fight.

Meeting again and again on the field of Dharm,
Against their will, one must kill preventing harm.

And even though the atma can never die,
Love can be destroyed, so we must try

To grasp this gold and silver paradox,
Whose words are keys that open all the locks,

For we are meant for sweet eternity,
Moksha, for every rule must set us free.

Arjuna, argentum[1], silver, that glistening ore,
Entwined with gold, they shine forevermore.

So, wear this necklace and hang from it a gem,
Inscribed with the Holy Names of both of them.

Nara-Narayan, their beauty weaves and blends
In a sacred friendship that never ends.

Krishna and Arjuna, the silver and gold,
A conversation in which Eternal Truth was told.

Jeffrey Armstrong | Kavindra Rishi

---

[1]Argentum means silver in Latin, hence the linguistic connection with Arjuna. It is the root of the word argument, which does not mean to quarrel but rather to make a subject brighter like silver.

Foreword

Nilesh Nilkanth Oak

I met Jeffrey Armstrong in Jabalpur, at the World Ramayana Conference in the winter of 2016. We became instant friends, and since then we have been in regular communication. Both he and Prof. Bal Ram Singh were originally the only two scholars who understood the true impact of my dating of the Mahabharata War. Although we hardly knew each other, Jeffrey was the first to express, in no uncertain terms, the importance of my research and why it mattered to his own work as a Vedic scholar and an Ayurvedic astrologer. He went on to explain why the comprehension of ancient Indian astronomy and the accurate historical dating of the Mahabharata (5561 BCE) is crucial for both Gita study and Vedic astrology.

Though we who study and research the Mahabharata and the Bhagavad Gita do not consider ourselves experts in all aspects of the Gita, I am frequently asked which English translation of the Bhagavad Gita I would recommend. Those who ask me always sense my hesitation to answer. I do not hesitate because I have not read them all. Rather, my hesitation is because the many I have read have all left me dissatisfied.

Against this background, if someone would have told me that they were publishing a new English translation of the Bhagavad Gita, I would have been more irritated than elated. I did not know that Jeffrey had been working on his Bhagavad Gita translation project for more than a decade. He explained the scope of the project and his rationale. I cannot explain why, but I was elated. My early elation turned into conviction that he was on the verge of solving my problem of which translation to recommend.

But the analyst in me needed some proof. So, I asked Jeffrey for his translation of a few specific verses—the verses that test the translator's *adhyatmic* (spiritual) acumen. In my assessment, Jeffrey passed with flying colours. Next, I requested he send me his complete translation, and I can assert that I have read no better English translation of the Bhagavad Gita.

The Mahabharata is the composition of the unparalleled genius of Krishna Dvaipayana Vyasa as he documented the *itihasa* (history) of the Kuru dynasty. The Bhagavad Gita is the pinnacle of Vyasa's *adhyatmic* (spiritual) teachings in which he has encoded the wisdom of Bhagavan's discussion with Arjuna in poetic verse. Whenever I refer to the Bhagavad Gita, I go to the original Sanskrit text, along with a very poetic translation into Marathi by the Acharya Vinoba Bhave. In the future, I will include Jeffrey's translation, *The Bhagavad Gita Comes Alive*, as a valuable part of my core Gita studies.

Jeffrey's translation focuses on conveying the essential, innate and root meaning of each verse of the Bhagavad Gita. He has taken the utmost care in his translation and has decided to keep many of the original Sanskrit words within the English verse where he felt that an English equivalent would only distort the Sanskrit meaning or do more harm. Where necessary, he has inserted short English definitions within the verse, but for non-translatable or deeply nuanced words he has provided in-depth definitions in a glossary, instead of lengthy purports.

Finally, and most important to this revolutionary translation, he has removed all the misleading, irrelevant, and toxic English words that have twisted and distorted all other translations. He has identified, corrected, and removed all the colonial and distorting terms which were intentionally used to diminish and subvert the liberating truths of the Gita.

The wisdom of the Bhagavad Gita has impressed oriental and occidental thought leaders alike. Many of them were not aware of the antiquity of this deep wisdom. My curiosity to validate impossible sounding astronomical descriptions of two celestial objects from the Mahabharata (Arundhati or Alcor and Vashishta or Mizar) led me to extract 300+ astronomical references from the grandest epic of humanity, which in turn determined 5561 BCE as the year of the Mahabharata War and 16 October 5561 BCE (Julian calendar reference) as the day of Gita Jayanti, the birth of the Bhagavad Gita.

Sage Yaskacharya defines *Sanatana Vedic Dharma* as 'Sanatano Nityanutana' (सनातनो न त्यनूतनः-यास्काचार्य) a dharma that is capable of, and insists on, refreshing itself in the light of changing circumstances, time, and place. This is the reason various acharyas wrote commentaries on the Bhagavad Gita, apt for the circumstances they envisioned. Jeffrey Armstrong's translation is in this very spirit and tradition.

It is my wish and desire to see Jeffrey's radical new translation, *The Bhagavad Gita Comes Alive*, on the bookshelf of every student of the Gita. We are all students of the Bhagavad Gita.

—*Nilesh Nilkanth Oak*
Author, *When did the Mahabharata War Happen?*
Adjunct Faculty, Institute of Advanced Sciences, Dartmouth,
MA, BS, MS (Chemical Engineering), EMBA

Preface

The Two Problems of Gita Translation

I have been working on this translation of the Bhagavad Gita for over a decade. In the beginning, I thought I was creating a translation not dissimilar to the rest—a one-to-one Sanskrit-English translation. However, the more I delved into the linguistics and semantics of the original Sanskrit and the many misleading English translations, the more convinced I became of the need for a thorough decolonizing of the Bhagavad Gita, in the translation and, through the process, in the text itself.

In working on this Sanskrit-to-English translation of the Bhagavad Gita—and reading through dozens of translations—two common yet profound problems have been consistently revealed.

Problem one, whether intentionally or not, every Bhagavad Gita translation has failed to bridge the intellectual gap between the unique and precise meanings of key Sanskrit words and the vague and distorted English words used incorrectly as synonyms to explain them. Consider these blatant and repetitive examples of inappropriately paired words found in almost all Gita translations: dharma to religion, Svarga Loka to heaven, isha to lord, papa to sin, tapasya to austerity, atma to soul, pranic to spiritual, Bhagavan to God, shraddha to faith, varna to caste, patala to hell, yajna to sacrifice, devas to gods or demi-gods, dana to charity, avatar to prophet, and at least a hundred others. Individually, the mistranslations are disconcerting and annoying.

Collectively, they are misleading and disastrous to the readers' understanding and growth.

In the process of leaning on false definitions and incorrect synonyms that colonize the text, translators inadvertently stop their readers from gaining a true and deeper understanding of these profound Sanskrit terms.

Christianized translations are so universal it feels as though the Gita is bumping into language guards who will not allow the truest Gita translation to cross international borders because the text's original meaning is simply too foreign for the West to grasp. I do not agree.

And so my passion and focus has been to excise the offending words and re-insert the Sanskrit words and, where necessary, clarify the Sanskrit meaning with definitions directly after the term (inside single quotation marks). For some key words, a more detailed definition is provided in the glossary at the back of the book.

Problem two flows from problem one. By choosing incorrect and often Christianized definitions for key Sanskrit words, translators have not insisted that students of the Bhagavad Gita undertake learning upwards of 200 essential Sanskrit words. The process of *not* learning these words renders the text far more generic and far less powerful, intellectually and spiritually. Learning the key words instils in the reader both a more precise understanding of the philosophy taught in the Gita and a vocabulary for expressing that understanding accurately.

Why are precise definitions leading back to the original Sanskrit so critical? The Vedic philosophy presented in the Gita teaches concepts that have *never* been taught or even fully expressed in Western culture and the English language. Thus, these profound Vedic concepts cannot be articulated by any single English word. And these Sanskrit terms make up a large part of the essence of the Bhagavad Gita.

And so it is my deepest hope that by delving into *The Bhagavad Gita Comes Alive*—a translation devoted to Sanskrit vidya—the English-speaking student will experience the unique, eternal, and original meaning of the Bhagavad Gita as its teachings were intended.

Jeffrey Armstrong | Kavindra Rishi

"In any translation from one language to another, one of two things will happen. Either the author is inconvenienced in favour of the reader, or the reader is inconvenienced in favour of the author."

Umberto Eco, European Scholar of Linguistics

About this Gita

In Jeffrey Armstrong | Kavindra Rishi's radical translation of India's sacred Bhagavad Gita, the text's eternal message has been revealed for all to contemplate, regardless of religious affiliation or intellectual background.

To get there, Kavindra Rishi utilized a lifetime of linguistic research and Vedic insight to explore the root of *every* Sanskrit word and its English counterpart used in this translation. He wrestled with myriad cultural and linguistic translation problems that have, over time, diminished and distorted the Gita's original and essential meaning through 'linguistic drift' and manipulative colonial influence.

There are no purports (text explanations) in this Gita, but the text itself reads so smoothly that they are not missed. Given such simplicity, one might wonder what took Jeffrey so long to put this translation together. But remember: As in martial arts, the Master makes all the moves look easy only after having been thrown to the mat ten thousand times to gain such skills. Jeffrey Armstrong is not only a scholar; he has been a daily spiritual practitioner for over 50 years and has been deeply affected by and absorbed in the Vedic *vidya*. He is also an accomplished poet and with his word-gifts he takes the Bhagavad Gita to a level of clarity that had until now been inaccessible for the English-speaking reader.

In the translation process, to maximize flow, Armstrong provides concise definitions of Sanskrit words carefully woven into the verses. However, many Sanskrit terms are too complex to be grasped without studying a more detailed definition. So,

Jeffrey has included an in-depth glossary of Sanskrit words and terms that he challenges the reader to learn. Indeed, he considers their memorization and understanding essential. Without such effort, one's advancement is greatly limited. So please, read the glossary—it is your friend. This "inconvenience" to the reader will be generously repaid when the deep and profound meanings of the Gita blossom in your heart and mind and *atma* like a beautiful garden.

Beyond the profound meanings of the Sanskrit words, the sacred Sanskrit language also carries the vibrations and frequencies of the transcendental realms (Akshar Brahman). This gift cannot be understated. In addition to comprehending the deeper meanings of these Vedic concepts that don't exist in the English language, the reader benefits from hearing and voicing these Sanskrit words. And so, I would encourage the reading of this book aloud, a chapter a day at the end of morning meditation, before tackling the challenges of the day. Remember, these words carry sacred healing vibrations.

Understanding these multiple layers of the Sanskrit language is an essential step for clarifying the universal Sanatana Dharma contained in the Gita and for making its message accessible and understandable to all English readers, be they Hindu youth, yoga practitioners, Vedic teachers, or the spiritually curious.

May you be as absorbed in and inspired by Jeffrey Armstrong's original and radical translation as we were by the process of uncovering it and bringing it to your eyes, your ears, and your hearts.

S. Graham, Director
VASA Publishing

Sanskrit Editor's Comments

One goal of this translation is to accelerate the migration of Sanskrit terms into the English language. Some words are already there, such as *yoga* and *yogi,* and they appear to have come in organically as a result of common everyday usage. However, this translation methodically manages the purposeful introduction of new Sanskrit words. It uses a particularly simplified style of spelling without complex diacritical marks and avoids certain awkward constructions that some texts have used, such as the doubled 'aa' for a long 'a' vowel. On the other hand, some Sanskrit letters seem naturally expressed as consonant blends, such as 'sh' or 'ch', which help pronunciation. Ultimately, the new word is forced to shed its precise Sanskrit grammatical forms to be able to co-exist with English words. For example, in Sanskrit the plural of *yogi* is *yoginah,* but in English we just add the usual 's' to form *yogis*.

Similarly, nominal declensions, which are also found in Latin and Greek, as well as modern German and Russian, add endings to a word according to its use in a sentence. These too are mostly abandoned. We hope the result will be a co-existence of English and Sanskrit words that convey appropriate meanings.

Reverential capitalization in English is the practice of capitalizing religious words that refer to a deity and/or divine being(s) in cases where the words would not otherwise have been capitalized. There is no capitalization in the Sanskrit language.

Additional Notes on this Translation

Verses have been given a number in addition to chapter and verse for easy reference.

Only Shri Bhagavan, Shri Krishna and Arjuna are the names used for the two main characters, although many names are used for them in the original Sanskrit. Their other names are listed in the appendix.

Where Sanskrit words have been embedded in the text, we have defined them within 'single quotation marks'.

Selected Sanskrit words with no English equivalent or with complex meanings have been defined in the glossary.

In certain verses, we have highlighted a series of Sanskrit words or concepts in list form as a learning tool for students.

Since the entire Bhagavad Gita is a dialogue, we have removed almost all quotation marks and instead used bold formatting to clearly distinguish who the speaker is.

Sanskrit words are not capitalized except where they start a sentence or are a proper name.

All 'forbidden' words and sexist language have been replaced or removed. He/his has been replaced by gender-neutral they, them, their, even though it sometimes results in awkward phrasing or sentence construction.

Introduction

The Bhagavad Gita presents itself to us as a historical event that took place in India a little over 7,500 years ago, according to astronomical calculations from the text of the Mahabharata. That moment in history and the events that preceded it are described in a larger work called the Mahabharata, an epic poem of over 100,000 verses, written in the ancient and sacred language of Sanskrit. The plot of the story concerns a royal family that was divided by a quarrel over leadership of the kingdom. The ensuing political struggle culminated in a battle of epic proportions in which over three million soldiers were killed in eighteen days.

The two branches of this dynasty were the Kauravas, headed by the selfish and dark-minded Duryodhana, and the Pandavas, led by Yudhishthira and his four brothers who were known for their virtuous and dharmic behaviour. The two branches of the family were first cousins, the children of two brothers. The Kauravas were descended from a blind king named Dhritarashtra, while the father of the five Pandavas was a valiant and honourable king named Pandu.

In the final analysis, the cause of the battle was twofold. First, Duryodhana was envious of his cousins' charisma and personal endowments, and so unjustly usurped their rightful half of the kingdom by coercion and deceit. Second and more important, he was by nature opposed to the view that creation is the manifestation of a divine will, intelligence, and purposefulness. Instead, he viewed the world as his personal property, meant for his own use and pleasure, without accountability to either the Supreme Being or the living beings under his control. The Pandavas were inclined to rule their kingdom as a sacred responsibility, with accountability to divine law and for the benefit of all living entities, whereas Duryodhana and his supporters were the classic tyrants with their abusive henchmen.

In the midst of this global struggle, a unique being was also present. The distinctive feature of India's (Bharat's) history and thought is the notion that from time to time, the Divine Intelligence or Supreme and Ultimate Being makes a personal appearance on Earth. The Sanskrit term for this process is *avatar*, which means a voluntary descent and appearance of the Ultimate Divine Being in a personal form, disguised as an ordinary human being. Thus, the Mahabharata explains that the Source of all existence, Bhagavan Shri Krishna, the Supreme Brahman Reality, Being and Person, appeared in India at this time as the cousin of both Duryodhana and his siblings, as well as Yudhishthira and his four brothers with their wife Draupadi.

An avatar is not a prophet, guru, teacher, angelic being, or so called demi-god. The avatar, unlike human beings, is neither forced to take birth nor born in ignorance, but rather, descends purposely in our midst at a specific, pre-planned historical moment in order to make a revelation of the transcendental reality that exists beyond our sight. The other reason for the *avatar's* coming is to adjust the affairs of humans, to restore balance to life on our planet, and to reaffirm and reveal the immortal truths that maintain all reality. Those truths are called *Sanatana Dharma*, that which is always true.

The Bhagavad Gita, meaning the Song of Bhagavan, was spoken on the battlefield where the armies of both sides had assembled for a final showdown. The Pandavas had spent the previous thirteen years in forced exile using diplomatic efforts to try to avoid an interfamilial conflict. When it was clear that the battle was inevitable, Arjuna went to Duryodhana one last time to ask him to cease hostilities and restore the peace. When the dark-minded king refused, Shri Krishna himself called one last meeting between Arjuna and Duryodhana, at which time He declared that, as the Supreme Being, He would not directly fight in the conflict. He proposed that one side receive His army and the other have Him as their advisor and chariot driver during the battle. Predictably, Arjuna chose Shri Krishna as his chariot driver, and Duryodhana was glad to have His army.

Soon thereafter, the two great armies assembled at a field called Kurukshetra. Kurukshetra is situated around 170 km north of what is now Delhi and is also known by many names like Brahmakshetra 'Land of Brahma', Uttaradevi, Brahmadevi, and Dharmakshetra 'the place where dharma was tested'. It was on that field of conflict, just as the fighting was about to begin, that Shri Krishna spoke the message of the Bhagavad Gita to Arjuna, His best friend and cousin. Unlike Duryodhana, Arjuna was able to recognize that Bhagavan Shri Krishna was the Supreme Being appearing in the human world to renew and revive our understanding of timeless truths and to lend support in the fight against asuric forces on Earth.

Many layers of meaning...

The Bhagavad Gita has many levels of significance for us as readers. On one level, Shri Krishna is making an appearance here in the realm of matter to remind us that we are really immortal beings who come from the transcendental realm of Brahman and are only visiting this world of darkness and death.

On another level, Shri Krishna represents the all-pervading divine intelligence that is the creator, maintainer and destroyer of this material world. As such, Shri Krishna stands for and is the source of the invisible laws of nature to which all beings are accountable. In this role, Shri Krishna is advocating what we would now call ecology and sustainability, and Duryodhana represents the destructive and unsustainable attitude toward nature which promotes the view that no one designed or is in control of the material world.

At another level, the battle that was acted out as a historical event 7,500 years ago, as described in the Mahabharata, continues in the form of global conflicts wherever sincere and caring people oppose the harmful and evil practices of the modern-day Duryodhanas. None of us is entirely free or safe from the effects of these seemingly unstoppable conflicts.

On another level, our bodies are in a constant state of conflict as our immune system fights against the invading hordes of entities trying to destroy the balance within our bodies. In this case, Duryodhana and his cohorts are cancer cells, anaerobic death-inflicting soldiers who bring darkness, dysfunction, and chaos into our balanced bodies.

Finally, on the level of our mind, the doubts that plague us, depress us, and lead us to despair are just as certainly the forces of evil who have overtaken the field of our manas 'our mind and heart', and would like to extinguish the light of our atma 'our true immortal self'. The struggle for existence of the human race is an apt metaphor for our position in the midst of the forces that swirl around us in the world of matter. We are either humans having a divine experience, or immortal beings having a human experience. As we will see, Krishna is the great light and Supreme friend who is forever in support of our existence as immortal beings. Therefore, His advice to Arjuna on the battlefield of Kurukshetra is relevant to anyone struggling against the forces of darkness, chaos, and destruction as long as the struggle for ultimate truth continues in this realm of matter and duality.

It is also important to remember that Bhagavan Shri Krishna

has two purposes for appearing before us. One of these is to be the driver of the chariot of our body and guide us safely through the struggle of life. The second and ultimately most important is to attract us back to the divine transcendental Brahman realm that is our true and immortal home. In fact, Krishna means the most beautiful and attractive Being.

In that capacity, it is important to remember that even though He is the Supreme, Shri Krishna has purposely taken the humble and menial task of being Arjuna's chariot driver. The reason for this humble posture is that in the Bhagavad Gita, the Supreme Being is not depicted as an angry, vengeful, judgmental or dangerous 'God'. Quite the contrary—Shri Krishna presents himself as Arjuna's very best friend, speaks with him in a sweet voice, smiling, and at the end of the book tells him kindly to do what he wants by using his free will. So in spite of the fact that the Gita appears to be a war story, it is in fact a love story—the story of love's struggle to exist in this difficult and challenging world, and the story of how love exists for eternity and never ends.

...thus dear reader, the story begins

It could be over 7,500 years ago in India, or right now, anywhere in the world. Arjuna, like many of us, is reluctant to fight against his own family and friends for any reason, yet he finds that an implacable evil exists in his world, just as it does today.

He has been chosen by destiny to lead the fight against the forces that would destroy the innocent and harm the world. He is, nonetheless, profoundly saddened at the struggle, being at heart a gentle, peace-loving being. He is sick at heart at the thought of the fight to come. If you have ever been depressed or afraid of facing the struggle of life, you can understand Arjuna's heart and mind.

And now...with the horses and elephants dressed for battle, bugles and conch shells sounding the battle cry, the blind king Dhritarashtra, father of Duryodhana, asks his servant Sanjaya, who has the power of remotely viewing the distant battlefield: "What is taking place on the battlefield of Kurukshetra in the conflict between my sons and the Pandavas, headed by Arjuna?"

Why Radical?

"The radical Bhagavad Gita—a translation for the Indic Renaissance"
—Nilesh Nilkanth Oak

1. Linguistics: denoting or relating to the roots of a word
2. Music: belonging to the root of a chord
3. Mathematics: of the root of a number or quantity

Adjective

1. "A radical overhaul of the existing regulatory framework." Relating to or affecting the fundamental nature of something; far-reaching or thorough, especially of change or action.
   Similar: thorough, complete, total, entire, absolute, utter, comprehensive, to reach out with roots and branches, sweeping, far-reaching, wide-ranging, extensive, profound, severe, serious, major.
   Similar: fundamental, basic, essential, quintessential, inherent, innate, structural, deep-seated, intrinsic, organic, constitutive, root.
2. Advocating or based on thorough or complete political or social change; representing or supporting an extreme or progressive section of a political party. "A radical activist."
   Similar: revolutionary, progressive, reforming, reformist, progressivist.
3. Slang: excellent, cool.

Source: *Oxford Dictionary Online, Merriam-Webster.com*

Part I

Chapter 1

The Agony of Arjuna

1 dhṛtarāṣṭra uvāca
dharmakṣetre kurukṣetre samavetā yuyutsavaḥ
Ch.1 v.1 māmakāḥ pāṇḍavāś caiva kim akurvata saṁjaya

The blind MAHARAJA DHRITARASHTRA asked his personal servant: O Sanjaya, when my sons and the sons of Pandu were assembled with their respective armies on the field of Kurukshetra, which is also the dharma kshetra 'where truth is determined', what did they do next?

2 saṁjaya uvāca
dṛṣṭvā tu pāṇḍavānīkaṁ vyūḍhaṁ duryodhanas tadā
Ch.1 v.2 ācāryam upasaṁgamya rājā vacanam abravīt

SANJAYA replied:
Upon seeing the army of the Pandavas arrayed in battle formation, Raja Duryodhana approached his acharya and martial arts master Drona and began to speak.

3 paśyaitāṁ pāṇḍuputrāṇām ācārya mahatīṁ camūm
Ch.1 v.3 vyūḍhāṁ drupadaputreṇa tava śiṣyeṇa dhīmatā

DURYODHANA said:
Just see, O Master, the mighty army of the sons of Pandu has been skilfully arranged into formidable battle formations by your student Dhrishtadyumna, the brilliant son of King Drupada.

4 atra śūrā maheṣvāsā bhīmārjunasamā yudhi
Ch.1 v.4 yuyudhāno virāṭaś ca drupadaś ca mahārathaḥ

In the Pandu army, there are amazing archers like Yuyudhana and Virata, who are equal in skill to Bhima and Arjuna. There is also the unstoppable Drupada.

5
Ch.1 v.5

dhṛṣṭaketuś cekitānaḥ kāśirājaś ca vīryavān
purujit kuntibhojaś ca śaibyaś ca narapuṁgavaḥ

There are also Dhristaketu, Chekitana, the heroic King of Kashi, and Purujit, Kuntibhoja, and Shaibya, all of whom are extraordinary fighters.

6
Ch.1 v.6

yudhāmanyuś ca vikrānta uttamaujāś ca vīryavān
saubhadro draupadeyāś ca sarva eva mahārathāḥ

The spirited Yudhamanyu, the bold Uttamauja, and the valiant sons of both Subhadra and Draupadi are all courageous and extraordinary warriors.

7
Ch.1 v.7

asmākaṁ tu viśiṣṭā ye tān nibodha dvijottama
nāyakā mama sainyasya saṁjñārthaṁ tān bravīmi te

O best among enlightened beings, now let me tell you the names of the distinguished leaders of our army, so you will know them well.

8
Ch.1 v.8

bhavān bhīṣmaś ca karṇaś ca kṛpaś ca samitiṁjayaḥ
aśvatthāmā vikarṇaś ca saumadattis tathaiva ca

With yourself at the forefront, there are also Bhishma, Karna, and Kripa, who are always victorious in battle, as well as the remarkable Ashvatthama, Vikarna, and the son of Somadatta.

9
Ch.1 v.9

anye ca bahavaḥ śūrā madarthe tyaktajīvitāḥ
nānāśastrapraharaṇāḥ sarve yuddhaviśāradāḥ

In addition, there are many other great heroic warriors who are skilled in warfare and ready to risk their lives by attacking all opposition with a variety of deadly weapons.

10
Ch.1 v.10

aparyāptaṁ tad asmākaṁ balaṁ bhīṣmābhirakṣitam
paryāptaṁ tv idam eteṣāṁ balaṁ bhīmābhirakṣitam

Our strength is far greater than theirs and it is guarded by the undefeatable grandfather Bhishma, while our opponent's army is far fewer in numbers and is protected by Bhima.

11
Ch.1 v.11

ayaneṣu ca sarveṣu yathābhāgam avasthitāḥ
bhīṣmam evābhirakṣantu bhavantaḥ sarva eva hi

And so, I am requesting all of you to give your attentive support to Bhishma and guard him by positioning yourselves at various strategic points in the divisions of our mighty army.

12
Ch.1 v.2

tasya saṁjanayan harṣaṁ kuruvṛddhaḥ pitāmahaḥ
siṁhanādaṁ vinadyoccaiḥ śaṅkhaṁ dadhmau pratāpavān

SANJAYA said:
At that moment, in order to enthuse Duryodhana, Bhishma blew his conch shell very powerfully, making a loud noise that resembled the roar of a lion.

13
Ch.1 v.13

tataḥ śaṅkhāś ca bheryaś ca paṇavānakagomukhāḥ
sahasaivābhyahanyanta sa śabdas tumulo 'bhavat

Immediately following that, conch shells, trumpets, drums, horns, and bugles were sounded on both sides. The combined tumult was uproarious.

14
Ch.1 v.14

tataḥ śvetair hayair yukte mahati syandane sthitau
mādhavaḥ pāṇḍavaś caiva divyau śaṅkhau pradadhmatuḥ

Then, across the battlefield, Shri Bhagavan and Arjuna, standing on a magnificent chariot pulled by four powerful white horses, sounded their divine conch shells.

15 pāñcajanyaṁ hṛṣīkeśo devadattaṁ dhanaṁjayaḥ
pauṇḍraṁ dadhmau mahāśaṅkhaṁ bhīmakarmā
vṛkodaraḥ

Ch.1 v.15

Shri Bhagavan blew his conch named Panchajanya, Arjuna sounded his conch named Devadatta, while the fierce Bhima roared forth on his great conch named Paundra.

16 anantavijayaṁ rājā kuntīputro yudhiṣṭhiraḥ
nakulaḥ sahadevaś ca sughoṣamaṇipuṣpakau

Ch.1 v.16

Then Maharaja Yudhishthira blew his conch, Anantavijaya, and Nakula and Sahadeva blew theirs, the Sughosa and Manipushpaka.

17 kāśyaś ca parameṣvāsaḥ śikhaṇḍī ca mahārathaḥ
dhṛṣṭadyumno virāṭaś ca sātyakiś cāparājitaḥ

Ch.1 v.17

Following this, the King of Kashi, the ultimate archer; the great chariot fighter Shikhandini; and the invincible warriors Dhrishtadyumna, Virata, and Satyaki who had never been conquered...

18 drupado draupadeyāś ca sarvaśaḥ pṛthivīpate
saubhadraś ca mahābāhuḥ śaṅkhān dadhmuḥ pṛthak
pṛthak

Ch.1 v.18

...along with Drupada, the five sons of Draupadi, and the strong-armed son of Subhadra, each blew upon their powerful conch shells.

19 sa ghoṣo dhārtarāṣṭrāṇāṁ hṛdayāni vyadārayat
nabhaś ca pṛthivīṁ caiva tumulo vyanunādayan

Ch.1 v.19

The tumultuous sounding of those instruments burst forth with a deafening roar that split the sky, shook the ground, and shattered the hearts of your sons.

20 atha vyavasthitān dṛṣṭvā dhārtarāṣṭrān kapidhvajaḥ
Ch.1 v.20 pravṛtte śastrasaṁpāte dhanur udyamya pāṇḍavaḥ

At that moment, standing upon his chariot with its flag bearing the image of the mighty Hanuman, and seeing the armies in formation with weapons already beginning to clash, Arjuna raised his bow and spoke to Shri Krishna.

21 hṛṣīkeśaṁ tadā vākyam idam āha mahīpate
Ch.1 v.21 senayor ubhayor madhye rathaṁ sthāpaya me 'cyuta

ARJUNA said to Shri Bhagavan:
O undefeatable one, please drive my chariot to the centre of the battlefield, in between both armies.

22 yāvad etān nirīkṣe 'haṁ yoddhukāmān avasthitān
Ch.1 v.22 kair mayā saha yoddhavyam asmin raṇasamudyame

Place me where I can see the faces of all those who have come here hungry to fight with us, from where they are standing in their battle formations.

23 yotsyamānān avekṣe 'haṁ ya ete 'tra samāgatāḥ
Ch.1 v.23 dhārtarāṣṭrasya durbuddher yuddhe priyacikīrṣavaḥ

I want to see close-up all those who have come here prepared to fight against us out of affection for the conniving and dark-minded Duryodhana.

24 evam ukto hṛṣīkeśo guḍākeśena bhārata
Ch.1 v.24 senayor ubhayor madhye sthāpayitvā rathottamam

O Dhritarashtra, hearing this request from Arjuna, Shri Bhagavan drove the chariot to a point in the middle of the field, directly in front of Bhishma and Drona, and exactly between both armies.

25 bhīṣmadroṇapramukhataḥ sarveṣāṁ ca mahīkṣitām
Ch.1 v.25 uvāca pārtha paśyaitān samavetān kurūn iti

There, in the presence of Bhishma, Drona, and the other kings of the world, SHRI KRISHNA said:
Look, Arjuna, all the Kurus are assembled here.

26 tatrāpaśyat sthitān pārthaḥ pitṝn atha pitāmahān
Ch.1 v.26 ācāryān mātulān bhrātṝn putrān pautrān sakhīṁs tathā

In the ranks of both armies, Arjuna could see his brothers, cousins, friends, sons, grandsons, uncles, fathers, grandfathers, and teachers.

27 śvaśurān suhṛdaś caiva senayor ubhayor api
Ch.1 v.27 tān samīkṣya sa kaunteyaḥ sarvān bandhūn avasthitān

In the two armies, he also saw fathers-in-law as well as dear companions, and contemplated all his kinsmen who were standing in battle formation.

28 kṛpayā parayāviṣṭo viṣīdann idam abravīt
Ch.1 v.28 dṛṣṭvemān svajanān kṛṣṇa yuyutsūn samavasthitān

Filled with deep sadness and profound empathy, Arjuna spoke:
O Krishna, seeing my own family and friends standing ready to fight against each other...

29 sīdanti mama gātrāṇi mukhaṁ ca pariśuṣyati
Ch.1 v.29 vepathuś ca śarīre me romaharṣaś ca jāyate

...my limbs have lost their strength, my mouth is dry, my body is trembling with empathy, and my hair is standing on end.

My dear Krishna, I do not
wish for victory, or to be a
ruler, or to enjoy royal
pleasures. O Bhagavan,
O beloved of all, what is the
use of power, enjoyment, or
even life itself, when all
those for whose benefit
we would rule, and with
whom we would share
abundance and pleasures,
are dressed for a battle in
which they will not only
lose their wealth, but their
very life-breath?–32-3

30 gāṇḍīvaṁ sraṁsate hastāt tvak caiva paridahyate
na ca śaknomy avasthātuṁ bhramatīva ca me manaḥ
Ch.1 v.30

My bow Gandiva has fallen from my hands; my skin is burning. I am unable to remain standing and my manas is unfocused and disturbed.

31 nimittāni ca paśyāmi viparītāni keśava
na ca śreyo 'nupaśyāmi hatvā svajanam āhave
Ch.1 v.31

O Bhagavan, I am perceiving many inauspicious signs, and I foresee only misfortune will be the outcome of destroying my beloved family and friends in this battle.

32 na kāṅkṣe vijayaṁ kṛṣṇa na ca rājyaṁ sukhāni ca
kiṁ no rājyena govinda kiṁ bhogair jīvitena vā
Ch.1 v.32

My dear Krishna, I do not wish for victory, or to be a ruler, or to enjoy royal pleasures. O Bhagavan, O beloved of all, what is the use of power, enjoyment, or even life itself...

33 yeṣām arthe kāṅkṣitaṁ no rājyaṁ bhogāḥ sukhāni ca
ta ime 'vasthitā yuddhe prāṇāṁs tyaktvā dhanāni ca
Ch.1 v.33

...when all those for whose benefit we would rule, and with whom we would share abundance and pleasures, are dressed for a battle in which they will not only lose their wealth, but their very life-breath?

34 ācāryāḥ pitaraḥ putrās tathaiva ca pitāmahāḥ
mātulāḥ śvaśurāḥ pautrāḥ syālāḥ saṁbandhinas tathā
Ch.1 v.34

These are all my dear ones: teachers, fathers, children, grandfathers, uncles, brothers-in-law, all my kinsmen, and friends.

35
Ch.1 v.35

etān na hantum icchāmi ghnato 'pi madhusūdana
api trailokyarājyasya hetoḥ kiṁ nu mahīkṛte

O Bhagavan, I do not wish to kill them, even if they are intent upon killing me. I would not harm them to become ruler of the trilokas 'three cosmic realms', what to speak of this tiny world.

36
Ch.1 v.36

nihatya dhārtarāṣṭrān naḥ kā prītiḥ syāj janārdana
pāpam evāśrayed asmān hatvaitān ātatāyinaḥ

O Krishna, how could we ever find pleasure in life again after killing the sons of Dhritarashtra? The darkness of papa 'activities which result in suffering' would cling to us after we killed such aggressors.

37
Ch.1 v.37

tasmān nārhā vayaṁ hantuṁ dhārtarāṣṭrān sabāndhavān
svajanaṁ hi kathaṁ hatvā sukhinaḥ syāma mādhava

Therefore, we cannot be justified in killing those sons of Dhritarashtra, who are our own kinsmen. O Krishna, how could we ever be joyful again after destroying our own family...

38
Ch.1 v.38

yady apy ete na paśyanti lobhopahatacetasaḥ
kulakṣayakṛtaṁ doṣaṁ mitradrohe ca pātakam

...even if they are overwhelmed by greed and cannot see the negative consequences that will be caused by the crime of committing treachery to friends and one's own kula 'extended family'?

39
Ch.1 v.39

kathaṁ na jñeyam asmābhiḥ pāpād asmān nivartitum
kulakṣayakṛtaṁ doṣaṁ prapaśyadbhir janārdana

Dearest Krishna, why should we engage in this battle since we know the flaws and negative reactions that will result from the destruction of family traditions?

40 kulakṣaye praṇaśyanti kuladharmāḥ sanātanāḥ
Ch.1 v.40 dharme naṣṭe kulaṁ kṛtsnam adharmo 'bhibhavaty uta

When the kula structures are destroyed, so also are the sanatana principles of family unity. Then chaos overwhelms all and the kula is fragmented.

41 adharmābhibhavāt kṛṣṇa praduṣyanti kulastriyaḥ
Ch.1 v.41 strīṣu duṣṭāsu vārṣṇeya jāyate varṇasaṁkaraḥ

O Krishna, when the vedic codes of kula dharma are overpowered by social chaos, the integrity of women which keeps the kula healthy is damaged. This disturbs the consistency of family values and the on-going performance of family responsibilities.

42 saṁkaro narakāyaiva kulaghnānāṁ kulasya ca
Ch.1 v.42 patanti pitaro hy eṣāṁ luptapiṇḍodakakriyāḥ

O Bhagavan, I have heard that those who destroy the kula dharma and thus stop the offerings to the departed ancestors go to Naraka 'the most painful and degraded realms of material existence' as a result of their disruptive actions.

43 doṣair etaiḥ kulaghnānāṁ varṇasaṁkarakārakaiḥ
Ch.1 v.43 utsādyante jātidharmāḥ kuladharmāś ca śāśvatāḥ

Because of the chaos caused by those who destroy the perpetual extended family structure, the class responsibilities in society are also destroyed. Finally, even the jati codes of professional conduct are compromised.

44
Ch.1 v.44

utsannakuladharmāṇāṁ manuṣyāṇāṁ janārdana
narake niyataṁ vāso bhavatīty anuśuśruma

O Bhagavan, we have heard again and again that the manushas 'human beings' who choose to destroy kula dharma are destined to reside in places of Naraka where they experience pain and suffering.

45
Ch.1 v.45

aho bata mahat pāpaṁ kartuṁ vyavasitā vayam
yad rājyasukhalobhena hantuṁ svajanam udyatāḥ

O dear Bhagavan, because of greed for royal pleasures, we are about to plunge into utter darkness through the papa of killing our own beloved relations.

46
Ch.1 v.46

yadi mām apratīkāram aśastraṁ śastrapāṇayaḥ
dhārtarāṣṭrā raṇe hanyus tan me kṣemataraṁ bhavet

Considering all these truths, I would be much happier if the sons of Dhritarashtra simply killed me, unarmed and without fighting or resistance.

47
Ch.1 v.47

evam uktvārjunaḥ saṁkhye rathopastha upāviśat
visṛjya saśaraṁ cāpaṁ śokasaṁvignamānasaḥ

After speaking in this way, there in the middle of the battlefield, Arjuna threw down his bow and arrows and sat down upon the chariot, his manas overcome with sorrow.

Chapter 2

A Concise Summary of the Bhagavad Gita

48
Ch.2 v.1

saṁjaya uvāca
taṁ tathā kṛpayāviṣṭam aśrupūrṇākulekṣaṇam
viṣīdantam idaṁ vākyam uvāca madhusūdanaḥ

SANJAYA said:
Seeing Arjuna overcome by pity, sorrow, and despair, with his eyes downcast and full of tears, Krishna began to speak.

49
Ch.2 v.2

śrībhagavān uvāca
kutas tvā kaśmalam idaṁ viṣame samupasthitam
anāryajuṣṭam asvargyam akīrtikaram arjuna

SHRI BHAGAVAN said:
My dear Arjuna, how has this unmanly weakness in the face of danger overtaken you? It will only lead to disgrace. It is unbefitting of a great aryan leader like yourself and will not lead you to Svarga Loka at the time of death.

50
Ch.2 v.3

klaibyaṁ mā sma gamaḥ pārtha naitat tvayy upapadyate
kṣudraṁ hṛdayadaurbalyaṁ tyaktvottiṣṭha paraṁtapa

Do not behave like a coward, Arjuna, acting in this weak and faint-hearted way. Instead, O mighty warrior, uttishta 'arise' and stand firm in battle.

51
Ch.2 v.4

arjuna uvāca
kathaṁ bhīṣmam ahaṁ saṁkhye droṇaṁ ca madhusūdana
iṣubhiḥ pratiyotsyāmi pūjārhāv arisūdana

ARJUNA replied:
O Krishna, how can I fire arrows in battle at Bhishma and Drona, who are both elders and mentors worthy of my veneration and respect?

52
Ch.2 v.5

gurūn ahatvā hi mahānubhāvāñ; śreyo bhoktuṁ bhaikṣam apīha loke
hatvārthakāmāṁs tu gurūn ihaiva; bhuñjīya bhogān rudhirapradigdhān

I am certain it would be more noble for me to live by begging than to satisfy my personal desires achieved by killing these great beings who are also my gurus. If they are destroyed, all that we gain will be spoiled by the spilling of their blood.

53
Ch.2 v.6

na caitad vidmaḥ kataran no garīyo; yad vā jayema yadi vā no jayeyuḥ
yān eva hatvā na jijīviṣāmas; te 'vasthitāḥ pramukhe dhārtarāṣṭrāḥ

It is difficult to say which would be a worse outcome, destroying them or being defeated by them. If I kill the sons of Dhritarashtra, I will not want to live. And yet, here they are, standing before me on the field of battle.

54
Ch.2 v.7

kārpaṇyadoṣopahatasvabhāvaḥ; pṛcchāmi tvāṁ dharmasaṁmūḍhacetāḥ
yac chreyaḥ syān niścitaṁ brūhi tan me; śiṣyas te 'haṁ śādhi māṁ tvāṁ prapannam

My thinking is filled with imperfections, pity has overcome my true nature, and I cannot discern how to follow the path of dharma with certainty. Therefore, I am now bowing at Your feet and am Your completely surrendered disciple. Please instruct me on the correct path of action.

na hi prapaśyāmi mamāpanudyād; yac chokam
55 ucchoṣaṇam indriyāṇām
Ch.2 v.8 avāpya bhūmāv asapatnam ṛddhaṁ; rājyaṁ surāṇām api
cādhipatyam

I can see no way, now or in the future, to remove this sorrow that is tormenting and debilitating my indriyas 'bodily senses', even if I become the ultimate maharaja of Bhumi Loka 'Mother Earth' herself, or achieve the supreme powers and enjoyments of the devas.

saṁjaya uvāca
56 evam uktvā hṛṣīkeśaṁ guḍākeśaḥ paraṁtapa
Ch.2 v.9 na yotsya iti govindam uktvā tūṣṇīṁ babhūva ha

As Dhritarashtra's curiosity increased regarding Arjuna's state of mind,
Sanjaya said:
Then, having accepted Shri Krishna as his guru, Arjuna said, "O Bhagavan, I will not fight." And with those words, he became silent.

57 tam uvāca hṛṣīkeśaḥ prahasann iva bhārata
Ch.2 v.10 senayor ubhayor madhye viṣīdantam idaṁ vacaḥ

At that moment, Shri Krishna, who had a look of bemusement and surprise on his face, started laughing and began to speak to the disheartened Arjuna.

58 śrībhagavān uvāca

Ch.2 v.11 aśocyān anvaśocas tvaṁ prajñāvādāṁś ca bhāṣase

gatāsūn agatāsūṁś ca nānuśocanti paṇḍitāḥ

SHRI BHAGAVAN said:
The words you speak appear to be full of profound meaning, but those who are wise do not grieve for those who are breathing or whose breath has gone.

59 na tv evāhaṁ jātu nāsaṁ na tvaṁ neme janādhipāḥ

Ch.2 v.12 na caiva na bhaviṣyāmaḥ sarve vayam ataḥ param

Never was there a time when I did not exist, nor you, nor all these kings, and from this time forward, none of us will ever cease to be.

60 dehino 'smin yathā dehe kaumāraṁ yauvanaṁ jarā

Ch.2 v.13 tathā dehāntaraprāptir dhīras tatra na muhyati

Just as a person grows within their deha 'perishable body' from childhood to youth to adulthood and then to old age, so at the death of the deha, their dehi 'immortal consciousness' migrates to another deha. One who understands this is not confused by these changes.

61 mātrāsparśās tu kaunteya śītoṣṇasukhaduḥkhadāḥ

Ch.2 v.14 āgamāpāyino 'nityās tāṁs titikṣasva bhārata

Listen Arjuna, material experiences like heat and cold or sukha 'pleasure' and dukha 'pain' come and go. They are temporary and one must learn to endure them.

62
Ch.2 v.15

yaṁ hi na vyathayanty ete puruṣaṁ puruṣarṣabha
samaduḥkhasukhaṁ dhīraṁ so 'mṛtatvāya kalpate

The person who is not disturbed by the fluctuations of sukha and dukha is eligible to reclaim their own indestructible and immortal nature.

63
Ch.2 v.16

nāsato vidyate bhāvo nābhāvo vidyate sataḥ
ubhayor api dṛṣṭo 'ntas tv anayos tattvadarśibhiḥ

That which is asat will not endure, while that which is sat can never cease to exist. Both these states of being are known by the seers as that which is tattva 'always true'.

64
Ch.2 v.17

avināśi tu tad viddhi yena sarvam idaṁ tatam
vināśam avyayasyāsya na kaś cit kartum arhati

Just try to see this tattva which is both indestructible and immortal. No one can accomplish the destruction of that unalterable reality.

65
Ch.2 v.18

antavanta ime dehā nityasyoktāḥ śarīriṇaḥ
anāśino 'prameyasya tasmād yudhyasva bhārata

O Arjuna, these dehas which must someday end and then be burned are inhabited by an undying, indestructible, immeasurable being. Therefore, you should join the battle.

66
Ch.2 v.19

ya enaṁ vetti hantāraṁ yaś cainaṁ manyate hatam
ubhau tau na vijānīto nāyaṁ hanti na hanyate

One who imagines that the immortal being can kill or be killed does not understand that no one can ever kill or be killed.

Never was there a time when
I did not exist, nor you, nor
all these kings, and from
this time forward, none of
us will ever cease to be.
Just as a person grows
within their deha 'perishable
body' from childhood to
youth to adulthood and
then to old age, so at the
death of the deha, their dehi
'immortal consciousness'
migrates to another deha.
One who understands
this is not confused by
these changes.–59-60

67
Ch.2 v.20

na jāyate mriyate vā kadā cin; nāyaṁ bhūtvā bhavitā vā na bhūyaḥ
ajo nityaḥ śāśvato 'yaṁ purāṇo; na hanyate hanyamāne śarīre

That being who was not born, can never die and who, having been, will always be. Unborn, undying, with no origin, this timeless being is not slain when the deha is destroyed.

68
Ch.2 v.21

vedāvināśinaṁ nityaṁ ya enam ajam avyayam
kathaṁ sa puruṣaḥ pārtha kaṁ ghātayati hanti kam

The true self is indestructible, timeless, and is neither born nor dies. So, then tell me Arjuna, how is that purusha going to be slain and who is able to kill them?

69
Ch.2 v.22

vāsāṁsi jīrṇāni yathā vihāya; navāni gṛhṇāti naro 'parāṇi
tathā śarīrāṇi vihāya jīrṇāny; anyāni saṁyāti navāni dehī

Just as the nara 'human being' throws away old garments that are tattered and worn, so the immortal dehi leaves one material body and simply moves on to another.

70
Ch.2 v.23

nainaṁ chindanti śastrāṇi nainaṁ dahati pāvakaḥ
na cainaṁ kledayanty āpo na śoṣayati mārutaḥ

That indestructible being cannot be cut by weapons or burned by fire. Water cannot make it wet and the wind cannot cause it to wither.

71
Ch.2 v.24

acchedyo 'yam adāhyo 'yam akledyo 'śoṣya eva ca
nityaḥ sarvagataḥ sthāṇur acalo 'yaṁ sanātanaḥ

This sanatana 'immortal' being cannot be cut into parts, destroyed by fire, drowned by water, or dried by wind. It is nitya 'everlasting', subtler than matter, always standing, and exists forever.

72 avyakto 'yam acintyo 'yam avikāryo 'yam ucyate
Ch.2 v.25 tasmād evaṁ viditvainaṁ nānuśocitum arhasi

That undying individual is invisible, inconceivable, and unchangeable. Therefore, you should not despair at the passing away of the bodily form.

73 atha cainaṁ nityajātaṁ nityaṁ vā manyase mṛtam
Ch.2 v.26 tathāpi tvaṁ mahābāho nainaṁ śocitum arhasi

So, Arjuna, either you believe that living beings are nitya 'immortal' and are reborn again and again, or you believe that they only live once and that their mrityu 'death' is final. In either case, you should not mourn their passing.

74 jātasya hi dhruvo mṛtyur dhruvaṁ janma mṛtasya ca
Ch.2 v.74 tasmād aparihārye 'rthe na tvaṁ śocitum arhasi

Whoever is janma 'born within matter' will experience mrityu 'the death of their deha', and the supposedly dead will always be reborn again. This process is inevitable, so you should never lament about it.

75 avyaktādīni bhūtāni vyaktamadhyāni bhārata
Ch.2 v.28 avyaktanidhanāny eva tatra kā paridevanā

All beings are unmanifest in the beginning, manifest for some time in the middle, and then unmanifest again at the end. Crying and complaining will not change this process.

76 āścaryavat paśyati kaś cid enam; āścaryavad vadati tathaiva cānyaḥ

Ch.2 v.29 āścaryavac cainam anyaḥ śṛṇoti; śrutvāpy enaṁ veda na caiva kaś cit

Some perceive this as amazing, some proclaim that this is amazing. Others hear about how amazing this is, but even after hearing about this process, it remains a mystery to them.

77 dehī nityam avadhyo 'yaṁ dehe sarvasya bhārata

Ch.2 v.30 tasmāt sarvāṇi bhūtāni na tvaṁ śocitum arhasi

O Arjuna, the dehi within the deha of all beings cannot be harmed in any way. Therefore, you should not grieve for the passing on of any being.

78 svadharmam api cāvekṣya na vikampitum arhasi

Ch.2 v.31 dharmyād dhi yuddhāc chreyo 'nyat kṣatriyasya na vidyate

Since your svadharma as a kshatriya is to fight to protect, honour, and support the lives of innocent beings, you should not fear or hesitate to fight in this battle.

79 yadṛcchayā copapannaṁ svargadvāram apāvṛtam

Ch.2 v.32 sukhinaḥ kṣatriyāḥ pārtha labhante yuddham īdṛśam

O Arjuna, the kshatriyas who give up their lives while fighting for a noble cause are very fortunate. They are immediately transferred through the door of Deva Loka, a sublime realm where they spend their next life in joyful pursuits.

80 atha cet tvam imaṁ dharmyaṁ saṁgrāmaṁ na kariṣyasi
Ch.2 v.33 tataḥ svadharmaṁ kīrtiṁ ca hitvā pāpam avāpsyasi

But if you do not fight on behalf of dharma in this conflict, you will go against your own svadharma and lose your fame and glory. At the same time, you will commit papa 'activities which produce pain' and that will lead to the bondage of negative cause and effect in future lives.

81 akīrtiṁ cāpi bhūtāni kathayiṣyanti te 'vyayām
Ch.2 v.34 saṁbhāvitasya cākīrtir maraṇād atiricyate

As a result of neglecting your svadharma, in the future people will only speak of your disgrace on the battlefield, which will ruin your reputation as an upholder of dharma. For an honourable person, such dishonour is a fate far worse than the death of their body.

82 bhayād raṇād uparataṁ maṁsyante tvāṁ mahārathāḥ
Ch.2 v.35 yeṣāṁ ca tvaṁ bahumato bhūtvā yāsyasi lāghavam

The great warriors who previously spoke highly of your character and abilities will assume you left the battlefield out of cowardice. They will deride you and never again speak of you with respect.

83 avācyavādāṁś ca bahūn vadiṣyanti tavāhitāḥ
Ch.2 v.36 nindantas tava sāmarthyaṁ tato duḥkhataraṁ nu kim

Your enemies will also ridicule you with harsh words and denigrate your ability. As a noble warrior and protector of truth, what could be more humiliating for you?

84
Ch.2 v.37

hato vā prāpsyasi svargaṁ jitvā vā bhokṣyase mahīm
tasmād uttiṣṭha kaunteya yuddhāya kṛtaniścayaḥ

Listen Arjuna! Either your body will be killed in battle and you will ascend to the joys of Deva Loka, or you will triumph in battle and establish an honourable life here on Bhumi Loka 'Mother Earth'. Therefore, uttishta 'stand up' and fight!

85
Ch.2 v.38

sukhaduḥkhe same kṛtvā lābhālābhau jayājayau
tato yuddhāya yujyasva naivaṁ pāpam avāpsyasi

Treat happiness and distress, gain and loss, victory and defeat as if they are all the same. Let this conflict be your yoga and you will not create papa.

86
Ch.2 v.39

eṣā te 'bhihitā sāṁkhye buddhir yoge tv imāṁ śṛṇu
buddhyā yukto yayā pārtha karmabandhaṁ prahāsyasi

This yoga of discernment that I am sharing with you is called sankhya, O Arjuna. Now hear from Me how through this buddhi yoga you can be freed from the binding effects of karma generated by action within matter.

87
Ch.2 v.40

nehābhikramanāśo 'sti pratyavāyo na vidyate
svalpam apy asya dharmasya trāyate mahato bhayāt

First of all, the results of buddhi yoga practice are never lost, in this or future lives. Even a little of this sanatana dharma action protects one from the dangers of future harmful karmic reactions.

88 vyavasāyātmikā buddhir ekeha kurunandana
Ch.2 v.41 bahuśākhā hy anantāś ca buddhayo 'vyavasāyinām

In this buddhi yoga process, the discerning faculty is constantly held with a one-pointed focus upon the atma, whereas the attention of unfocused persons is many-branched and wanders endlessly upon the temporary pathways of material thought.

89 yām imāṁ puṣpitāṁ vācaṁ pravadanty avipaścitaḥ
Ch.2 v.42 vedavādaratāḥ pārtha nānyad astīti vādinaḥ

Most humans mistake the ultimate purpose of the vedic knowledge. They become confused by the flowery and poetic language, taking symbols and metaphors in a literal way and then conclude that rituals for material gain and harmony with nature are the final and ultimate vedic truth.

90 kāmātmānaḥ svargaparā janmakarmaphalapradām
Ch.2 v.43 kriyāviśeṣabahulāṁ bhogaiśvaryagatiṁ prati

Because their atma is still distorted by the karmas of unfulfilled material desires on Earth, they perform a variety of superficial vedic rituals, hoping to achieve their wished-for goal of intense pleasures in Svarga Loka, which is merely a higher material realm.

91 bhogaiśvaryaprasaktānāṁ tayāpahṛtacetasām
Ch.2 v.44 vyavasāyātmikā buddhiḥ samādhau na vidhīyate

For those attached to enjoying material pleasures, their immortal potential is distorted and stolen away. As a result, they do not have the discernment to see their atma or taste the greater pleasures of the highest states of transcendental samadhi.

92
Ch.2 v.45

traiguṇyaviṣayā vedā nistraiguṇyo bhavārjuna
nirdvaṁdvo nityasattvastho niryogakṣema ātmavān

The vedic rituals are mostly concerned with the three gunas and with managing our relationship with matter to achieve temporary material comfort. O Arjuna, redirect your desires from this acquisitive hunger for superficial pleasure. Instead, free yourself from duality, be true to your atma, and live in the world as an immortal being.

93
Ch.2 v.46

yāvān artha udapāne sarvataḥ saṁplutodake
tāvān sarveṣu vedeṣu brāhmaṇasya vijānataḥ

Just as there is no need to dig a well when fresh water is flowing everywhere, so one who knows the pleasures of Brahman 'the transcendental realm beyond matter from where we come' does not need to seek material pleasure separately through means of the vedic rituals.

94
Ch.2 v.47

karmaṇy evādhikāras te mā phaleṣu kadā cana
mā karmaphalahetur bhūr mā te saṅgo 'stv akarmaṇi

Because you have free will, you can control your actions, but you are never in control of the fruit or ultimate outcome of what you do. Therefore, never let attachment to the fruits be the ultimate reason for your actions. Conversely, do not simply retreat into a state of detached inaction.

95
Ch.2 v.48

yogasthaḥ kuru karmāṇi saṅgaṁ tyaktvā dhanaṁjaya
siddhyasiddhyoḥ samo bhūtvā samatvaṁ yoga ucyate

Instead, perform all your actions in a state of yogic awareness, without attachment to the result, undisturbed by pursuing siddhis 'perfections' or avoiding asiddhi 'imperfection' in whatever you do. It is said that such balanced consciousness is called karma yoga.

96 Ch.2 v.49
dūreṇa hy avaraṁ karma buddhiyogād dhanaṁjaya
buddhau śaraṇam anviccha kṛpaṇāḥ phalahetavaḥ

Listen, Arjuna, buddhi yoga is greatly superior to mere material actions. Take refuge in loving surrender to the wise discernment of the buddhi faculty. Those whose karmas are only based on the logic of obtaining the fruits of material action are selfish and become kripanas 'miserly beings clinging to inert matter'.

97 Ch.2 v.50
buddhiyukto jahātīha ubhe sukṛtaduṣkṛte
tasmād yogāya yujyasva yogaḥ karmasu kauśalam

One who is permanently linked to the buddhi faculty goes beyond the relativity of sukha and dukha as the determiner of what they do. Therefore, connect with your atma through yoga, and that yoga will restore harmony and balance to all your actions.

98 Ch.2 v.51
karmajaṁ buddhiyuktā hi phalaṁ tyaktvā manīṣiṇaḥ
janmabandhavinirmuktāḥ padaṁ gacchanty anāmayam

Those wise yogis who always act in the discernment of buddhi yoga and who have released their attachment to the karma phala 'results of their actions' are mukta 'liberated from the bondage to continued rebirth'. Their consciousness resides forever in that transcendental pada 'realm' of Mine where hunger is never felt again.

99 Ch.2 v.52
yadā te mohakalilaṁ buddhir vyatitariṣyati
tadā gantāsi nirvedaṁ śrotavyasya śrutasya ca

When the clarity of your awakened buddhi carries you beyond the dense forest of material illusions, then you will no longer be disturbed by what you have heard in the past or will hear in the future.

100
Ch.2 v.53

śrutivipratipannā te yadā sthāsyati niścalā
samādhāv acalā buddhis tadā yogam avāpsyasi

When your buddhi remains steady and unwavering in meditation upon your atma 'true self', you will no longer be distracted with the details of vedic rituals. Then, absorbed in samadhi, you will directly perceive your true nature and achieve the perfection of buddhi yoga.

101
Ch.2 v.54

arjuna uvāca
sthitaprajñasya kā bhāṣā samādhisthasya keśava
sthitadhīḥ kiṁ prabhāṣeta kim āsīta vrajeta kim

ARJUNA enquired:
Tell me, O Krishna, how do we recognize someone who has direct realization of this yogic awareness of the transcendental Brahman and who is unwavering in deep samadhi? How do they sit, how do they speak, and how do they move through life?

102
Ch.2 v.55

śrībhagavān uvāca
prajahāti yadā kāmān sarvān pārtha manogatān
ātmany evātmanā tuṣṭaḥ sthitaprajñas tadocyate

SHRI BHAGAVAN replied:
When one is completely unaffected by any material desires resulting from the thoughts of their manas, when their atma is entirely satisfied simply by being the atma, then it is said that their self-realization is steady.

103
Ch.2 v.56

duḥkheṣv anudvignamanāḥ sukheṣu vigataspṛhaḥ
vītarāgabhayakrodhaḥ sthitadhīr munir ucyate

A person whose manas is not disturbed in times of dukha 'pain'; who is not controlled by the need for sukha 'pleasure'; who has overcome all attachment, fear, and anger; and whose focus upon their atma is always steady is called a muni.

104 yaḥ sarvatrānabhisnehas tat tat prāpya śubhāśubham
Ch.2 v.57 nābhinandati na dveṣṭi tasya prajñā pratiṣṭhitā

One who is immune to desires for all material things, whether pleasing or displeasing, and who neither likes nor dislikes anything is steady in prajna 'the unfluctuating awareness of both the atma and Brahman'.

105 yadā saṁharate cāyaṁ kūrmo 'ṅgānīva sarvaśaḥ
Ch.2 v.58 indriyāṇīndriyārthebhyas tasya prajñā pratiṣṭhitā

When the muni can completely withdraw the dasha indriyas 'ten senses' from their desired objects, just like a turtle pulls its limbs into its shell, then they are firmly established in prajna.

106 viṣayā vinivartante nirāhārasya dehinaḥ
Ch.2 v.59 rasavarjaṁ raso 'py asya paraṁ dṛṣṭvā nivartate

When the objects of the senses no longer compel a person to have contact with them, still the memory of past pleasures and experiences remains. But even that memory is removed for one who has had a direct vision of the Supreme reality.

107 yatato hy api kaunteya puruṣasya vipaścitaḥ
Ch.2 v.60 indriyāṇi pramāthīni haranti prasabhaṁ manaḥ

Listen Arjuna, the hungry, turbulent, and insatiable indriyas 'senses' can carry away the manas even of a wise person who is striving to control them.

108 tāni sarvāṇi saṁyamya yukta āsīta matparaḥ
Ch.2 v.61 vaśe hi yasyendriyāṇi tasya prajñā pratiṣṭhitā

Therefore, disciplined in yoga, one should sit and meditate upon me as the Parama 'Ultimate and Highest Supreme'. The possessor of prajna should stand firm, controlling their indriyas 'senses'.

109 Ch.2 v.62
dhyāyato viṣayān puṁsaḥ saṅgas teṣūpajāyate
saṅgāt saṁjāyate kāmaḥ kāmāt krodho 'bhijāyate

While contemplating the objects of the senses, attachment to them is born. From such attachment, intense desires arise. From unfulfilled desires, the seeds of anger appear.

110 Ch.2 v.63
krodhād bhavati saṁmohaḥ saṁmohāt smṛtivibhramaḥ
smṛtibhraṁśād buddhināśo buddhināśāt praṇaśyati

From unrestrained anger, delusion arises. From this delusion, memory is lost. When memory is lost, discernment is lost. When discernment is lost, this leads to harmful or destructive actions.

111 Ch.2 v.64
rāgadveṣaviyuktais tu viṣayān indriyaiś caran
ātmavaśyair vidheyātmā prasādam adhigacchati

When the atma controls the indriyas 'material senses' and when one no longer experiences compulsive attachment or aversion to the objects of the senses, then the atma attains a tranquil, divine state known as prasada.

112 Ch.2 v.65
prasāde sarvaduḥkhānāṁ hānir asyopajāyate
prasannacetaso hy āśu buddhiḥ paryavatiṣṭhate

That state of prasada removes all pain and misery, and from it, a deep sense of tranquillity arises. In that balanced state of manas, the buddhi stands steady always.

113 Ch.2 v.66
nāsti buddhir ayuktasya na cāyuktasya bhāvanā
na cābhāvayataḥ śāntir aśāntasya kutaḥ sukham

When the buddhi is not connected with the atma, and when the manas is not steady, there is no shanti. Without shanti, how can there be lasting sukha?

114 indriyāṇāṁ hi caratāṁ yan mano 'nuvidhīyate
Ch.2 v.67 tad asya harati prajñāṁ vāyur nāvam ivāmbhasi

When the manas runs after the objects of the wandering indriyas 'senses', they carry away one's prajna, exactly as a ship on the water is driven by a strong wind.

115 tasmād yasya mahābāho nigṛhītāni sarvaśaḥ
Ch.2 v.68 indriyāṇīndriyārthebhyas tasya prajñā pratiṣṭhitā

Therefore, Arjuna, one who can restrain the indriyas from the compelling attraction of the objects of the senses is able to stand firm in their prajna 'unfluctuating awareness of both the atma and Brahman'.

116 yā niśā sarvabhūtānāṁ tasyāṁ jāgarti saṁyamī
Ch.2 v.69 yasyāṁ jāgrati bhūtāni sā niśā paśyato muneḥ

Those who can control their indriyas are enlightened and aware, while those with uncontrolled senses are still asleep to what is happening. And so, even when the uncontrolled appear to be awake, the wise muni knows that they are asleep, dreaming, and unconsciously driven by matter.

āpūryamāṇam acalapratiṣṭhaṁ; samudram āpaḥ
117 praviśanti yadvat
Ch.2 v.70 tadvat kāmā yaṁ praviśanti sarve; sa śāntim āpnoti na
kāmakāmī

Just as the ocean remains undisturbed by the constant flood of rivers, so one who has achieved shanti is unaffected by the influx of external material desires, while the unrestrained are always disturbed by endless currents of kama 'sense desires'.

118 vihāya kāmān yaḥ sarvān pumāṁś carati niḥspṛhaḥ
Ch.2 v.71 nirmamo nirahaṁkāraḥ sa śāntim adhigacchati

The person who sheds all material kama, whose actions are not determined by material longings, who says 'nothing is mine and I am not from matter,' that person attains shanti.

119 eṣā brāhmī sthitiḥ pārtha naināṁ prāpya vimuhyati
Ch.2 v.72 sthitvāsyām antakāle 'pi brahmanirvāṇam ṛcchati

O Arjuna, if one does not become steady in Brahman realization, then they will continue to be confused by matter. But if a yogi is standing as a being of Brahman when they leave their body, then they achieve the state of Brahman nirvana.

Chapter 3

Karma Yoga as Correct Action in the World

120
Ch.3 v.1

arjuna uvāca
jyāyasī cet karmaṇas te matā buddhir janārdana
tat kiṁ karmaṇi ghore māṁ niyojayasi keśava

ARJUNA said:
O Krishna, if it is your opinion that enlightened introspection through the discerning use of buddhi is the best process of yoga, then why do you ask me to engage in this ghastly conflict?

121
Ch.3 v.2

vyāmiśreṇaiva vākyena buddhiṁ mohayasīva me
tad ekaṁ vada niścitya yena śreyo 'ham āpnuyām

Your contradictory instructions have confused my buddhi. Tell me the one best path of yoga by which I can attain the highest outcome.

122
Ch.3 v.3

śrībhagavān uvāca
loke 'smin dvividhā niṣṭhā purā proktā mayānagha
jñānayogena sāṁkhyānāṁ karmayogena yoginām

SHRI BHAGAVAN said:
There are two methods of achieving self-perfection that I have taught since time immemorial. The first is jnana yoga of the sankhya darshan, which is pursued by those inclined to analytical thinking. The second is karma yoga, which is pursued by those inclined to action.

123
Ch.3 v.4

na karmaṇām anārambhān naiṣkarmyaṁ puruṣo 'śnute
na ca saṁnyasanād eva siddhiṁ samadhigacchati

One cannot avoid karma simply by giving up action, nor does one attain perfection by taking sannyasa and entering into a monastery.

124 na hi kaś cit kṣaṇam api jātu tiṣṭhaty akarmakṛt
Ch.3 v.5 kāryate hy avaśaḥ karma sarvaḥ prakṛtijair guṇaiḥ

No one can exist even for a moment without acting and receiving the karma of their actions. Everyone is within the grasp of prakriti and is forced to act because of the constant fluctuations of the gunas.

125 karmendriyāṇi saṁyamya ya āste manasā smaran
Ch.3 v.6 indriyārthān vimūḍhātmā mithyācāraḥ sa ucyate

One who controls the karma indriyas 'active senses' by practice of the yamas 'restraining oneself from all harmful actions', but whose manas still remembers the past pleasures of the indriya arthas 'sense objects', has only partially perfected their yoga.

126 yas tv indriyāṇi manasā niyamyārabhate 'rjuna
Ch.3 v.7 karmendriyaiḥ karmayogam asaktaḥ sa viśiṣyate

However, O Arjuna, one who also controls the karma indriyas 'active senses' with the manas by means of the niyamas 'behaviours that lead to self-realization' and without attachment to the results of their actions is a superior practitioner of karma yoga.

127 niyataṁ kuru karma tvaṁ karma jyāyo hy akarmaṇaḥ
Ch.3 v.8 śarīrayātrāpi ca te na prasidhyed akarmaṇaḥ

Therefore, perform the karmas 'actions' appropriate to your particular nature and stage of life, for action is better than inaction. After all, without working, you cannot even maintain your body.

128
Ch.3 v.9

yajñārthāt karmaṇo 'nyatra loko 'yaṁ karmabandhanaḥ
tadarthaṁ karma kaunteya muktasaṅgaḥ samācara

And remember, Arjuna, all karmas that are not performed as yajna 'actions dedicated to universal co-operation' lead to karma bandhana 'bondage due to negative cause and effect resulting from action'. Therefore, perform all actions as a yajna and you will be freed from the bondage of cause and effect.

129
Ch.3 v.10

sahayajñāḥ prajāḥ sṛṣṭvā purovāca prajāpatiḥ
anena prasaviṣyadhvam eṣa vo 'stv iṣṭakāmadhuk

At the beginning of the universe, Prajapati 'the first created being', who is also known as Brahma/Saraswati, created everything and then educated humans about the methods of yajna 'the process of give and take between humans and devas to effect balance in the context of the laws of nature'. At that time, Prajapati said, "May this co-operative process of divine yajna be an ishta kamadhuk 'desire-fulfilling cow of plenty' giving you all that you need for material life."

130
Ch.3 v.11

devān bhāvayatānena te devā bhāvayantu vaḥ
parasparaṁ bhāvayantaḥ śreyaḥ param avāpsyatha

Prajapati continued, "If you show your appreciation to and work in harmony with the devas who are the maintainers of the laws of nature through this interactive process of yajna 'sacred offering', then those devas will endow you with health, well-being, and everything beneficial. May humans and devas cherish and foster one another."

131 iṣṭān bhogān hi vo devā dāsyante yajñabhāvitāḥ
Ch.3 v.12 tair dattān apradāyaibhyo yo bhuṅkte stena eva saḥ

The devas are nourished when humans perform yajna of all kinds, just as human desires for material pleasures are fulfilled by those ishas or devas. But those humans who receive the benefits of material nature without performing yajna are certainly behaving as thieves.

132 yajñaśiṣṭāśinaḥ santo mucyante sarvakilbiṣaiḥ
Ch.3 v.13 bhuñjate te tv aghaṁ pāpā ye pacanty ātmakāraṇāt

Those who eat food that was first offered to the ishas as a yajna do not receive the negative reactions from the harm and suffering caused by obtaining the food. But the selfish who prepare food only for their own pleasure also unknowingly eat the negative reactions caused by obtaining the food.

133 annād bhavanti bhūtāni parjanyād annasaṁbhavaḥ
Ch.3 v.14 yajñād bhavati parjanyo yajñaḥ karmasamudbhavaḥ

From food, all human beings come into existence; from rain, all food comes to be. Rainfall is produced by the performance of yajna to the devas, and yajnas were designed to balance human consumption of natural resources with their production by the devas.

134 karma brahmodbhavaṁ viddhi
Ch.3 v.15 brahmākṣarasamudbhavam
tasmāt sarvagataṁ brahma nityaṁ yajñe pratiṣṭhitam

The rules of dharmic actions emanate from Brahman as the vedas. That all-pervading Brahman is continuously established through vedic yajna which aligns with the ritam. Therefore, the immortal Brahman is perpetually manifesting within prakriti through the performance of yajna.

Whatever actions are
performed by a great
dharmic leader or Acharya
'one who lives the noble
truths that they teach',
people are inspired to
imitate their actions,
and whatever standards
they set by their personal
example, the whole
world pursues.–140

135 evaṁ pravartitaṁ cakraṁ nānuvartayatīha yaḥ
Ch.3 v.16 aghāyur indriyārāmo moghaṁ pārtha sa jīvati

If one lives on Bhumi Loka 'Mother Earth', O Arjuna, receiving benefits from the turning wheel of the seasons, but does not give back to restore the ecological balance of nature, they live only to please their indriyas 'senses'. They are selfish and ungrateful, and they eventually cause harm to themselves and the world.

136 yas tv ātmaratir eva syād ātmatṛptaś ca mānavaḥ
Ch.3 v.17 ātmany eva ca saṁtuṣṭas tasya kāryaṁ na vidyate

One who is atma rati 'in a state of divine pleasure from their true self' and is atma tripta 'enlightened from within', as well as atma santushta 'entirely content with their own self' is no longer compelled to any external material action.

137 naiva tasya kṛtenārtho nākṛteneha kaś cana
Ch.3 v.18 na cāsya sarvabhūteṣu kaś cid arthavyapāśrayaḥ

Their internal experience of satisfaction does not depend upon anyone or anything external, so they are not compelled to any action as the source of their pleasure.

138 tasmād asaktaḥ satataṁ kāryaṁ karma samācara
Ch.3 v.19 asakto hy ācaran karma param āpnoti pūruṣaḥ

Therefore, always engage in the action that is appropriate to the situation with no attachment to the outcome. The person who performs their karmas in this way eventually goes to the param dhama 'supreme and ultimate abode, Brahman'.

139 karmaṇaiva hi saṁsiddhim āsthitā janakādayaḥ
Ch.3 v.20 lokasaṁgraham evāpi saṁpaśyan kartum arhasi

In previous times, the great ruler Maharaja Janaka, and after him many other noble leaders, achieved perfection by performing karma yoga. Like them, everyone should act unselfishly for the sake of loka samgraha 'holding the world together for the well-being of all'.

140 yad yad ācarati śreṣṭhas tat tad evetaro janaḥ
Ch.3 v.21 sa yat pramāṇaṁ kurute lokas tad anuvartate

Whatever actions are performed by a great dharmic leader or acharya 'one who lives the noble truths that they teach', people are inspired to imitate their actions, and whatever standards they set by their personal example, the whole world pursues.

141 na me pārthāsti kartavyaṁ triṣu lokeṣu kiṁ cana
Ch.3 v.22 nānavāptam avāptavyaṁ varta eva ca karmaṇi

My dear Arjuna, in all the trilokas 'three cosmic realms', there is no object that I seek to attain and there is nothing that I am compelled to do. Still, I continue to act.

142 yadi hy ahaṁ na varteyaṁ jātu karmaṇy atandritaḥ
Ch.3 v.23 mama vartmānuvartante manuṣyāḥ pārtha sarvaśaḥ

If I refused to act for the benefit of all, even though as the Supreme Being I have the power to do so, then manushas 'human beings' everywhere would follow My example.

143
Ch.3 v.24

utsīdeyur ime lokā na kuryāṁ karma ced aham
saṁkarasya ca kartā syām upahanyām imāḥ prajāḥ

If I did not perform the necessary and balanced karmas 'actions', then all these lokas would collapse. I would be the cause of great confusion and all living beings would perish.

144
Ch.3 v.25

saktāḥ karmaṇy avidvāṁso yathā kurvanti bhārata
kuryād vidvāṁs tathāsaktaś cikīrṣur lokasaṁgraham

Listen Arjuna, those who do not understand, perform their karmas attached to a selfish and limited outcome, while those who practice karma yoga do not cling to a particular self-serving result. Therefore, whenever you act on your own behalf, also remain focused on loka samgraha 'the greater well-being of all living entities'.

145
Ch.3 v.26

na buddhibhedaṁ janayed ajñānāṁ karmasaṅginām
joṣayet sarvakarmāṇi vidvān yuktaḥ samācaran

In addition, an enlightened practitioner of karma yoga should not disrupt or argue with those whose buddhi is still fragmented and attached only to selfish outcomes. Instead, they should encourage and teach others by the personal example of their own unselfish actions.

146
Ch.3 v.27

prakṛteḥ kriyamāṇāni guṇaiḥ karmāṇi sarvaśaḥ
ahaṁkāravimūḍhātmā kartāham iti manyate

All actions instigated by human beings within prakriti are impelled first by the forces of the three gunas. This is because when the atma is bewildered by the faculty of ahamkara, they mistakenly think, "I am my body, and I am the sole creator and controller of the final results of my actions."

147 tattvavit tu mahābāho guṇakarmavibhāgayoḥ
Ch.3 v.28 guṇā guṇeṣu vartanta iti matvā na sajjate

O Arjuna, one who understands how the three gunas function within matter also realizes that the compulsive attractions of our body for desirable objects are in fact created by the gunas. Therefore, those who are thoughtful say to themselves, 'The truth is, the gunas of my senses are merely attracted by the gunas of their objects.' As a result, they themselves remain detached from such material compulsions.

148 prakṛter guṇasaṁmūḍhāḥ sajjante guṇakarmasu
Ch.3 v.29 tān akṛtsnavido mandān kṛtsnavin na vicālayet

Those who are sincere but are still unaware of the distorting effects of the gunas continue to act by compulsion. Therefore, those who do understand should be careful in educating those who do not yet understand, so that the necessary actions and responsibilities of their lives are not disrupted.

149 mayi sarvāṇi karmāṇi saṁnyasyādhyātmacetasā
Ch.3 v.30 nirāśīr nirmamo bhūtvā yudhyasva vigatajvaraḥ

Dedicate all your actions to Me, meditate upon Me as the original and all-pervading Supreme Atma, give up all desires and selfish motives, declare that nothing material belongs to you, and with the fever and confusion caused by this conflict entirely gone, abandon your lethargy—act in your svadharma and fight!

150 ye me matam idaṁ nityam anutiṣṭhanti mānavāḥ
Ch.3 v.31 śraddhāvanto 'nasūyanto mucyante te 'pi karmabhiḥ

When human beings remain constant in this teaching of mine, standing steady for it, always seeing Me everywhere while focused in a state of shraddha and never resenting My supreme influence, then they are released from the negative karmic reactions from all they do.

151 ye tv etad abhyasūyanto nānutiṣṭhanti me matam
Ch.3 v.32 sarvajñānavimūḍhāṁs tān viddhi naṣṭān acetasaḥ

But those who are against this jnana that I am teaching, and do not put it into practice in their lives, have lost their discernment and live in a state of constant confusion.

152 sadṛśaṁ ceṣṭate svasyāḥ prakṛter jñānavān api
Ch.3 v.33 prakṛtiṁ yānti bhūtāni nigrahaḥ kiṁ kariṣyati

Every being within matter has a specific prakriti, a body type that must be expressed. No amount of knowledge can change this intrinsic genetic structure. What, then, will one gain by fighting against their unique material nature?

153 indriyasyendriyasyārthe rāgadveṣau vyavasthitau
Ch.3 v.34 tayor na vaśam āgacchet tau hy asya paripanthinau

By our nature, the senses are automatically raga or dvesha 'attracted to or repulsed by' various material objects. One should not come under the control of either of these impulses.

154 śreyān svadharmo viguṇaḥ paradharmāt svanuṣṭhitāt
Ch.3 v.35 svadharme nidhanaṁ śreyaḥ paradharmo bhayāvahaḥ

It is better to follow your own svadharma imperfectly than to follow another's path perfectly. Death as the result of being true to one's svadharma is preferable to any outcome that might be achieved by going against it.

155 arjuna uvāca
Ch.3 v.36 atha kena prayukto 'yaṁ pāpaṁ carati pūruṣaḥ
anicchann api vārṣṇeya balād iva niyojitaḥ

ARJUNA then asked:
O Krishna, what is the force that compels a person to perform actions that are papa 'in violation of the laws of nature'?

156 śrībhagavān uvāca
Ch.3 v.37 kāma eṣa krodha eṣa rajoguṇasamudbhavaḥ
mahāśano mahāpāpmā viddhy enam iha vairiṇam

SHRI BHAGAVAN replied:
When unfulfilled desire is transformed into krodha 'anger' and is fuelled by the hungers of raja guna, it produces an all-consuming and destructive force that drives humans to cause papa. Know this to be the unseen enemy of all.

157 dhūmenāvriyate vahnir yathādarśo malena ca
Ch.3 v.38 yatholbenāvṛto garbhas tathā tenedam āvṛtam

Just as a fire is covered by smoke, a mirror is covered by dust, or an embryo is covered by the womb, so varying degrees of material energy constantly distort the discerning faculty of human perception.

158 āvṛtaṁ jñānam etena jñānino nityavairiṇā
Ch.3 v.39 kāmarūpeṇa kaunteya duṣpūreṇānaleṇa ca

O Arjuna, even the wisest of jnana yogis are sometimes overcome by kama rupa 'the endless forms of material desire' that are the perpetual enemy of all truth seekers and which are as insatiable as a blazing fire.

159 indriyāṇi mano buddhir asyādhiṣṭhānam ucyate
Ch.3 v.40 etair vimohayaty eṣa jñānam āvṛtya dehinam

The indriyas, the manas, and the buddhi are the hiding places of these distorted desires which bewilder the dehi 'immortal self', obscure its true nature, and act as its enemy by compelling it to perform degrading and self-destructive material behaviours.

160 tasmāt tvam indriyāṇy ādau niyamyanamerṣabha
Ch.3 v.41 pāpmānaṁ prajahihy enaṁ jñānavijñānanāśanam

Therefore, Arjuna, you must first assert control over the bodily senses by the enlightening principles of the niyamas. Then, you must systematically remove any desires that could lead to committing papa, which eventually causes the destruction of both jnana and vijnana.

161 indriyāṇi parāṇy āhur indriyebhyaḥ paraṁ manaḥ
Ch.3 v.42 manasas tu parā buddhir yo buddheḥ paratas tu saḥ

The bodily senses are superior to matter; manas is superior to the bodily senses; buddhi is superior to manas; and the true self is superior to buddhi.

162
Ch.3 v.43

evaṁ buddheḥ paraṁ buddhvā saṁstabhyātmānam ātmanā
jahi śatruṁ mahābāho kāmarūpaṁ durāsadam

In this way, use your atma's discernment to strengthen your buddhi; then use your atma to steady your atma. And finally, O mighty-armed Arjuna, with that strength, destroy the insatiable enemy kama rupa 'the endless forms of material desire'.

Chapter 4

Creation, Yugas and the Descent of Vedic Wisdom

163
Ch.4 v.1

śrībhagavān uvāca
imaṁ vivasvate yogaṁ proktavān aham avyayam
vivasvān manave prāha manur ikṣvākave 'bravīt

SHRI BHAGAVAN said:
I originally spoke this knowledge to Vivasvan, the current deva of Surya 'the Sun'. Vivasvan then taught it to his son Vaivasvata, the current Manu, who in turn spoke it to the ancient human king, Ikshvaku.

164
Ch.4 v.2

evaṁ paramparāprāptam imaṁ rājarṣayo viduḥ
sa kāleneha mahatā yogo naṣṭaḥ paraṁtapa

In this way, Arjuna, this supreme knowledge of yoga was passed down from one generation to the next by human kings who were both leaders and seers of the vedic knowledge. But over a long period of time, these yogic teachings were lost.

165
Ch.4 v.3

sa evāyaṁ mayā te 'dya yogaḥ proktaḥ purātanaḥ
bhakto 'si me sakhā ceti rahasyaṁ hy etad uttamam

Therefore, today I am again transmitting that ancient body of yogic knowledge to you, because you have chosen to hear from me in the mood of bhakti 'devotion' and because you are My very dear friend. This rahasya 'secret' teaching is also uttama 'from beyond the realms of matter'.

166
Ch.4 v.4

arjuna uvāca
aparaṁ bhavato janma paraṁ janma vivasvataḥ
katham etad vijānīyāṁ tvam ādau proktavān iti

ARJUNA enquired:
O Bhagavan, the deva of the Sun, Vivasvan, came into being millions of years ago. How is it possible that you spoke this vedic knowledge to him at that time?

167 śrībhagavān uvāca
bahūni me vyatītāni janmāni tava cārjuna
Ch.4 v.5 tāny ahaṁ veda sarvāṇi na tvaṁ vettha paraṁtapa

SHRI BHAGAVAN replied:
O Arjuna, both you and I have had many, many births. The difference between us is that I, as the Supreme Being, remember the details of all of them, whereas you cannot.

168 ajo 'pi sann avyayātmā bhūtānām īśvaro 'pi san
Ch.4 v.6 prakṛtiṁ svām adhiṣṭhāya saṁbhavāmy ātmamāyayā

I am never born. Instead, I merely appear within matter as My immortal self. Because I am the Supreme Master of all beings and the Supreme Atma, I appear at will because I have complete control over prakriti 'the material energy'.

169 yadā yadā hi dharmasya glānir bhavati bhārata
Ch.4 v.7 abhyutthānam adharmasya tadātmānaṁ sṛjāmy aham

O Arjuna, whenever there is a dramatic decline in dharma and a dangerous increase in adharma, I descend and manifest myself within matter as an avatar.

170 paritrāṇāya sādhūnāṁ vināśāya ca duṣkṛtām
Ch.4 v.8 dharmasaṁsthāpanārthāya saṁbhavāmi yuge yuge

From yuga to yuga, I descend to Earth in various forms in order to protect those who are seekers of truth, to destroy the malicious and harmful beings, and to re-establish the principles of dharma. By so doing, I restore the balance of material nature for the benefit of all beings on Earth.

171
Ch.4 v.9

janma karma ca me divyam evaṁ yo vetti tattvataḥ
tyaktvā dehaṁ punarjanma naiti mām eti so 'rjuna

Listen, Arjuna, anyone who understands and accepts the truth of My descent immediately comes to Me at the death of their body and is never forced to take birth again.

172
Ch.4 v.10

vītarāgabhayakrodhā manmayā mām upāśritāḥ
bahavo jñānatapasā pūtā madbhāvam āgatāḥ

Those who have overcome the effects of compulsive material desires, fear, and anger; whose manas is focused entirely upon Me; and who are completely purified by jnana and tapasya attain to mad bhava 'the state of being that is the same as My divine nature'.

173
Ch.4 v.11

ye yathā māṁ prapadyante tāṁs tathaiva bhajāmy aham
mama vartmānuvartante manuṣyāḥ pārtha sarvaśaḥ

In whatever state of being a person approaches Me, bhajami aham 'I reciprocate and establish a relationship with them in that mood'. In fact, everyone already has a relationship with Me, even if they are unaware of its exact nature.

174
Ch.4 v.12

kāṅkṣantaḥ karmaṇāṁ siddhiṁ yajanta iha devatāḥ
kṣipraṁ hi mānuṣe loke siddhir bhavati karmajā

Those humans who are only hungry for material benefits perform a yajna of some kind, making an offering to the devas, but only motivated to perfect their material condition. Those ritualized actions do result in success and bring them material fulfillment quickly.

175 cāturvarṇyaṁ mayā sṛṣṭaṁ guṇakarmavibhāgaśaḥ
Ch.4 v.13 tasya kartāram api māṁ viddhy akartāram avyayam

The four varnas were originally created by me as a way of distributing responsibility and material empowerment throughout the social body. Each person is suited for a specific occupation according to their energetic state and inherent abilities. Even though I originally created this system, I am not directly involved in the details of its workings.

176 na māṁ karmāṇi limpanti na me karmaphale spṛhā
Ch.4 v.14 iti māṁ yo 'bhijānāti karmabhir na sa badhyate

My karma 'action within material nature' does not bind me in any way because I am not attached to the results of what I do. Therefore, anyone who acts in the same way that I do will no longer be bound by the stringent rules of karma.

177 evaṁ jñātvā kṛtaṁ karma pūrvair api mumukṣubhiḥ
Ch.4 v.15 kuru karmaiva tasmāt tvaṁ pūrvaiḥ pūrvataraṁ kṛtam

Since the very beginning of human life, the ancients seeking moksha 'ultimate freedom from the reactions to their karma' acted in this way. Therefore, perform your actions just as the ancients did.

178 kiṁ karma kim akarmeti kavayo 'py atra mohitāḥ
Ch.4 v.16 tat te karma pravakṣyāmi yaj jñātvā mokṣyase 'śubhāt

What is karma 'action' and what is akarma 'inaction'? Even the ancient seers who compiled the vedas were sometimes confused on this subject. So, now I will explain karma to you so that you achieve moksha 'freedom from the negative reactions to all your actions'.

179 karmaṇo hy api boddhavyaṁ boddhavyaṁ ca vikarmaṇaḥ
Ch.4 v.17 akarmaṇaś ca boddhavyaṁ gahanā karmaṇo gatiḥ

The intricacies of karma are difficult to understand. One should be able to discern the subtle differences between correct action, inaction, and forbidden action.

180 karmaṇy akarma yaḥ paśyed akarmaṇi ca karma yaḥ
Ch.4 v.18 sa buddhimān manuṣyeṣu sa yuktaḥ kṛtsnakarmakṛt

One who perceives inaction in action, and action in inaction, has mastered the subtleties of material cause and effect. This state of awakened buddhi 'highly refined discernment' is characteristic of a perfected yogi.

181 yasya sarve samārambhāḥ kāmasaṁkalpavarjitāḥ
Ch.4 v.19 jñānāgnidagdhakarmāṇaṁ tam āhuḥ paṇḍitaṁ budhāḥ

When a person's actions are free of selfish desires and ulterior motives, the reactions to their actions are immediately burned up in the fire of perfected knowing. Those who have achieved this state are known as pandita buddha.

182 tyaktvā karmaphalāsaṅgaṁ nityatṛpto nirāśrayaḥ
Ch.4 v.20 karmaṇy abhipravṛtto 'pi naiva kiṁ cit karoti saḥ

One who no longer clings to the fruits of their actions, who is always satisfied and is not dependent upon circumstance, even when apparently acting, in fact does nothing at all.

183 nirāśīr yatacittātmā tyaktasarvaparigrahaḥ
Ch.4 v.21 śārīraṁ kevalaṁ karma kurvan nāpnoti kilbiṣam

If one sees themself as the atma, performing all actions as if they are merely done by the body, with no desires, clear discernment, not grasping anything, and without acquisitive motives, then no karmic reactions are created.

184 yadṛcchālābhasaṁtuṣṭo dvaṁdvātīto vimatsaraḥ
Ch.4 v.22 samaḥ siddhāv asiddhau ca kṛtvāpi na nibadhyate

One who is satisfied with whatever they gain, who is unaffected by opposites within matter, who is not envious of others, and who is balanced in success or failure is not bound by the outcome of action.

185 gatasaṅgasya muktasya jñānāvasthitacetasaḥ
Ch.4 v.23 yajñāyācarataḥ karma samagraṁ pravilīyate

In this way, one who is freed from bondage to material cause and effect, who is established in the knowledge of their true self, and whose every action has become a yajna, also identifies themself with the supreme and ultimate state of being.

186 brahmārpaṇaṁ brahmahavir brahmāgnau brahmaṇā hutam
Ch.4 v.24 brahmaiva tena gantavyaṁ brahmakarmasamādhinā

Whatever is offered into agni 'the sacred fire' is Brahman. The ghee that is offered into the fire is Brahman. The fire itself is an extension of Brahman. The hutam 'smoke arising from the sacred offering' is also Brahman. And Brahman is what is attained by one who sees Brahman in everything they do.

187 daivam evāpare yajñaṁ yoginaḥ paryupāsate
brahmāgnāv apare yajñaṁ yajñenaivopajuhvati

Ch.4 v.25

Some yoga practitioners make a sacred offering to agni to please the devas. Others make a symbolic offering of their own atma into the immortal fire of Brahman itself.

188 śrotrādīnīndriyāṇy anye saṁyamāgniṣu juhvati
śabdādīn viṣayān anya indriyāgniṣu juhvati

Ch.4 v.26

Others build a fire within themselves by restraining their bodily senses, and there they burn the residues created by hearing and other sensory activities. Still others build a fire in their senses and burn sound and other objects of the senses as an offering to Brahman, represented by the agni burning within their body.

189 sarvāṇīndriyakarmāṇi prāṇakarmāṇi cāpare
ātmasaṁyamayogāgnau juhvati jñānadīpite

Ch.4 v.27

Other yogis offer all the activities of the ten senses, along with the vital prana from breathing, into the blazing fire of their own atma, whose sacred flames are constantly rekindled by the sparks of vedic knowledge.

190 dravyayajñās tapoyajñā yogayajñās tathāpare
svādhyāyajñānayajñāś ca yatayaḥ saṁśitavratāḥ

Ch.4 v.28

Some perform yajna by giving material substances to those in need. Some observe tapasya 'correct practices' in the diligent performance of ashtanga yoga as their yajna. Still others perform yajna through a vow of svadhyaya 'knowing one's true self through study of vedic knowledge'.

191 apāne juhvati prāṇaṁ prāṇe 'pānaṁ tathāpare
Ch.4 v.29 prāṇāpānagatī ruddhvā prāṇāyāmaparāyaṇāḥ

Some yogis perform yajna by offering the inhalation of prana 'breath' into the exhalation, and then the exhalation into the inhalation. They eventually achieve perfection through this pranayama yajna 'restraining the life force through breath control'.

192 apare niyatāhārāḥ prāṇān prāṇeṣu juhvati
Ch.4 v.30 sarve 'py ete yajñavido yajñakṣapitakalmaṣāḥ

Still others restrict their intake of food while offering each breath into the next, living directly on prana 'the universal life force'. All these yogic practitioners know and utilize the principles of yajna to remove the imperfections in their being.

193 yajñaśiṣṭāmṛtabhujo yānti brahma sanātanam
Ch.4 v.31 nāyaṁ loko 'sty ayajñasya kuto 'nyaḥ kurusattama

Those who only consume that which has first been offered to the devas eat amrita 'the nectar of immortality' and thereby enter into the timeless realm of Brahman. O Arjuna, even here on Bhumi Loka 'Mother Earth', no one can achieve material success without performing yajna and co-operating with the laws of nature, what to speak of attaining the ultimate destination.

194 evaṁ bahuvidhā yajñā vitatā brahmaṇo mukhe
Ch.4 v.32 karmajān viddhi tān sarvān evaṁ jñātvā vimokṣyase

Thus, through the many kinds of yajna, a wide variety of offerings are placed into the mouth of the transcendental Brahman. They are all born of various human actions. One who understands this will achieve moksha 'freedom from bondage to matter' through the performance of yajna.

Even if in the past you
were the most degraded
and hurtful person, lost
in ignorance and darkness,
this ship of yogic wisdom
will carry you to safety.–198

Therefore, with the sword
of divine knowledge and
the skills of yoga, cut away
the bonds of ignorance
and the doubts that have
occupied your heart.
Uttishta 'stand up'
O Arjuna, stand strong
as your true self
–the atma!–204

195 śreyān dravyamayād yajñāj jñānayajñaḥ paraṁtapa
Ch.4 v.33 sarvaṁ karmākhilaṁ pārtha jñāne parisamāpyate

But listen carefully, Arjuna, the yajna of cultivating jnana 'knowledge of the Supreme reality' is the ultimate yajna 'the offering of one's self to the Divine'. Such cultivation of jnana produces results that are far beyond what is possible through any material offering.

196 tad viddhi praṇipātena paripraśnena sevayā
Ch.4 v.34 upadekṣyanti te jñānaṁ jñāninas tattvadarśinaḥ

Just know this, O Arjuna, bow to the rishis and gurus who know the ultimate truth. Enquire from them with respectful questions, serve their efforts to share divine knowledge with the world, and through this process they will teach you jnana because they have tattva darshin 'the ability to see the truths that would otherwise remain unseen'.

197 yaj jñātvā na punar moham evaṁ yāsyasi pāṇḍava
Ch.4 v.35 yena bhūtāny aśeṣeṇa drakṣyasy ātmany atho mayi

Once you achieve that knowledge, you will never again fall into delusion. You will see all beings and yourself as the immortal atma and you will see that they are all within Me.

198 api ced asi pāpebhyaḥ sarvebhyaḥ pāpakṛttamaḥ
Ch.4 v.36 sarvaṁ jñānaplavenaiva vṛjinaṁ saṁtariṣyasi

Even if in the past you were the most degraded and hurtful person, lost in ignorance and darkness, this ship of yogic wisdom will carry you to safety.

199 yathaidhāṁsi samiddho 'gnir bhasmasāt kurute 'rjuna
Ch.4 v.37 jñānāgniḥ sarvakarmāṇi bhasmasāt kurute tathā

O Arjuna, just as a flame reduces firewood to ashes, so this jnana agni 'fire of transcendental knowledge' burns away the karmas resulting from material action.

200 na hi jñānena sadṛśaṁ pavitram iha vidyate
Ch.4 v.38 tat svayaṁ yogasaṁsiddhaḥ kālenātmani vindati

There is nothing in this world that compares to the healing and purifying effect of this vedic knowledge. One who perfects this yoga comes over the course of time to know their true self as the immortal atma.

201 śraddhāvāṁl labhate jñānaṁ tatparaḥ saṁyatendriyaḥ
Ch.4 v.39 jñānaṁ labdhvā parāṁ śāntim acireṇādhigacchati

One who with shraddha 'directly sees, remains focused upon, and trusts that life is pervaded by divine purpose, and constantly remains focused upon that knowledge', valuing it above all else, quickly attains the ultimate state of balanced knowing of Parama Brahman.

202 ajñaś cāśraddadhānaś ca saṁśayātmā vinaśyati
Ch.4 v.40 nāyaṁ loko 'sti na paro na sukhaṁ saṁśayātmanaḥ

One who is ajna 'ignorant', who does not have shraddha 'the ability to directly perceive the intelligence and purpose that pervades all of existence', and thus even doubts that life has a deeper meaning will not be able to achieve sukha and fulfillment on this loka 'plane of reality' or the next.

203
Ch.4 v.41

yogasaṁnyastakarmāṇaṁ jñānasaṁchinnasaṁśayam
ātmavantaṁ na karmāṇi nibadhnanti dhanaṁjaya

O Arjuna, one who is immune to the karmas of their actions through the practice of yoga and whose doubts have been cut away by the sharp blade of divine jnana always sees the immortal atma as their true self, and thus their actions no longer cause them bondage.

204
Ch.4 v.42

tasmād ajñānasaṁbhūtaṁ hṛtsthaṁ jñānāsinātmanaḥ
chittvainaṁ saṁśayaṁ yogam ātiṣṭhottiṣṭha bhārata

Therefore, with the sword of divine knowledge and the skills of yoga, cut away the bonds of ignorance and the doubts that have occupied your heart. Uttishta 'stand up' O Arjuna, stand strong as your true self—the atma!

Chapter 5

The Atma and the City of Nine Gates

205
Ch.5 v.1

arjuna uvāca
saṁnyāsaṁ karmaṇāṁ kṛṣṇa punar yogaṁ ca śaṁsasi
yac chreya etayor ekaṁ tan me brūhi suniścitam

ARJUNA said:
O Shri Krishna, on one hand you recommend the yoga of discernment, giving up action in the world in favour of detachment from matter. On the other, you advise the practice of karma yoga 'correct actions performed as service to the Supreme'. Now please tell me definitively, which of the two is the most effective form of yoga?

206
Ch.5 v.2

śrībhagavān uvāca
saṁnyāsaḥ karmayogaś ca niḥśreyasakarāv ubhau
tayos tu karmasaṁnyāsāt karmayogo viśiṣyate

SHRI BHAGAVAN replied:
Both buddhi yoga 'the yoga of cultivation of the knowledge of worldly categories contrasted with Brahman' and karma yoga 'the yoga of action with no attachment to the fruit' lead to the highest state of perfected being. However, yoga that is practiced through action is superior to that yoga which gives up all action only to cultivate knowledge.

207
Ch.5 v.3

jñeyaḥ sa nityasaṁnyāsī yo na dveṣṭi na kāṅkṣati
nirdvaṁdvo hi mahābāho sukhaṁ bandhāt pramucyate

One who neither hates nor covets matter and is indifferent both to sukha and dukha is known to have permanently disassociated their atma from prakriti and is thereby freed from all forms of material bondage.

208 sāṁkhyayogau pṛthag bālāḥ pravadanti na paṇḍitāḥ
Ch.5 v.4 ekam apy āsthitaḥ samyag ubhayor vindate phalam

It would be foolish to assert that sankhya yoga and karma yoga are opposed to each other, when in truth they are two different methods of approaching the same ultimate goal. Though both employ different techniques, the phala 'outcome' is the same.

209 yat sāṁkhyaiḥ prāpyate sthānaṁ tad yogair api gamyate
Ch.5 v.5 ekaṁ sāṁkhyaṁ ca yogaṁ ca yaḥ paśyati sa paśyati

That which is attained through karma yoga is also attained through the practice of sankhya or jnana yoga. The two methods lead to the same destination. One who sees this perceives correctly.

210 saṁnyāsas tu mahābāho duḥkham āptum ayogataḥ
Ch.5 v.6 yogayukto munir brahma nacireṇādhigacchati

O Arjuna, detachment from matter is extremely difficult to attain without yoga. But the muni who is steady in yogic practice attains Brahman very quickly.

211 yogayukto viśuddhātmā vijitātmā jitendriyaḥ
Ch.5 v.7 sarvabhūtātmabhūtātmā kurvann api na lipyate

One who is irrevocably connected to the practice of yoga, whose atma is cleansed of past impurities, who is self-contained and has completely controlled their senses, who sees that all living entities are also atmas, then even while acting in the world, such a yogi is no longer entangled in material reactions.

A perfected yogi gives up attachment to the results of their actions and thereby becomes balanced and tranquil, while those who are still attached to enjoying the fruit of their actions remain in bondage to their desires.–216

212
Ch.5 v.8

naiva kiṁ cit karomīti yukto manyeta tattvavit
paśyañ śṛṇvan spṛśañ jighrann aśnan gacchan svapañ
śvasan

While seeing, hearing, touching, smelling, eating, walking, sleeping, and breathing, one who knows these yogic truths, their manas steady in yoga, says, "I am not the doer of these actions."

213
Ch.5 v.9

pralapan visṛjan gṛhṇann unmiṣan nimiṣann api
indriyāṇīndriyārtheṣu vartanta iti dhārayan

While talking, defecating, grasping, opening and closing their eyes, they know that all of these are merely the interactions of the material senses with their material objects. They know that they are the atma and that therefore they are only the observer of all these activities.

214
Ch.5 v.10

brahmaṇy ādhāya karmāṇi saṅgaṁ tyaktvā karoti yaḥ
lipyate na sa pāpena padmapatram ivāmbhasā

One who performs all actions without attachment to the outcome, offering all they do into the ultimate reality of Brahman, is like a padma patra 'lotus leaf'. They stand untouched above the mud of matter and do not generate future karmic reactions.

215
Ch.5 v.11

kāyena manasā buddhyā kevalair indriyair api
yoginaḥ karma kurvanti saṅgaṁ tyaktvātmaśuddhaye

Yogis act through their body, indriyas, manas, and buddhi, performing the necessary activities of life with no attachment to the outcome. They act merely to refine their atma.

216
Ch.5 v.12

yuktaḥ karmaphalaṁ tyaktvā śāntim āpnoti naiṣṭhikīm
ayuktaḥ kāmakāreṇa phale sakto nibadhyate

A perfected yogi gives up attachment to the results of their actions and thereby becomes balanced and tranquil, while those who are still attached to enjoying the fruit of their actions remain in bondage to their desires.

217 sarvakarmāṇi manasā saṁnyasyāste sukhaṁ vaśī
Ch.5 v.13 navadvāre pure dehī naiva kurvan na kārayan

By controlling the manas faculty and using it to release attachment to the results of all actions, the dehi or atma sits happily within the body as the ruler of the nava dvara pura 'city of nine gates', neither acting nor controlling the outcome of action.

218 na kartṛtvaṁ na karmāṇi lokasya sṛjati prabhuḥ
Ch.5 v.14 na karmaphalasaṁyogaṁ svabhāvas tu pravartate

That ruler of the city of nine gates, though the prabhu 'master of the temporary body', does not determine the ultimate outcome of actions occurring in the world around them. Neither do they have the power to completely compel the behaviour of other beings, nor do they have final control over outcomes that arise from complex actions in the world. All final outcomes are governed by the laws of material nature.

219 nādatte kasya cit pāpaṁ na caiva sukṛtaṁ vibhuḥ
Ch.5 v.15 ajñānenāvṛtaṁ jñānaṁ tena muhyanti jantavaḥ

As the Vibhu 'the all-pervading Supreme Being Paramatma', I do not compel human actions, and I do not receive the positive or negative effects resulting from the choices made by deluded and unconscious beings.

220
Ch.5 v.16

jñānena tu tad ajñānaṁ yeṣāṁ nāśitam ātmanaḥ
teṣām ādityavaj jñānaṁ prakāśayati tatparam

However, when one is finally enlightened by jnana 'ultimate knowledge' and their ignorance is destroyed, then the luminous nature of Brahman reality shines within them, just like the rising sun lights up the world.

221
Ch.5 v.17

tadbuddhayas tadātmānas tanniṣṭhās tatparāyaṇāḥ
gacchanty apunarāvṛttiṁ jñānanirdhūtakalmaṣāḥ

When one's buddhi, manas, and atma are all fixed upon and absorbed in that supreme knowledge of the reality of Brahman, then one's past vrittis are all removed. In that state they proceed straight on the path of moksha and are never born within matter again.

222
Ch.5 v.18

vidyāvinayasaṁpanne brāhmaṇe gavi hastini
śuni caiva śvapāke ca paṇḍitāḥ samadarśinaḥ

Those who have direct perception of the Brahman nature of the atma see a learned brahmin, a cow, an elephant, a dog, or an unevolved human as essentially the same.

223
Ch.5 v.19

ihaiva tair jitaḥ sargo yeṣāṁ sāmye sthitaṁ manaḥ
nirdoṣaṁ hi samaṁ brahma tasmād brahmaṇi te sthitāḥ

Even while still living here on Earth, those whose manas is established in Brahman realization become flawless and impartial like Brahman, and they have already overcome the apparently endless process of reincarnation.

224 na prahṛṣyet priyaṁ prāpya nodvijet prāpya cāpriyam
Ch.5 v.20 sthirabuddhir asaṁmūḍho brahmavid brahmaṇi sthitaḥ

One who does not rejoice upon receiving what is pleasing and is not disturbed by receiving what is unpleasant, whose buddhi is steady and free of delusion, is firmly established in the vidya of Brahman and has become the same in quality as Brahman.

225 bāhyasparśeṣv asaktātmā vindaty ātmani yat sukham
Ch.5 v.21 sa brahmayogayuktātmā sukham akṣayam aśnute

One who is unaffected by external sense perceptions, who derives joy only from direct perception of their own atma, and who as the atma is united with and situated within the energy of Brahman, ultimately achieves the highest state of transcendental sukha 'happiness'.

226 ye hi saṁsparśajā bhogā duḥkhayonaya eva te
Ch.5 v.22 ādyantavantaḥ kaunteya na teṣu ramate budhaḥ

The pleasures that arise from contact with the material senses are just like yonis 'material wombs' which give birth to us, leading to material pleasures, but also inevitably lead us to pain and suffering. Arjuna, this is because all material pleasures have a beginning and an end. Therefore, one who is truly discerning does not seek delight in them.

227 śaknotīhaiva yaḥ soḍhuṁ prāk śarīravimokṣaṇāt
Ch.5 v.23 kāmakrodhodbhavaṁ vegaṁ sa yuktaḥ sa sukhī naraḥ

The person who is able to overcome the vegas 'urges of the senses' and the krodha 'anger' that arises when they are not fulfilled, is established in yoga and experiences a steady state of transcendental sukha.

228 yo 'ntaḥsukho 'ntarārāmas tathāntarjyotir eva yaḥ
Ch.5 v.24 sa yogī Brahmanirvāṇaṁ brahmabhūto 'dhigacchati

Those yogis who only pursue pleasure within, who experience antarama 'ecstatic inner delight' and are always antarjyoti 'enlightened by an illuminating brilliance from within' have achieved Brahman nirvana. They no longer claim ownership over anything and identify themselves to be the same in essence as Brahman.

229 labhante Brahmanirvāṇam ṛṣayaḥ kṣīṇakalmaṣāḥ
Ch.5 v.25 chinnadvaidhā yatātmānaḥ sarvabhūtahite ratāḥ

Those who have achieved Brahman nirvana go beyond the dualistic logic of matter so their material flaws are all removed. They become a rishi 'seer enlightened by the luminous nature of Brahman'. In that enlightened state, they see all living beings as their dearest friend.

230 kāmakrodhaviyuktānāṁ yatīnāṁ yatacetasām
Ch.5 v.26 abhito Brahmanirvāṇaṁ vartate viditātmanām

Those yogis who roam freely throughout the world and who no longer experience kama and krodha, their thoughts controlled and focused only upon their atma, experience the joy of Brahman nirvana at all times.

231 sparśān kṛtvā bahir bāhyāṁś cakṣuś caivāntare bhruvoḥ
Ch.5 v.27 prāṇāpānau samau kṛtvā nāsābhyantaracāriṇau

Ignoring all outer sensory stimulation, focusing intently upon the spot between the eyebrows, a yogi breathes with a slow and equal balance between the incoming and outgoing breath as it passes through the nostrils.

232 yatendriyamanobuddhir munir mokṣaparāyaṇaḥ
Ch.5 v.28 vigatecchābhayakrodho yaḥ sadā mukta eva saḥ

When the senses, manas, and buddhi are controlled and turned within, when fear, kama, and krodha have all disappeared, then the muni is released from bondage to the impermanent and achieves moksha 'the ultimate state of complete freedom'.

233 bhoktāraṁ yajñatapasāṁ sarvalokamaheśvaram
Ch.5 v.29 suhṛdaṁ sarvabhūtānāṁ jñātvā māṁ śāntim ṛcchati

One who experiences Me as the eater of what is offered in a yajna; one who feels Me as the fire in the body that burns away impurities while performing tapasya; one who sees Me as the ultimate ruler of all the planets in the universe; and one who knows Me as the one who is seated in the heart of all living entities, desiring only what is best for them—that person finally reaches Me and achieves the delightful and harmonious state of shanti.

Chapter 6

The Secrets of Ashtanga Yoga

234
Ch.6 v.1

śrībhagavān uvāca
anāśritaḥ karmaphalaṁ kāryaṁ karma karoti yaḥ
sa saṁnyāsī ca yogī ca na niragnir na cākriyaḥ

SHRI BHAGAVAN spoke:
The person who performs the karmas that are appropriate to their own nature and stage of life, without attachment to the results of those actions, is a true yogi and a sannyasi. But one who simply gives up all actions and responsibilities is neither a sannyasi nor a yogi.

235
Ch.6 v.2

yaṁ sannyāsam iti prāhur yogaṁ taṁ viddhi pāṇḍava
na hy asaṁnyastasaṁkalpo yogī bhavati kaś cana

What is called sannyasa 'casting off all selfish desire for the results of action within matter' is exactly the same state of being as is practiced in yoga. Without taking a vow to give up all attachment to the results of material actions within matter, one cannot be a yogi.

236
Ch.6 v.3

ārurukṣor muner yogaṁ karma kāraṇam ucyate
yogārūḍhasya tasyaiva śamaḥ kāraṇam ucyate

For one who is just learning the practice of the eight-limbed ashtanga yoga, disciplined action within matter is the recommended means of perfecting oneself. For one who has achieved perfection in this yoga, the best course of action is to remain detached and balanced in all material situations.

237 yadā hi nendriyārtheṣu na karmasv anuṣajjate
sarvasaṁkalpasamnyāsī yogārūḍhas tadocyate
Ch.6 v.4

When a yogi does not cling to their actions within matter or to the objects of the senses, and gives up all results, detaching their self from all material goals, then with single-minded purpose that yogi becomes yoga arudha 'flies free from the bondage of matter upon the wings of yoga'.

238 uddhared ātmanātmānaṁ nātmānam avasādayet
ātmaiva hy ātmano bandhur ātmaiva ripur ātmanaḥ
Ch.6 v.5

One should use the divine strength of their atma to uplift their own atma and should not use their power to degrade the atma. The atma is the atma's own best friend, and only the atma can become the atma's own worst enemy.

239 bandhur ātmātmanas tasya yenātmaivātmanā jitaḥ
anātmanas tu śatrutve vartetātmaiva śatruvat
Ch.6 v.6

For one who has controlled their atma with their atma, the atma acts as their atma's best friend. But for one who has not been able to discipline their atma, their atma remains their own worst enemy.

240 jitātmanaḥ praśāntasya paramātmā samāhitaḥ
śītoṣṇasukhaduḥkheṣu tathā mānāvamānayoḥ
Ch.6 v.7

One who is victorious in being the atma achieves the ultimate state of balance and becomes united in yoga with Paramatma 'the all-pervading Supreme Being who resides within the heart'. In this way, one remains steady and unwavering in heat or cold, pleasure or pain, honour or dishonour.

241 jñānavijñānatṛptātmā kūṭastho vijitendriyaḥ
Ch.6 v.8 yukta ity ucyate yogī samaloṣṭāśmakāñcanaḥ

The yogi who has attained jnana of their atma and achieved vijnana 'has realized it' as well, who is self-satisfied and unwavering in yogic practice, has subdued their indriyas 'senses'. To them, a lump of clay, a stone, or a piece of gold all appear to be of the same value.

242 suhṛnmitrāryudāsīnamadhyasthadveṣyabandhuṣu
Ch.6 v.9 sādhuṣv api ca pāpeṣu samabuddhir viśiṣyate

One who is objective and equipoised with dear friends, casual associates and opponents; who stands in the same steady state with both family members or enemies; who is undisturbed in the presence of both the seekers for the divine as well as the harmful and malicious—that person is distinguished as one whose awakened buddhi has made them impartial and perfectly balanced.

243 yogī yuñjīta satatam ātmānaṁ rahasi sthitaḥ
Ch.6 v.10 ekākī yatacittātmā nirāśīr aparigrahaḥ

The yogi should always focus upon and stay connected with their own atma, steady in solitude, controlling and focusing their consciousness unwaveringly upon their own atma. In this way, the yogi perfects aparigraha 'not grasping or clinging to anything material'.

244 śucau deśe pratiṣṭhāpya sthiram āsanam ātmanaḥ
Ch.6 v.11 nātyucchritaṁ nātinīcaṁ cailājinakuśottaram

When practicing yoga [in a forest], one should choose a clean and stable location in which to sit that is neither too high nor too low. The yogi should then cover the ground with a layer of kusha grass, cover that with the skin of a deer, and upon that, place a soft cloth of natural fibres.

245 tatraikāgraṁ manaḥ kṛtvā yatacittendriyakriyaḥ
Ch.6 v.12 upaviśyāsane yuñjyād yogam ātmaviśuddhaye

There, assuming an appropriate asana, the yogi should focus the manas upon a single intention. Completely restraining both the thoughts and the senses, the yogi should remain entirely fixed upon their own atma in order to become purified of any misconceptions regarding the true nature of their self.

246 samaṁ kāyaśirogrīvaṁ dhārayann acalaṁ sthiraḥ
Ch.6 v.13 saṁprekṣya nāsikāgraṁ svaṁ diśaś cānavalokayan

Holding the body, neck, and head in correct alignment, motionless, gazing neither entirely outward nor completely within, the yogi does not allow their attention to wander and remains steady in their dharana 'one-pointed meditation within'.

247 praśāntātmā vigatabhīr brahmacārivrate sthitaḥ
Ch.6 v.14 manaḥ saṁyamya maccitto yukta āsīta matparaḥ

Entirely satisfied within their own atma, all fears completely removed, established in a vow of brahmacharya 'restraint and correct circulation of their sexual energies', with the manas faculty calm and attentive, the yogi should meditate upon Me as the ultimate reality.

248 yuñjann evaṁ sadātmānaṁ yogī niyatamānasaḥ
Ch.6 v.15 śāntiṁ nirvāṇaparamāṁ matsaṁsthām adhigacchati

By constantly disciplining their atma in this way, the yogi gradually subdues and focuses all the faculties of manas, achieving complete tranquillity, and by so doing reaches the state of parama nirvana 'becoming both enlightened to their own true nature and detached from all forms of material reality'. Eventually, through this process, the yogi connects directly with Me and we remain together, permanently linked in that perfect yogic union.

249 nātyaśnatas tu yogo 'sti na caikāntam anaśnataḥ
Ch.6 v.16 na cātisvapnaśīlasya jāgrato naiva cārjuna

To practice this yoga, one must establish a balance in relation to all material activities, neither eating nor sleeping too much or too little.

250 yuktāhāravihārasya yuktaceṣṭasya karmasu
Ch.6 v.17 yuktasvapnāvabodhasya yogo bhavati duḥkhahā

Yoga means to be moderate in sattvic eating and recreation; yoga is to remain equipoised while performing all actions; yoga is finding the right balance between times spent awake and asleep. One who lives as a yogi carefully removes all sources of disturbance from their life.

251 yadā viniyataṁ cittam ātmany evāvatiṣṭhate
Ch.6 v.18 niḥspṛhaḥ sarvakāmebhyo yukta ity ucyate tadā

When the consciousness of the atma is entirely free from all material longings and desires, one's yoga finally becomes perfect.

252 yathā dīpo nivātastho neṅgate sopamā smṛtā
Ch.6 v.19 yogino yatacittasya yuñjato yogam ātmanaḥ

Just as a lamp in a windless place does not waver, so a yogi who has focused the chit faculties of conscious awareness entirely upon their own atma is once again restored to their true nature by perfecting this yoga of transcendental self-knowing.

253 yatroparamate cittaṁ niruddhaṁ yogasevayā
Ch.6 v.20 yatra caivātmanātmānaṁ paśyann ātmani tuṣyati

When the chit faculty stops interacting with matter and is entirely engaged in yogic practice, and when the atma sees the atma by means of the atma, the yogi becomes completely content.

254 sukham ātyantikaṁ yat tad buddhigrāhyam atīndriyam
Ch.6 v.21 vetti yatra na caivāyaṁ sthitaś calati tattvataḥ

When the buddhi is finally established in an unending state of ecstatic happiness that carries the yogi beyond the material senses, then, abiding permanently in that joyful consciousness, the yogi never again deviates from that truth.

255 yaṁ labdhvā cāparaṁ lābhaṁ manyate nādhikaṁ tataḥ
Ch.6 v.22 yasmin sthito na duḥkhena guruṇāpi vicālyate

Having attained that level of awareness, the yogi directly realizes that no greater state of being can be achieved. While abiding steadily in that sublime joyful state, even the heaviest material loss cannot cause distress.

256 taṁ vidyād duḥkhasaṁyogaviyogaṁ yogasaṁjñitam
Ch.6 v.23 sa niścayena yoktavyo yogo 'nirviṇṇacetasā

Let it be known that true yoga is the dissolution of our long-time union with the pain and suffering of matter. The yogi must re-establish their self as the atma with great determination and with the certainty that they are not related to matter.

257 saṁkalpaprabhavān kāmāṁs tyaktvā sarvān aśeṣataḥ
manasaivendriyagrāmaṁ viniyamya samantataḥ
Ch.6 v.24

Setting their unwavering resolve to entirely abandon all desires that arise from association with matter, and completely restraining the needs of the indriyas by controlling the manas...

258 śanaiḥ śanair uparamed buddhyā dhṛtigṛhītayā
ātmasaṁsthaṁ manaḥ kṛtvā na kiṁ cid api cintayet
Ch.6 v.25

... step by step, the yogi should withdraw their focus from matter by focusing their buddhi faculty entirely upon the atma. A dedicated yogi should not meditate upon anything else.

259 yato yato niścarati manaś cañcalam asthiram
tatas tato niyamyaitad ātmany eva vaśaṁ nayet
Ch.6 v.26

The manas faculty is chanchala 'restless and flitting from one thing to another', but a determined yogi should immediately bring it back under control of the atma.

260 praśāntamanasaṁ hy enaṁ yoginaṁ sukham uttamam
upaiti śāntarajasaṁ brahmabhūtam akalmaṣam
Ch.6 v.27

The yogi who has calmed the manas and overcome the powerful drives of the desires created by rajas reclaims their Brahman nature and attains ultimate joy.

261 yuñjann evaṁ sadātmānaṁ yogī vigatakalmaṣaḥ
sukhena brahmasaṁsparśam atyantaṁ sukham aśnute
Ch.6 v.28

Thus, through the constant practice of the yoga of seeing oneself as the atma, the yogi becomes calm and goes beyond the reach of all harmful material influences. Now in direct contact with the reality of Brahman, the yogi achieves a state of joyfulness that has no limitations.

262 sarvabhūtastham ātmānaṁ sarvabhūtāni cātmani
Ch.6 v.29 īkṣate yogayuktātmā sarvatra samadarśanaḥ

One permanently yoked in such yogic practices sees an atma inside of all incarnated beings. An atma yoked through yoga sees all other beings as atmas, exactly resembling their own immortal self.

263 yo māṁ paśyati sarvatra sarvaṁ ca mayi paśyati
Ch.6 v.30 tasyāhaṁ na praṇaśyāmi sa ca me na praṇaśyati

For one who also sees Me pervading all that is, and sees that all beings are within Me, I am never again invisible to them and they are never again separated from Me.

264 sarvabhūtasthitaṁ yo māṁ bhajaty ekatvam āsthitaḥ
Ch.6 v.31 sarvathā vartamāno 'pi sa yogī mayi vartate

The yogi who sees Me as present within all beings, who is perfectly established in a one-pointed and unbreakable intimate and affectionate relationship with Me, and who is absorbed in a fervent state of loving adoration for Me dwells within Me wherever they go.

265 ātmaupamyena sarvatra samaṁ paśyati yo 'rjuna
Ch.6 v.32 sukhaṁ vā yadi vā duḥkhaṁ sa yogī paramo mataḥ

O Arjuna, one who continually sees the atma in all living entities as in essence the same as their own atma, even while experiencing dukha 'material miseries and pains' or sukha 'the joys and pleasures of matter', is said to have attained the peak of yogic perfection.

At a certain point, upon
hearing the vedic sound
vibrations that lead to
Brahman realization, the
yogi is re-awakened to
the intense desire for
self-realization that was
cultivated in their previous
life. Once re-awakened,
they are compelled to
continue their journey of
yogic realization.

Eventually, by persevering
in their yogic practice, with
their manas fully controlled
and all material tendencies
removed, the process of
self-realization that they
have pursued over many
lifetimes finally leads
the yogi to attain the
param gati 'ultimate
destination'.–277-278

266 arjuna uvāca
Ch.6 v.33
yo 'yaṁ yogas tvayā proktaḥ sāmyena madhusūdana
etasyāhaṁ na paśyāmi cañcalatvāt sthitiṁ sthirām

ARJUNA said:
O Shri Krishna, the method of yoga that you have described seems impossible to attain. The faculty of manas is chanchala 'inherently unstable and fickle', and I do not see how even yoga can achieve the steadiness you are describing.

267 cañcalaṁ hi manaḥ kṛṣṇa pramāthi balavad dṛḍham
Ch.6 v.34 tasyāhaṁ nigrahaṁ manye vāyor iva suduṣkaram

ARJUNA continued:
Not only is the manas faculty chanchala, it is also turbulent, unyielding, and powerful. In my experience, it would be easier to control the wind than to control the unsteadiness of manas.

268 śrībhagavān uvāca
Ch.6 v.35
asaṁśayaṁ mahābāho mano durnigrahaṁ calam
abhyāsena tu kaunteya vairāgyeṇa ca gṛhyate

SHRI KRISHNA replied:
You are right, O mighty Arjuna, the manas is very restless and unsteady, and it is extremely difficult to become free from its grasp, but with constant practice and vairagya 'complete determination and indifference to material objects', it can finally be controlled.

269 asaṁyatātmanā yogo duṣprāpa iti me matiḥ
Ch.6 v.36 vaśyātmanā tu yatatā śakyo 'vāptum upāyataḥ

I agree that yoga is difficult to perfect if the atma is not disciplined, but it is My opinion that any atma who practices yoga with great determination will reach the goal.

270
Ch.6 v.37

arjuna uvāca
ayatiḥ śraddhayopeto yogāc calitamānasaḥ
aprāpya yogasaṁsiddhiṁ kāṁ gatiṁ kṛṣṇa gacchati

ARJUNA asked:
O Shri Krishna, what is the destination of a yogi who pursues the goals of yoga with great conviction and determination but does not attain perfection in one lifetime? Where does such a person take birth in their next life?

271
Ch.6 v.38

kaccin nobhayavibhraṣṭaś chinnābhram iva naśyati
apratiṣṭho mahābāho vimūḍho brahmaṇaḥ pathi

Are they simply dispersed like a small cloud in a windy sky? It would seem that they have failed to enjoy this world and have also failed to find the path to Brahman. Having attained neither, it appears to me that they would be completely lost, with nowhere to stand in either realm.

272
Ch.6 v.39

etan me saṁśayaṁ kṛṣṇa chettum arhasy aśeṣataḥ
tvad anyaḥ saṁśayasyāsya chettā na hy upapadyate

O Shri Krishna, this is my deepest doubt and I ask you to remove it. No one other than You can possibly remove this disabling doubt.

273
Ch.6 v.40

śrībhagavān uvāca
pārtha naiveha nāmutra vināśas tasya vidyate
na hi kalyāṇakṛt kaś cid durgatiṁ tāta gacchati

SHRI BHAGAVAN said:
My dear friend Arjuna, any person who performs actions that are beneficial to their self and all beings is never degraded, not in this life or the next.

274 Ch.6 v.41
prāpya puṇyakṛtāṁl lokān uṣitvā śāśvatīḥ samāḥ
śucīnāṁ śrīmatāṁ gehe yogabhraṣṭo 'bhijāyate

Yogis who have not finished perfecting their yoga take their next birth on Svarga Loka 'the beautiful realm of the devas'. There they live amid radiance and splendour for many delightful years. In their next life, they return to Earth, where they take birth in a beneficial family.

275 Ch.6 v.42
atha vā yoginām eva kule bhavati dhīmatām
etad dhi durlabhataraṁ loke janma yad īdṛśam

Or they take their next birth in a family of yoga practitioners. Such an enlightened birth is rare and very difficult to achieve.

276 Ch.6 v.43
tatra taṁ buddhisaṁyogaṁ labhate paurvadehikam
yatate ca tato bhūyaḥ saṁsiddhau kurunandana

O Arjuna, in either of those enlightened or beneficial family environments, the yogi eventually resumes the pursuit of self-perfection through yoga at the same level of achievement they had attained in their previous life.

277 Ch.6 v.44
pūrvābhyāsena tenaiva hriyate hy avaśo 'pi saḥ
jijñāsur api yogasya śabdabrahmātivartate

At a certain point, upon hearing the vedic sound vibrations that lead to Brahman realization, the yogi is re-awakened to the intense desire for self-realization that was cultivated in their previous life. Once re-awakened, they are compelled to continue their journey of yogic realization.

278 prayatnād yatamānas tu yogī saṁśuddhakilbiṣaḥ
Ch.6 v.45 anekajanmasaṁsiddhas tato yāti parāṁ gatim

Eventually, by persevering in their yogic practice, with their manas fully controlled and all material tendencies removed, the process of self-realization that they have pursued over many lifetimes finally leads the yogi to attain the param gati 'ultimate destination'.

279 tapasvibhyo 'dhiko yogī jñānibhyo 'pi mato 'dhikaḥ
Ch.6 v.46 karmibhyaś cādhiko yogī tasmād yogī bhavārjuna

A perfected yogi is greater than those who only perform tapasya. They are more advanced than those who only pursue jnana. The perfected yogi also goes beyond those who perform the vedic rituals only for material gain. Therefore, Arjuna, in all circumstances strive to be a perfected yogi.

280 yoginām api sarveṣāṁ madgatenāntarātmanā
Ch.6 v.47 śraddhāvān bhajate yo māṁ sa me yuktatamo mataḥ

And of all yogis, those who are completely dedicated to Me, who have joined their atma with Me in a deep and loving relationship in the mood of bhakti yoga 'divine loving service'—those yogis are the most connected to Me.

Chapter 7

The Perpetual Quest for Ultimate Knowing

281
Ch.7 v.1

śrībhagavān uvāca
mayy āsaktamanāḥ pārtha yogaṁ yuñjan madāśrayaḥ
asaṁśayaṁ samagraṁ māṁ yathā jñāsyasi tac chṛṇu

Shri Bhagavan said:
O Arjuna, now hear what occurs when the thinking, feeling, willing, and memory faculties of manas are completely focused upon Me, and the yogi is fully absorbed in the practice of yoga, taking shelter only in Me, with no doubts remaining regarding My existence.

282
Ch.7 v.2

jñānaṁ te 'haṁ savijñānam idaṁ vakṣyāmy aśeṣataḥ
yaj jñātvā neha bhūyo 'nyaj jñātavyam avaśiṣyate

I will explain in detail the jnana 'sacred knowledge' from which you will achieve vijnana 'ultimate knowing and perfect discernment'. Knowing this, nothing greater remains to be known in this world.

283
Ch.7 v.3

manuṣyāṇāṁ sahasreṣu kaś cid yatati siddhaye
yatatām api siddhānāṁ kaś cin māṁ vetti tattvataḥ

Among thousands of human beings, few are consistently searching for siddhi 'ultimate self-perfection'. Even among those who are seeking such siddhis, very few are aware of My true nature.

284
Ch.7 v.4

bhūmir āpo 'nalo vāyuḥ khaṁ mano buddhir eva ca
ahaṁkāra itīyaṁ me bhinnā prakṛtir aṣṭadhā

My prakriti is composed of eight energies. The first five are the tangible energies: earth, water, fire, air, and space. The three intangible energies are: manas, which consists of the thinking, feeling, willing, and memory faculties; buddhi, the analytical faculty that discerns one thing from another; and ahamkara, the faculty that misidentifies the consciousness of the atma with the minute particles of matter.

285 apareyam itas tv anyāṁ prakṛtiṁ viddhi me parām
Ch.7 v.5 jīvabhūtāṁ mahābāho yayedaṁ dhāryate jagat

These eight unconscious energies constitute My apara prakriti 'unconscious nature' that is manifest as the realm of matter. Beyond that, and distinct from it, is My param 'fully conscious and immortal nature'. The countless atmas or jiva bhutas are manifestations of My param energy and are the moving force within every jagat 'material universe'.

286 etadyonīni bhūtāni sarvāṇīty upadhāraya
Ch.7 v.6 ahaṁ kṛtsnasya jagataḥ prabhavaḥ pralayas tathā

Try to understand that all beings have originally descended into this apara world from the para realm of Brahman, entering through the portal of My cosmic yoni 'womb'. I am the creator of and ultimately the destroyer of every material universe.

287 mattaḥ parataraṁ nānyat kiṁ cid asti dhanaṁjaya
Ch.7 v.7 mayi sarvam idaṁ protaṁ sūtre maṇigaṇā iva

O Arjuna, there is nothing greater than Me or beyond Me. All that exists is held in place by Me, just like the jewels strung on a necklace are held together by invisible threads.

288 raso 'ham apsu kaunteya prabhāsmi śaśisūryayoḥ
Ch.7 v.8 praṇavaḥ sarvavedeṣu śabdaḥ khe pauruṣaṁ nṛṣu

O Arjuna

1. I am the taste of water.
2. I am the radiance of the Moon and the Sun.
3. I am the vedas emerging from the original sound of aum.
4. I am the vibrations carried by akasha 'space'.
5. I am the ability in all persons.

289 puṇyo gandhaḥ pṛthivyāṁ ca tejaś cāsmi vibhāvasau
Ch.7 v.9 jīvanaṁ sarvabhūteṣu tapaś cāsmi tapasviṣu

6. I am the sacred smell of the earth.
7. I am the radiant energy emanating from fire.
8. I am the life force in all beings.
9. I am the focus and correct practice of those who endeavor to perfect themselves.

290 bījaṁ māṁ sarvabhūtānāṁ viddhi pārtha sanātanam
Ch.7 v.10 buddhir buddhimatām asmi tejas tejasvinām aham

O Arjuna

10. I am the seed that gives rise to all beings.
11. I am that which always exists.
12. I am the discernment of those who see everything as it truly exists.
13. I am the brilliant energy of those who are radiant and powerful.

291 balaṁ balavatāṁ cāhaṁ kāmarāgavivarjitam
Ch.7 v.11 dharmāviruddho bhūteṣu kāmo 'smi bharatarṣabha

And Arjuna

14. I am the strength of the powerful who are not corrupted by material attachment and selfish desires.
15. I am the desire for pleasure and beauty in all beings that does not violate the codes of dharma.

292 Ch.7 v.12
ye caiva sāttvikā bhāvā rājasās tāmasāś ca ye
matta eveti tān viddhi na tv ahaṁ teṣu te mayi

The three gunas 'dynamic states of matter'—sattvic, rajasic, and tamasic—emanate from Me. Yet, though they come from Me, I am neither produced from them nor am I under their influence in any way.

293 Ch.7 v.13
tribhir guṇamayair bhāvair ebhiḥ sarvam idaṁ jagat
mohitaṁ nābhijānāti mām ebhyaḥ param avyayam

Because of the deluding influence of these trigunas, those under their influence cannot see Me, even though I am timeless and always visible beyond the wall of matter.

294 Ch.7 v.14
daivī hy eṣā guṇamayī mama māyā duratyayā
mām eva ye prapadyante māyām etāṁ taranti te

This gunamayi 'illusory divine energy of Mine', which I personally designed using My divine and mystical intelligence, is exceedingly difficult to transcend and go beyond. Only those who completely take shelter in Me can go beyond the deluding influence of the three gunas of prakriti.

295 Ch.7 v.15
na māṁ duṣkṛtino mūḍhāḥ prapadyante narādhamāḥ
māyayāpahṛtajñānā āsuraṁ bhāvam āśritāḥ

Therefore, those whose actions are harmful to others, who are low-minded and unevolved, who are deluded and confused, whose jnana has been subverted by delusion, and who are dedicated to the path of tamas leading to darkness and destruction cannot see Me.

After many, many births in
pursuit of divine knowledge,
one finally surrenders unto
Me alone, saying: Vasudeva
sarvam iti 'Vasudeva
is the vast source of all and
is everything'. Such a
mahatma is very rare.–299

296 caturvidhā bhajante māṁ janāḥ sukṛtino 'rjuna
Ch.7 v.16 ārto jijñāsur arthārthī jñānī ca bharatarṣabha

Listen Arjuna, there are four kinds of humans who are already devoted to me and act for the benefit of all beings:

1. arto—they feel the miseries around them and ask Me for help
2. jijnasu—they are curious and seek higher knowledge from Me
3. artharthi—they seek wealth from Me for idealistic reasons to alleviate distress in society
4. jnani—their strongest desire is to acquire self-actualizing wisdom by which to know Me.

297 teṣāṁ jñānī nityayukta ekabhaktir viśiṣyate
Ch.7 v.17 priyo hi jñānino 'tyartham ahaṁ sa ca mama priyaḥ

Of these four, the person who is dedicated to acquiring knowledge about Me and engages directly in My service with eka bhakti 'single-minded devotion' is most affectionately linked to Me. They are extremely priya 'beloved' to Me, and I think of them constantly.

298 udārāḥ sarva evaite jñānī tv ātmaiva me matam
Ch.7 v.18 āsthitaḥ sa hi yuktātmā mām evānuttamāṁ gatim

All four of these noble aspirants are highly evolved, but the persons who live only for jnana are just like My own Atma 'My very own Self'. Indeed, the jiva atma whose yoga is unwavering forever abides in Me and finally attains Me as their ultimate and final destination.

299 bahūnāṁ janmanām ante jñānavān māṁ prapadyate
vāsudevaḥ sarvam iti sa mahātmā sudurlabhaḥ
Ch.7 v.19

After many, many births in pursuit of divine knowledge, one finally surrenders unto Me alone, saying: Vasudeva sarvam iti 'Vasudeva is the vast source of all and is everything'. Such a mahatma is very rare.

300 kāmais tais tair hṛtajñānāḥ prapadyante 'nyadevatāḥ
tam̐ tam̐ niyamam āsthāya prakṛtyā niyatāḥ svayā
Ch.7 v.20

Conversely, those whose discernment has been stolen by their hunger for pleasure make offerings to the lesser devas of material nature, seeking benefits from them. The deva they choose to adore reflects the bias of their own unique material nature.

301 yo yo yāṁ yāṁ tanuṁ bhaktaḥ śraddhayārcitum icchati
tasya tasyācalāṁ śraddhāṁ tām eva vidadhāmy aham
Ch.7 v.21

When a human being becomes attracted to a particular deva and sees them as worthy of their devotion, I steady their attention so they can please that deva with their offerings.

302 sa tayā śraddhayā yuktas tasyā rādhanam īhate
labhate ca tataḥ kāmān mayaiva vihitān hi tān
Ch.7 v.22

Anyone who invests their shraddha upon a lesser divine being or upon an object whatever they desire eventually receives the result they are seeking, but that result is in fact given by Me.

303 antavat tu phalaṁ teṣāṁ tad bhavaty alpamedhasām
Ch.7 v.23 devān devayajo yānti madbhaktā yānti mām api

Those who hold a smaller vision of what is possible try to please one of the devas. As a result, after leaving their present body, they take birth on the material loka of the deva to whom they were attracted. The result is pleasurable but temporary, whereas those who adore and serve Me come to live with Me forever.

304 avyaktaṁ vyaktim āpannaṁ manyante mām abuddhayaḥ
Ch.7 v.24 paraṁ bhāvam ajānanto mamāvyayam anuttamam

Those who have not yet developed the discernment of buddhi think that because I make an appearance within matter as an avatar, I too have come under matter's laws and control. They do not understand that I am beyond the three gunas of prakriti and exist permanently outside the control of time.

305 nāhaṁ prakāśaḥ sarvasya yogamāyāsamāvṛtaḥ
Ch.7 v.25 mūḍho 'yaṁ nābhijānāti loko mām ajam avyayam

I am not visible to those who are still deluded by matter and have not yet cultivated yogic discernment. My true nature is purposely hidden from them by my yoga maya 'mystical Brahman energies that act like a veil, protecting my true identity from those who are not yet qualified to see Me'.

306 vedāhaṁ samatītāni vartamānāni cārjuna
Ch.7 v.26 bhaviṣyāṇi ca bhūtāni māṁ tu veda na kaś cana

O Arjuna, I know the departed beings and those who are still living, as well as those who are not yet manifest, but no one knows Me entirely or grasps the full extent of My endless being.

307 icchādveṣasamutthena dvaṁdvamohena bhārata
Ch.7 v.27 sarvabhūtāni saṁmohaṁ sarge yānti paraṁtapa

O Arjuna, just because of the moha 'overwhelming and deluding power' generated by My prakriti, all beings who are born are influenced by hatred and perverted desires to some degree.

308 yeṣāṁ tv antagataṁ pāpaṁ janānāṁ puṇyakarmaṇām
Ch.7 v.28 te dvaṁdvamohanirmuktā bhajante māṁ dṛḍhavratāḥ

Those who have reached the end of their long evolutionary journey through matter, who no longer generate papa and instead perform punya, finally overcome the delusion and duality of matter. In that state of moksha, they serve and adore Me constantly with sacred vows that always remain steady.

309 jarāmaraṇamokṣāya mām āśritya yatanti ye
Ch.7 v.29 te brahma tad viduḥ kṛtsnam adhyātmaṁ karma cākhilam

That state of moksha protects them from the effects of old age and death, and now they completely take shelter in Me. Remembering their own Brahman nature, they now direct all their actions toward Me as Adhyatma 'the Supreme and ultimate Atma'.

310 sādhibhūtādhidaivaṁ māṁ sādhiyajñaṁ ca ye viduḥ
Ch.7 v.30 prayāṇakāle 'pi ca māṁ te vidur yuktacetasaḥ

They also know Me as Adhibhuta 'the Supreme among all beings,' Adhidaiva 'the origin of all divine beings', and Adhiyajna 'the one who ultimately receives all sacred offerings'. They know Me perfectly in the steady focus of their yoga, even at the final moment when they leave their body.

Chapter 8

The Process of Attaining Knowledge of Brahman

311
Ch.8 v.1

arjuna uvāca
kiṁ tad brahma kim adhyātmaṁ kiṁ karma puruṣottama
adhibhūtaṁ ca kiṁ proktam adhidaivaṁ kim ucyate

ARJUNA said:
O Purusha Uttama 'Ultimate Person'

1. What is Brahman?
2. What is adhyatma?
3. What is karma?
4. What is adhibhuta?
5. What is adhidaiva?

312
Ch.8 v.2

adhiyajñaḥ kathaṁ ko 'tra dehe 'smin madhusūdana
prayāṇakāle ca kathaṁ jñeyo 'si niyatātmabhiḥ

6. Who is Adhiyajna?
7. Where does Adhiyajna reside within the body?
8. How is a dedicated yogi to meditate upon Adhiyajna at the moment of the death of their body?

313
Ch.8 v.3

śrībhagavān uvāca
akṣaraṁ brahma paramaṁ svabhāvo 'dhyātmam ucyate
bhūtabhāvodbhavakaro visargaḥ karmasaṁjñitaḥ

SHRI BHAGAVAN said:

1. The immortal, imperishable and always brilliant supreme reality from which everything arises, and within which it exists, is called Brahman.
2. That immortal being who resides in the body is known as Adhyatma.
3. Karma is the reaction generated by the atma's use of free will, by which they put in motion the chains of cause and effect that manifest from life to life.

314 adhibhūtaṁ kṣaro bhāvaḥ puruṣaś cādhidaivatam
Ch.8 v.4 adhiyajño 'ham evātra dehe dehabhṛtāṁ vara

4. Adhibhuta is the totality of prakriti 'the realm of matter' functioning as a single cosmic being whose body is the entire universe.
5. Adhidaiva is the Supreme Being who is pervading the entire universe.
6. Adhiyajna is Me, present in the hridaya 'heart' of every living being from where I receive all offerings of love and adoration.

315 antakāle ca mām eva smaran muktvā kalevaram
Ch.8 v.5 yaḥ prayāti sa madbhāvaṁ yāti nāsty atra saṁśayaḥ

And at the final moment of leaving the body, anyone who remembers only Me is removed from the process of reincarnation and achieves moksha. They are reinstated in their original nature like My own and come to live in My Brahman abode. Of this, there is no doubt.

316 yaṁ yaṁ vāpi smaran bhāvaṁ tyajaty ante kalevaram
Ch.8 v.6 taṁ tam evaiti kaunteya sadā tadbhāvabhāvitaḥ

Whatever state of being one envisions through smaranam 'remembrance' at the time of leaving their body, determines their next state of being and the destination to which they will be transported for their next birth.

317 tasmāt sarveṣu kāleṣu mām anusmara yudhya ca
Ch.8 v.7 mayy arpitamanobuddhir mām evaiṣyasy asaṁśayaḥ

Therefore, always remember Me through yogic smaranam. With your manas and buddhi completely focused upon Me, fight on behalf of dharma, acting for the well-being of all. In this way, you will come to Me without a doubt.

318 abhyāsayogayuktena cetasā nānyagāminā
Ch.8 v.8 paramaṁ puruṣaṁ divyaṁ yāti pārthānucintayan

One who is constantly disciplined in yogic practices, meditating upon Me as the Parama Purusha 'Supreme and Ultimate Person', whose thoughts do not wander to anything else comes directly to Me.

319 kaviṁ purāṇam anuśāsitāram; aṇor aṇīyāṁsam anusmared yaḥ
Ch.8 v.9 sarvasya dhātāram acintyarūpam; ādityavarṇaṁ tamasaḥ parastāt

One should meditate upon the Parama Purusha as

1. Kavi—the original poet seer
2. Purana—the most ancient
3. Anushasitara—the controller of all
4. Anor Aniyamsa—more minute than the atom
5. Sarvasya Dhatara—the supporter of all
6. Achintya Rupa—one whose form is inconceivable
7. Aditya Varna—one who is golden and luminous like the Sun
8. Tamasah Parastat—one who is beyond the darkness of matter.

320 prayāṇakāle manasācalena; bhaktyā yukto yogabalena caiva
Ch.8 v.10 bhruvor madhye prāṇam āveśya samyak; sa taṁ paraṁ puruṣam upaiti divyam

At the exact moment of leaving the body, the yogi should steady their manas, holding an unwavering focus and united in deep devotional connection with Me. Held steady by the power of yoga, one should direct their focus between the eyebrows, leading the prana 'life force' in that direction. In this way, they are certain to ascend to the supreme realm of the Parama Purusha.

321 yad akṣaraṁ vedavido vadanti; viśanti yad yatayo vītarāgāḥ
Ch.8 v.11 yad icchanto brahmacaryaṁ caranti; tat te padaṁ saṁgraheṇa pravakṣye

I will now briefly explain the path and process that is followed by those who know the conclusion of the vedic knowledge, who have withdrawn from sensual pleasures, who no longer have material attachments, and who are constantly performing tapasya in order to return to the ultimate realm of the Akshara Brahman 'imperishable abode'.

322 sarvadvārāṇi saṁyamya mano hṛdi nirudhya ca
Ch.8 v.12 mūrdhny ādhāyātmanaḥ prāṇam āsthito yogadhāraṇām

Having withdrawn their awareness from all sources of external sensory experience, the yogi controls and closes the nine gates of the body. This confines the faculties of manas entirely within the hridaya 'heart'. Next, the yogi focuses their atma prana 'life force of the atma' on the topmost point of the head and thus becomes completely established in dharana 'the yogic process of one-pointed focus'.

323 om ity ekākṣaraṁ brahma vyāharan mām anusmaran
Ch.8 v.13 yaḥ prayāti tyajan dehaṁ sa yāti paramāṁ gatim

In order to re-enter into Akshara Brahman, the yogi constantly chants the sacred one-syllabled mantra aum and remembers Me in every moment. Removing any sense of identification with the five-element body, the yogi at last reaches param gati 'the final and ultimate destination'.

324 ananyacetāḥ satataṁ yo māṁ smarati nityaśaḥ
tasyāhaṁ sulabhaḥ pārtha nityayuktasya yoginaḥ
Ch.8 v.14

O Arjuna, for one whose thoughts do not wander to anything else, who remembers Me at all times, who is always striving for yogic union with Me, I am very easy to reach.

325 mām upetya punarjanma duḥkhālayam aśāśvatam
nāpnuvanti mahātmānaḥ saṁsiddhiṁ paramāṁ gatāḥ
Ch.8 v.15

By approaching Me for a loving relationship, these yogis become mahatmas 'great immortal and liberated beings' who have aspired toward and finally gone to the place of final perfection. They are never forced to take birth again within prakriti, the home of all misery and suffering.

326 ā brahmabhuvanāl lokāḥ punarāvartino 'rjuna
mām upetya tu kaunteya punarjanma na vidyate
Ch.8 v.16

If, at the moment of death, one goes to any loka 'realm' within prakriti, even to the very abode of the creator Brahma, they are still forced to reincarnate again. But one who reaches Me in My immortal abode, O Arjuna, never takes birth again.

327 sahasrayugaparyantam ahar yad brahmaṇo viduḥ
rātriṁ yugasahasrāntāṁ te 'horātravido janāḥ
Ch.8 v.17

In the vedas it is said that Brahma, the creator of each material universe, lives for 100 of his own cosmic years. It is said that one day and night of his life lasts for 8,640,000,000 Earth years. Persons who have studied the vedic science of time understand these immense cosmic cycles.

328 avyaktād vyaktayaḥ sarvāḥ prabhavanty aharāgame
Ch.8 v.18 rātryāgame pralīyante tatraivāvyaktasaṁjñake

All manifestations within prakriti come into being at the start of Brahma's day and are dissolved into an unmanifest state at the beginning of his night. The ultimate source of their coming into being is the transcendental Brahman realm which cannot be directly seen by those living within the realms of matter.

329 bhūtagrāmaḥ sa evāyaṁ bhūtvā bhūt
Ch.8 v.19 ātryāgame 'vaśaḥ pārtha prabhavaty aharāgame

O Arjuna, when the night of Brahma arrives, the bodies of the countless beings living within matter are destroyed, along with the lokas on which they live. When the day of Brahma arrives, the atmas reincarnate and resume their evolutionary journey within matter, continuing exactly where they had been interrupted by the previous cycle of destruction.

330 paras tasmāt tu bhāvo 'nyo 'vyakto 'vyaktāt sanātanaḥ
Ch.8 v.20 yaḥ sa sarveṣu bhūteṣu naśyatsu na vinaśyati

Beyond this duality of the manifest and unmanifest realms of material existence within prakriti, there is another realm of existence that is of a different nature. While everything within matter fluctuates, this luminous Brahman realm remains steady.

331 avyakto 'kṣara ity uktas tam āhuḥ paramāṁ gatim
Ch.8 v.21 yaṁ prāpya na nivartante tad dhāma paramaṁ mama

That avyakta 'unmanifest' and akshara 'indestructible' place is the param gati 'ultimate destination'. That place is the final goal and ultimate abode from which one never returns. It is My param dhama 'the beautiful realm where liberated immortal beings perpetually reside in their highest state of perfection'.

O Arjuna, this final
and supreme stage of
self-perfection is only
achieved when the
embodied atma focuses
its entire being upon
achieving an intimate
relationship of joyful bhakti
yoga with Me, and this is
the final stage of loving
existence. That ecstatic
love is the mysterious force
by which all the universes
are pervaded.–332

332 puruṣaḥ sa paraḥ pārtha bhaktyā labhyas tv ananyayā
Ch.8 v.22 yasyāntaḥsthāni bhūtāni yena sarvam idaṁ tatam

O Arjuna, this final and supreme stage of self-perfection is only achieved when the embodied atma focuses its entire being upon achieving an intimate relationship of joyful bhakti yoga with Me, and this is the final stage of loving existence. That ecstatic love is the mysterious force by which all the universes are pervaded.

333 yatra kāle tv anāvṛttim āvṛttiṁ caiva yoginaḥ
Ch.8 v.23 prayātā yānti taṁ kālaṁ vakṣyāmi bharatarṣabha

And now, Arjuna, I will explain the times of the year that are favourable or unfavourable for yogis to leave their body, and to successfully leave the realm of prakriti and re-enter the transcendental realm of Brahman.

334 agnir jyotir ahaḥ śuklaḥ ṣaṇmāsā uttarāyaṇam
Ch.8 v.24 tatra prayātā gacchanti brahma brahmavido janāḥ

Those yogis who know Brahman and leave their body during the day, in the fortnight from new moon to full moon, and when the sun travels in the north from the winter solstice to the summer solstice, which is known as the time when fire and light rule the sky, go immediately to Brahman and are not ever forced to return to rebirth within matter.

335 dhūmo rātris tathā kṛṣṇaḥ ṣaṇmāsā dakṣiṇāyanam
Ch.8 v.25 tatra cāndramasaṁ jyotir yogī prāpya nivartate

On the other hand, those yogis who know Brahman but leave their body at night, in the dark fortnight from full moon to new moon, and when the sun travels in the south, from the summer solstice to the winter solstice, when smoke and darkness rule the sky, are reborn once again within prakriti in order to complete their yogic practice.

336 śuklakṛṣṇe gatī hy ete jagataḥ śāśvate mate
Ch.8 v.26 ekayā yāty anāvṛttim anyayāvartate punaḥ

These are the two paths leading to two different destinations: one of light and one of darkness. Following one path, the yogi returns to prakriti for one final birth. Following the other path, one is not forced to return to prakriti again.

337 naite sṛtī pārtha jānan yogī muhyati kaś cana
Ch.8 v.27 tasmāt sarveṣu kāleṣu yogayukto bhavārjuna

By understanding these two paths, a yogi is never bewildered. Therefore, O Arjuna, remain disciplined and steady in yoga under all circumstances.

338 vedeṣu yajñeṣu tapaḥsu caiva; dāneṣu yat puṇyaphalaṁ pradiṣṭam
Ch.8 v.28 atyeti tat sarvam idaṁ viditvā; yogī paraṁ sthānam upaiti cādyam

By knowing this process, the yogi goes beyond the study of the vedas, beyond offering yajna to the devas, beyond the performance of tapasya and other methods of personal perfection, and beyond dana 'the distribution of the benefits of material life to those in need'. Surpassing all these indirect processes, the perfected yogi goes directly to the supreme and ultimate abode of Brahman.

Chapter 9

The Secrets of Dharma and Devotion

339
Ch.9 v.1

śrībhagavān uvāca
idaṁ tu te guhyatamaṁ pravakṣyāmy anasūyave
jñānaṁ vijñānasahitaṁ yaj jñātvā mokṣyase 'śubhāt

Shri Bhagavan spoke to Arjuna:
Because you are never jealous of my opulence and you are sincere, I will share these guhyatama 'supreme secrets' with you. By realizing this divine knowledge, you will become immune to anything that could otherwise cause you harm.

340
Ch.9 v.2

rājavidyā rājaguhyaṁ pavitram idam uttamam
pratyakṣāvagamaṁ dharmyaṁ susukhaṁ kartum avyayam

This is the raja vidya raja guhya 'secret knowledge that is primarily given to those who rule'. It is the knowledge that empowers leaders to truly protect all beings and serve in a way that is pure and beyond the corruption of tamas. This knowledge is clear, always supports dharma, brings joy to all, and is always true.

341
Ch.9 v.3

aśraddadhānāḥ puruṣā dharmasyāsya paraṁtapa
aprāpya māṁ nivartante mṛtyusaṁsāravartmani

Those persons who cannot stay in a state of shraddha and focus upon the invisible yet essential truths of dharma cannot attain a permanent connection with Me, so they stay on the path that leads to repeated birth and death through samsara.

342
Ch.9 v.4

mayā tatam idaṁ sarvaṁ jagad avyaktamūrtinā
matsthāni sarvabhūtāni na cāhaṁ teṣv avasthitaḥ

This entire jagat is pervaded by My invisible murti 'nonmaterial transcendental form'. All beings are standing within Me, but I am not contained by or encompassed within them.

343 na ca matsthāni bhūtāni paśya me yogam aiśvaram
Ch.9 v.5 bhūtabhṛn na ca bhūtastho mamātmā bhūtabhāvanaḥ

This is the immense power of My yoga, created by My Atma. Behold, even though all beings reside within Me and are Mine, I am also a separate, individual being entirely apart from them.

344 yathākāśasthito nityaṁ vāyuḥ sarvatrago mahān
Ch.9 v.6 tathā sarvāṇi bhūtāni matsthānīty upadhāraya

Try to understand this, Arjuna. Just as vayu 'the mighty wind', blowing everywhere, is always resting within akasha 'space', so all created beings are always standing within Me.

345 sarvabhūtāni kaunteya prakṛtiṁ yānti māmikām
Ch.9 v.7 kalpakṣaye punas tāni kalpādau visṛjāmy aham

Just see, Arjuna, at the end of one kalpa 'a day for the creator Brahma', I withdraw all beings into an unmanifest state within My prakriti. Then, by My unlimited energy, as the next day of Brahma begins, I bring them all back into manifestation again, exactly where they left off, ready for the next kalpa.

346 prakṛtiṁ svām avaṣṭabhya visṛjāmi punaḥ punaḥ
Ch.9 v.8 bhūtagrāmam imaṁ kṛtsnam avaśaṁ prakṛter vaśāt

The whole of material existence is resting upon My prakriti and by My will, the entire multitude of living beings are first withdrawn and then sent forth into manifestation again.

This is the raja vidya raja
guhya 'secret knowledge
that is primarily given to
those who rule'. It is the
knowledge that empowers
leaders to truly protect all
beings and serve in a way
that is pure and beyond
the corruption of tamas.
This knowledge is clear,
always supports dharma,
brings joy to all,
and is always true.–340

347 na ca māṁ tāni karmāṇi nibadhnanti dhanaṁjaya
Ch.9 v.9 udāsīnavad āsīnam asaktaṁ teṣu karmasu

But none of those activities constrain Me in any way. O Arjuna, I sit apart from them in My own asana, unattached to all these actions.

348 mayādhyakṣeṇa prakṛtiḥ sūyate sacarācaram
Ch.9 v.10 hetunānena kaunteya jagad viparivartate

With Me as the witness and overseer, prakriti produces all things, both moving and non-moving, that are required to manifest life by hetu 'the rules and logic of cosmic cause and effect', impelling the universal manifestation to renew itself again and again.

349 avajānanti māṁ mūḍhā mānuṣīṁ tanum āśritam
Ch.9 v.11 paraṁ bhāvam ajānanto mama bhūtamaheśvaram

Those who are deluded treat Me with contempt when I descend within matter as an avatar assuming a human-like form. They do not know My ultimate and supreme nature as the controller of all beings, for I am Bhuta Maha Ishvara 'the ultimate source and controller of all beings'.

350 moghāśā moghakarmāṇo moghajñānā vicetasaḥ
Ch.9 v.12 rākṣasīm āsurīṁ caiva prakṛtiṁ mohinīṁ śritāḥ

Those whose future hopes are deluded, whose actions produce an undesirable result, and whose knowledge is flawed and harmful are called asuras and rakshasas. They darken the world and devour the life force of those with whom they interact.

351 mahātmānas tu māṁ pārtha daivīṁ prakṛtim āśritāḥ
Ch.9 v.13 bhajanty ananyamanaso jñātvā bhūtādim avyayam

But those atmas who embrace Me become mahatma and have a nature like that of the devas. They always dwell in Me and bhajanti 'adore Me with single-minded devotion', and they know Me as the immortal and imperishable source of all beings.

352 satataṁ kīrtayanto māṁ yatantaś ca dṛḍhavratāḥ
Ch.9 v.14 namasyantaś ca māṁ bhaktyā nityayuktā upāsate

Those who are satatam kirtayanto mam 'always chanting and singing My names', who desire to serve Me, and who bow before Me with dedication and affection are linked to Me in a timeless yoga of intense devotion.

353 jñānayajñena cāpy anye yajanto mām upāsate
Ch.9 v.15 ekatvena pṛthaktvena bahudhā viśvatomukham

Other yogis light the sacred fire of knowledge within themselves and make offerings to Me as the one ultimate Being whose vishvata mukha 'unlimited faces' are manifesting in every direction as the light shining across the universe.

354 ahaṁ kratur ahaṁ yajñaḥ svadhāham aham auṣadham
Ch.9 v.16 mantro 'ham aham evājyam aham agnir ahaṁ hutam

O Arjuna

1. aham kratu—I am the ceremony.
2. aham yajna—I am the process of sacred offering.
3. aham svadha—I am the intention of one who offers.
4. aham aushadha—I am the fragrant healing herbs.
5. aham mantra—I am the sacred words spoken with the offering.

6. aham evajya—I am the ghee 'clarified butter' poured into the fire.
7. aham agni—I am the deva Agni as the fire itself.
8. aham hutam—I am the offering which is placed into the fire and the smoke arising from it.

355 pitāham asya jagato mātā dhātā pitāmahaḥ
Ch.9 v.17 vedyaṁ pavitram oṁkāra ṛk sāma yajur eva ca

9. aham pita asya jagat—I am the father of this jagat.
10. aham mata—I am the mother of this jagat.
11. aham dhata—I am the support of this jagat.
12. aham pitamaha—I am the grandfather of this jagat.
13. aham vedya—I am all that can be known.
14. aham pavitra—I am that which purifies everything.
15. aham omkara—I am aum, the original sound from which everything has manifested.
16. aham rik sama yajur—I am the Rig, Sama, and Yajur Vedas.

356 gatir bhartā prabhuḥ sākṣī nivāsaḥ śaraṇaṁ suhṛt
Ch.9 v.18 prabhavaḥ pralayaḥ sthānaṁ nidhānaṁ bījam avyayam

17. aham gati—I am the destination.
18. aham bharta—I am the sustainer.
19. aham prabhu—I am the master.
20. aham sakshi—I am the witness who sees all.
21. aham nivasa—I am the final abode.
22. aham sharana—I am the greatest shelter.
23. aham suhrit—I am the most-dear friend.
24. aham prabhava—I am the origin of everything.
25. aham pralaya—I am the destroyer of all.
26. aham sthana—I am the support of all.
27. aham nidhana—I am that upon which everything rests.
28. aham bija avyaya—I am the undying seed.

357 tapāmy aham ahaṁ varṣaṁ nigṛhṇāmy utsṛjāmi ca
Ch.9 v.19 amṛtaṁ caiva mṛtyuś ca sadasac cāham Arjuna

29. aham tapami—From My tapasya I generate the fire.
30. aham varsham nigrihnami utsrijami—I withhold the rains or cause them to pour forth.
31. aham amrita cha eva mrityu cha—Both death and immortality come from My being.
32. aham sat asat cha—I am that which is immortal and that which is temporary.

traividyā māṁ somapāḥ pūtapāpā; yajñair iṣṭvā svargatiṁ
358 prārthayante
Ch.9 v.20 te puṇyam āsādya surendralokam; aśnanti divyān divi devabhogān

Those who follow the vedic path of yajna 'ritual offerings into the sacred fire to show gratitude to the devas' adore Me indirectly through those offerings. Purified of the papa arising from their harmful human actions, they drink the celestial nectar that flows from the gratitude of the devas, which in turn gives them great joy. They take their next birth in the deva realms and there continue to enjoy divine delights.

te taṁ bhuktvā svargalokaṁ viśālaṁ; kṣīṇe puṇye martyalokaṁ
359 viśanti
Ch.9 v.21 evaṁ trayīdharmam anuprapannā; gatāgataṁ kāmakāmā labhante

In this way, by following the dharma presented in the Rig, Sama, and Yajur Vedas, they spend many years enjoying the refined and sublime pleasures of the Deva Loka realm. But when the karmas that elevated them to Svarga Loka have expired, they again descend to Bhumi Loka and reincarnate once more.

360 ananyāś cintayanto māṁ ye janāḥ paryupāsate
Ch.9 v.22 teṣāṁ nityābhiyuktānāṁ yogakṣemaṁ vahāmy aham

On the other hand, when yoga practitioners constantly adore Me and their thoughts are focused upon Me in a state of perpetual yogic awareness, then I take a personal interest in their life and its needs.

361 ye 'py anyadevatā bhaktā yajante śraddhayānvitāḥ
Ch.9 v.23 te 'pi mām eva kaunteya yajanty avidhipūrvakam

You see Arjuna, even though they may not understand the entire process, those who make offerings of devotion to the devas are also indirectly giving those offerings to Me.

362 ahaṁ hi sarvayajñānāṁ bhoktā ca prabhur eva ca
Ch.9 v.24 na tu mām abhijānanti tattvenātaś cyavanti te

Indeed, I am the ultimate recipient of all sacred offerings, but those who do not consciously understand this truth must return again and take birth within matter.

363 yānti devavratā devān pitṝn yānti pitṛvratāḥ
Ch.9 v.25 bhūtāni yānti bhūtejyā yānti madyājino 'pi mām

Those who make their offering to the devas, go to live with the devas. Those who make their offering to their departed ancestors, go to live on the lokas where those ancestors reside. Those who make their offering to ghosts and disembodied beings, go to wherever they are, while those who make their sacred offering to Me, come to live with Me.

364 patraṁ puṣpaṁ phalaṁ toyaṁ yo me bhaktyā prayacchati
Ch.9 v.26 tad ahaṁ bhaktyupahṛtam aśnāmi prayatātmanaḥ

If anyone offers Me, with love and devotion, a leaf, a flower, a fruit, or some water, I accept their offering as an act of love.

365 yat karoṣi yad aśnāsi yaj juhoṣi dadāsi yat
Ch.9 v.27 yat tapasyasi kaunteya tat kuruṣva madarpaṇam

Therefore, Arjuna, whatever you do, whatever you eat, whatever you distribute and circulate as dana to others, whatever you offer into the sacred fire of a yajna as an offering to the devas, and whatever tapasya you perform to perfect yourself, just do all of these as a sacred offering directly to Me.

366 śubhāśubhaphalair evaṁ mokṣyase karmabandhanaiḥ
Ch.9 v.28 saṁnyāsayogayuktātmā vimukto mām upaiṣyasi

If you perform this sannyasa yoga, you will achieve moksha 'release from the bondage of karma resulting from your actions within matter', and your atma will come directly to Me.

367 samo 'haṁ sarvabhūteṣu na me dveṣyo 'sti na priyaḥ
Ch.9 v.29 ye bhajanti tu māṁ bhaktyā mayi te teṣu cāpy aham

I am within all beings and view them all the same way. None is disliked by Me or is dearer to Me than the others. But those who adore Me directly, and who constantly show their dedication through acts performed in the serving moods of bhakti yoga are in Me, and I am in them. I always reciprocate and think of them just as they think of Me.

368 api cet sudurācāro bhajate mām ananyabhāk
Ch.9 v.30 sādhur eva sa mantavyaḥ samyag vyavasito hi saḥ

Even if a person purposely causes harm to others and their actions are still flawed, but they are trying to be devoted to Me in bhakti yoga, I consider them to be on the right path, in spite of their imperfections.

369 kṣipraṁ bhavati dharmātmā śaśvacchāntiṁ nigacchati
Ch.9 v.31 kaunteya pratijānīhi na me bhaktaḥ praṇaśyati

You should know for certain, Arjuna, that any atma who is dedicated to My loving service quickly becomes steady in dharmic living and soon achieves the balanced state of shanti. No bhakta of Mine is ever lost for long, and none is ultimately lost or destroyed.

370 māṁ hi pārtha vyapāśritya ye 'pi syuḥ pāpayonayaḥ
Ch.9 v.32 striyo vaiśyās tathā śūdrās te 'pi yānti parāṁ gatim

O Arjuna, those born from compromised situations or in corrupted families; those born female and who were not given freedom or education; those who work in businesses that harm their character; and those who work in compromising occupations can still have a relationship with Me through the practice of bhakti yoga and eventually they will reach the param gati 'ultimate destination'.

371 kiṁ punar brāhmaṇāḥ puṇyā bhaktā rājarṣayas tathā
Ch.9 v.33 anityam asukhaṁ lokam imaṁ prāpya bhajasva mām

How easy is it then, for those who know Brahman, who are dharmic rulers, and who know that this world is temporary and full of miseries, to become engaged in loving service to me?

372

Ch.9 v.34

manmanā bhava madbhakto madyājī māṁ namaskuru
mām evaiṣyasi yuktvaivam ātmānaṁ matparāyaṇaḥ

Just focus your thinking, feeling, willing, and memory upon Me in a state of intense adoration. Offer everything you possess to Me with sincere humility, uniting with Me in the mood of endearing devotion. Then, when you are steady in your meditation, you will come to Me.

I am the source of everything;
from Me the entire creation flows.
Knowing this, the wise adore Me
with all their hearts.

◆

Their thoughts dwell in Me,
their lives are surrendered unto Me.
They derive great satisfaction and bliss
enlightening one another
and conversing about Me.

◆

To those who are constantly devoted
and adore Me with purest love,
I give the understanding by which
they may come to Me.

◆

Out of compassion for them,
I, who am dwelling within their hearts,
destroy the darkness born of ignorance
with the shining lamp of knowledge.

These are known as the four core verses—the heart—of the Bhagavad Gita. 380–383

Chapter 10

The Heart and Majesty of Bhagavan

373 śrībhagavān uvāca
Ch.10 v.1 bhūya eva mahābāho śṛṇu me paramaṁ vacaḥ
yat te 'haṁ prīyamāṇāya vakṣyāmi hitakāmyayā

SHRI BHAGAVAN spoke:
O Arjuna, because you are so very dear to Me, listen closely as I reveal for your ultimate well-being the most confidential knowledge of My param nature.

374 na me viduḥ suragaṇāḥ prabhavaṁ na maharṣayaḥ
Ch.10 v.2 aham ādir hi devānāṃ maharṣīṇāṁ ca sarvaśaḥ

Neither the devas nor the greatest rishis completely understand My true nature for I am the source of the devas and the maharishis.

375 yo mām ajam anādiṁ ca vetti lokamaheśvaram
Ch.10 v.3 asaṁmūḍhaḥ sa martyeṣu sarvapāpaiḥ pramucyate

One who knows Me as the Loka Maha Ishvara 'the greatest being who is the ruler of all the realms', who realizes that I am unborn and without beginning, goes beyond the delusions, limitations, and confusion of ordinary human knowledge. That person, although still living among mortals, is completely released from all papa.

376 buddhir jñānam asaṁmohaḥ kṣamā satyaṁ damaḥ śamaḥ
Ch.10 v.4 sukhaṁ duḥkhaṁ bhavo 'bhāvo bhayaṁ cābhayam eva ca

The qualities of

1. buddhi—discernment between matter and the atma
2. jnana—knowledge of both prakriti and Brahman
3. asammoha—undeluded awareness

4. kshama—patience
5. satya—truthfulness
6. dama—control of the senses
7. shama—equanimity and tranquility
8. sukha—pleasure
9. dukha—pain
10. bhava—the state of embodied being
11. abhava—the state of disembodiment
12. bhaya—fear
13. abhaya—courage

377 ahiṁsā samatā tuṣṭis tapo dānaṁ yaśo 'yaśaḥ
Ch.10 v.5 bhavanti bhāvā bhūtānāṁ matta eva pṛthagvidhāḥ

14. ahimsa—performance of one's dharma while causing the least harm
15. samata—sameness, equality with all beings
16. tushti—self-contentment
17. tapas—self-improvement by correct practice
18. dana—circulation of resources in society
19. yasha—fame, and
20. ayasha—infamy

are qualities and states of existence that are present in varying degrees in every living being, and all have their origin in Me.

378 maharṣayaḥ sapta pūrve catvāro manavas tathā
Ch.10 v.6 madbhāvā mānasā jātā yeṣāṁ loka imāḥ prajāḥ

The vedas say that in ancient times, there were seven great rishis and four great manus who were the source of the various lokas in the universe and who were responsible for populating those planets with human beings. Those rishis and manus were created from my imagination.

379 etāṁ vibhūtiṁ yogaṁ ca mama yo vetti tattvataḥ
so 'vikampena yogena yujyate nātra saṁśayaḥ
Ch.10 v.7

All this universal beauty, glory, and power is merely vibhuti yoga 'the wonders manifested by Me through My unlimited and inconceivable powers of yoga'. One who fully understands this becomes forever united with Me by means of the unwavering connection of their yoga.

380 ahaṁ sarvasya prabhavo mattaḥ sarvaṁ pravartate
iti matvā bhajante māṁ budhā bhāvasamanvitāḥ
Ch.10 v.8

I am the source of everything; from Me the entire creation flows. Knowing this, the wise adore Me with all their hearts.

381 maccittā madgataprāṇā bodhayantaḥ parasparam
kathayantaś ca māṁ nityaṁ tuṣyanti ca ramanti ca
Ch.10 v.9

Their thoughts dwell in Me, their lives are surrendered unto Me, and they derive great satisfaction and bliss enlightening one another and conversing about Me.

382 teṣāṁ satatayuktānāṁ bhajatāṁ prītipūrvakam
dadāmi buddhiyogaṁ taṁ yena mām upayānti te
Ch.10 v.10

To those who are constantly devoted and adore Me with purest love, I give the understanding by which they may come to Me.

383 teṣām evānukampārtham aham ajñānajaṁ tamaḥ
nāśayāmy ātmabhāvastho jñānadīpena bhāsvatā
Ch.10 v.11

Out of compassion for them, I, who am dwelling within their hearts, destroy the darkness born of ignorance with the shining lamp of knowledge.

384 paraṁ brahma paraṁ dhāma pavitraṁ paramaṁ bhavān
Ch.10 v.12 puruṣaṁ śāśvataṁ divyam ādidevam ajaṁ vibhum

ARJUNA said:

O Krishna, You are

1. Param Brahma—the ultimate manifestation of Brahman
2. Param Dhama—the supreme abode within Brahman
3. Pavitra—that Being whose association purifies everyone
4. Paramam Bhavan—the ultimate and Supreme Being
5. Purusha Shashvata Divya—the Ultimate Divine Person
6. Adideva—the original deva
7. Aja—that Being who is never born but merely appears
8. Vibhu—the Supreme Being who pervades everything.

385 āhus tvām ṛṣayaḥ sarve devarṣir nāradas tathā
Ch.10 v.13 asito devalo vyāsaḥ svayaṁ caiva bravīṣi me

All the greatest rishis among the devas and the humans, including Narada, Asita, Devala, and Vyasa, have explained who You are, and now You are personally explaining yourself to me.

386 sarvam etad ṛtaṁ manye yan māṁ vadasi keśava
Ch.10 v.14 na hi te bhagavan vyaktiṁ vidur devā na dānavāḥ

O Shri Krishna, I know that all the wisdom You are giving me contains the deepest truths on which the ritam of this world rests. O Bhagavan, neither the devas nor the asuras truly understand how You are manifest within all that exists.

387 svayam evātmanātmānaṁ vettha tvaṁ puruṣottama
Ch.10 v.15 bhūtabhāvana bhūteśa devadeva jagatpate

O greatest Atma, only You truly know Yourself with Your own Atma, for You are

1. Purusha Uttama—the greatest person who exists beyond the influence of the gunas
2. Bhuta Bhavana—the source of well-being for all living beings
3. Bhutesha—the ultimate ruler above all living beings
4. Devadeva—the Supreme Deva to whom all other devas must answer, and
5. Jagatpati—the master, controller, and source of all the universes.

388 vaktum arhasy aśeṣeṇa divyā hy ātmavibhūtayaḥ
Ch.10 v.16 yābhir vibhūtibhir lokān imāṁs tvaṁ vyāpya tiṣṭhasi

Now please describe without any reservations how the countless divine wonders of existence emanate from Your own Atma, pervading and abiding within every one of the countless lokas.

389 kathaṁ vidyām ahaṁ yogiṁs tvāṁ sadā paricintayan
Ch.10 v.17 keṣu keṣu ca bhāveṣu cintyo 'si bhagavan mayā

How should I see and know You, O greatest yogi, constantly meditating upon You in a myriad of ways? O Shri Bhagavan, in what forms, aspects and states of being should I contemplate the countless wonders of Your being?

390 vistareṇātmano yogaṁ vibhūtiṁ ca janārdana
Ch.10 v.18 bhūyaḥ kathaya tṛptir hi śṛṇvato nāsti me 'mṛtam

O Shri Krishna, please explain the many details of how You bring forth this amazing manifestation through the power of Your own yoga. I never tire of hearing the amrita 'life restoring nectar' of Your immortal words.

391 śrībhagavān uvāca
Ch.10 v.19 hanta te kathayiṣyāmi divyā hy ātmavibhūtayaḥ
prādhānyataḥ kuruśreṣṭha nāsty anto vistarasya me

Shri Bhagavan said:
Listen Arjuna, as I reveal to you the atma vibhuti 'divine process by which all that exists is manifest from My own Atma'. But since there is no limit to My endless expansions, I will only describe those that are most prominent.

392 aham ātmā guḍākeśa sarvabhūtāśayasthitaḥ
Ch.10 v.20 aham ādiś ca madhyaṁ ca bhūtānām anta eva ca

O Arjuna, I am the

1. atma—the true self residing in the heart of all beings
2. adi—the beginning
3. madhya—the middle, and
4. anta bhutana—the end of life of all beings.

393 ādityānām ahaṁ viṣṇur jyotiṣāṁ ravir aṁśumān
Ch.10 v.21 marīcir marutām asmi nakṣatrāṇām ahaṁ śaśī

Shri Krishna continued:

5. Among the Adityas, I am Vishnu.
6. Of lights, I am Ravi, the radiant Sun.

7. Of the Maruts, I am Marici.
8. Among nakshatras 'the twenty-seven constellations', I am Shashi, the Moon.

394 vedānāṁ sāmavedo 'smi devānām asmi vāsavaḥ
Ch.10 v.22 indriyāṇāṁ manaś cāsmi bhūtānām asmi cetanā

9. Among the vedas, I am the Sama Veda.
10. Of devas, I am Vasava or Indra.
11. Among the indriyas, I am the manas faculty.
12. I am chetana 'the conscious awareness of the atma in each being'.

395 rudrāṇāṁ śaṁkaraś cāsmi vitteśo yakṣarakṣasām
Ch.10 v.23 vasūnāṁ pāvakaś cāsmi meruḥ śikhariṇām aham

13. Of the Rudras, I am Shankara.
14. Of the Yakshas and Rakshas, I am Vittesha or Kuvera.
15. Of the Vasus, I am Pavaka.
16. Of mountains, I am Meru.

396 purodhasāṁ ca mukhyaṁ māṁ viddhi pārtha bṛhaspatim
Ch.10 v.24 senānīnām ahaṁ skandaḥ sarasām asmi sāgaraḥ

You should know, Arjuna

17. Of the purohits 'wise performers of sacred rituals', I am Brihaspati.
18. Of military commanders, I am Skanda.
19. Of bodies of water, I am Sagara, the ocean.

397 maharṣīṇāṁ bhṛgur ahaṁ girām asmy ekam akṣaram
Ch.10 v.25 yajñānāṁ japayajño 'smi sthāvarāṇāṁ himālayaḥ

20. Of great rishis, I am Brighu.
21. Of all words, I am the single-syllabled sound vibration of aum.
22. Of all yajnas, I am japa, the chanting of mantras on a mala.
23. Of immovable things, I am the Himalaya mountains.

398 aśvatthaḥ sarvavṛkṣāṇāṁ devarṣīṇāṁ ca nāradaḥ
Ch.10 v.26 gandharvāṇāṁ citrarathaḥ siddhānāṁ kapilo muniḥ

24. Of trees, I am ashvattha, the peepul tree (Ficus religiosa).
25. Among the deva rishis, I am Naraḍa.
26. Among the Gandharvas 'deva musicians', I am Chitraratha.
27. Of siddha munis, I am Kapila, the founder of sankhya darshan 'the branch of vedic knowledge that gave us modern science'.

399 uccaiḥśravasam aśvānāṁ viddhi mām amṛtodbhavam
Ch.10 v.27 airāvataṁ gajendrāṇāṁ narāṇāṁ ca narādhipam

28. Of horses, I am Ucchaishravas, the seven-headed horse of the deva Indra that was born from the churning of the milk ocean.
29. Of elephants, I am Airavata, the four-headed elephant of Indra who was also born from the milk ocean.
30. Among humans, I am the ruler.

400 āyudhānām ahaṁ vajraṁ dhenūnām asmi kāmadhuk
Ch.10 v.28 prajanaś cāsmi kandarpaḥ sarpāṇām asmi vāsukiḥ

31. Among weapons of war, I am the vajra 'thunderbolt wielded by the deva Indra'.
32. Of cows that reside in the transcendental realm of Brahman,

I am Kamadhuk, the Surabhi cow who, when milked, gives anything one desires.

33. I am Kandarpa or Kama Deva, that being who excites humans with sensual and sexual desires.
34. Of sarpas 'serpents', I am Vasuki, the deva ruler of all such beings.

401 anantaś cāsmi nāgānāṁ varuṇo yādasām aham
Ch.10 v.29 pitṝṇām aryamā cāsmi yamaḥ saṁyamatām aham

35. Among all the nagas 'celestial serpents', I am Ananta Shesha, the thousand-headed serpent and the resting-place of Vishnu.
36. Among the yadasas, the beings who live in water, I am the deva Varuna.
37. Among ancestors or original progenitors of human beings, I am Aryaman.
38. Of those devas who exercise control over others, I am Yama, the deva presiding over the process of samsara 'repeated birth and death'.

402 prahlādaś cāsmi daityānāṁ kālaḥ kalayatām aham
Ch.10 v.30 mṛgāṇāṁ ca mṛgendro 'haṁ vainateyaś ca pakṣiṇām

39. Among the asuras of ancient history, I am the devoted Prahlada.
40. Among those who observe and calculate cycles of time, I am kala 'time itself'.
41. Among all creatures of the animal kingdom, I am the mrigendra 'lion'.
42. Of feathered beings, I am Vainateya or Garuda 'the son of Vinata and the carrier of Vishnu'.

403 pavanaḥ pavatām asmi rāmaḥ śastrabhṛtām aham
Ch.10 v.31 jhaṣāṇāṁ makaraś cāsmi srotasām asmi jāhnavī

43. Among all things that purify, I am Pavana or Vayu 'the deva of the wind'.
44. Of all warriors bearing weapons, I am Rama, the seventh avatar of Vishnu.
45. Of all creatures that live in the ocean, I am makara 'the sea-dragon', the greatest guardian creature of the deep oceans.
46. Of all rivers, I am Jahnavi, also known as the Ganga.

404 sargāṇām ādir antaś ca madhyaṁ caivāham Arjuna
Ch.10 v.32 adhyātmavidyā vidyānāṁ vādaḥ pravadatām aham

O Arjuna
47. Of all manifest things, I am the creator, maintainer, and destroyer.
48. I am adhyatma vidya, the science by which one knows oneself as the atma.
49. Of those who discuss and debate the ultimate truths that can be known, I am the logic of the irrefutable conclusion.

405 akṣarāṇām akāro 'smi dvaṁdvaḥ sāmāsikasya ca
Ch.10 v.33 aham evākṣayaḥ kālo dhātāhaṁ viśvatomukhaḥ

50. Of aksharas, the letters in the Sanskrit alphabet, I am akara, the letter 'a'.
51. I am that principle in grammar that joins two words together as a dual compound.
52. I am immeasurable time.
53. I am Vishvata Mukha, that Being who is facing all directions in the universe.

406 mṛtyuḥ sarvaharaś cāham udbhavaś ca bhaviṣyatām
Ch.10 v.34 kīrtiḥ śrīr vāk ca nārīṇāṁ smṛtir medhā dhṛtiḥ kṣamā

54. I am all-devouring death.
55. I am Udbhava Bhavishyata 'the generating principle', the cause of everything that is and is yet to be.
56. Of all the excellent qualities of naris 'females', I am
    - kirti—honourable reputation
    - shri—the one who creates well-being
    - vak—elegant speech
    - smriti—memory
    - medha—intelligence that makes life possible
    - dhriti—constancy, determination, faithfulness, dedication, fortitude, endurance, and
    - kshama—patience.

407 bṛhatsāma tathā sāmnāṁ gāyatrī chandasām aham
Ch.10 v.35 māsānāṁ mārgaśīrṣo 'ham ṛtūnāṁ kusumākaraḥ

57. Among vedic melodies, I am the brihatsama.
58. Of poetic meters, I am gayatri chandas 'the gayatri meter'.
59. Of masas 'months', I am margashirsha 'the nakshatra bridging November and December'.
60. Of ritus 'seasons', I am kusuma kara 'springtime when the flowers bloom'.

408 dyūtaṁ chalayatām asmi tejas tejasvinām aham
Ch.10 v.36 jayo 'smi vyavasāyo 'smi sattvaṁ sattvavatām aham

61. Among cheaters, I am gambling.
62. Of extraordinary people, I am their tejas 'brilliance and charisma'.
63. I am jaya 'the moment of triumph'.

64. I am vyavasaya 'unbreakable determination'.
65. Of sattvavats 'those who are dedicated to the truth', I am their purity.

409 vṛṣṇīnāṁ vāsudevo 'smi pāṇḍavānāṁ dhanaṁjayaḥ
Ch.10 v.37 munīnām apy ahaṁ vyāsaḥ kavīnām uśanā kaviḥ

66. In the Vrishni dynasty, I am Shri Krishna, the son of Vasudeva.
67. Of the Pandavas, I am Dhananjaya, or you, Arjuna.
68. Among munis 'sages', I am Vyasadeva.
69. Among kavis 'great poets', I am Ushana.

410 daṇḍo damayatām asmi nītir asmi jigīṣatām
Ch.10 v.38 maunaṁ caivāsmi guhyānāṁ jñānaṁ jñānavatām aham

70. I am the power and right of rulers to punish.
71. I am the ethical and strategic advice given to those who are meant to be victorious.
72. I am the unrevealed secrets kept in silence.
73. I am the knowing of those who are the most knowledgeable.

411 yac cāpi sarvabhūtānāṁ bījaṁ tad aham Arjuna
Ch.10 v.39 na tad asti vinā yat syān mayā bhūtaṁ carācaram

O Arjuna, I am the source of the seeds from which all living beings arise. Without Me, none of these beings, either moving or unmoving, would have arisen.

412 nānto 'sti mama divyānāṁ vibhūtīnāṁ paraṁtapa
Ch.10 v.40 eṣa tūddeśataḥ prokto vibhūter vistaro mayā

There is no end to My divine manifestations, O mighty Arjuna. I have shared these examples with you merely as a small example of the vistas of My unlimited opulence manifest by My personal energies.

413 yad yad vibhūtimat sattvaṁ śrīmad ūrjitam eva vā
tat tad evāvagaccha tvaṁ mama tejoṁśasaṁbhavam
Ch.10 v.41

Whenever you see anything that is shrimad 'a splendid, powerful, prosperous, truthful, glorious reality, full of vigor and powerful urges to greatness', just try to understand that in every case, every being or object is merely endowed with just a tiny spark of My unlimited being and energies.

414 atha vā bahunaitena kiṁ jñātena tavārjuna
viṣṭabhyāham idaṁ kṛtsnam ekāṁśena sthito jagat
Ch.10 v.42

O Arjuna, what is the need for sharing all this detailed knowledge with you, since with a single fragment of Myself, I support everything that exists?

Chapter 11

Cosmic Time and the Universal Form

415
Ch.11 v.1

madanugrahāya paramaṁ guhyam adhyātmasaṁjñitam
yat tvayoktaṁ vacas tena moho 'yaṁ vigato mama

ARJUNA said:
Out of kindness and affection for me, You have just revealed the ultimate guhya 'secret knowledge' concerning Your nature as Adyatmika 'the Supreme Being and the source of all that is'. Because of Your words, my moha 'delusion' has now been removed.

416
Ch. 11 v. 2

bhavāpyayau hi bhūtānāṁ śrutau vistaraśo mayā
tvattaḥ kamalapatrākṣa māhātmyam api cāvyayam

O kamala patra akshi 'O lotus-eyed One whose eyes are as beautiful as the petals of a blooming lotus', I have heard from You in detail about how the countless beings are manifested within matter and then dissolved again and again. I have also learned that You are the greatest Atma who pervades all and can never be destroyed.

417
Ch.11 v.3

evam etad yathāttha tvam ātmānaṁ parameśvara
draṣṭum icchāmi te rūpam aiśvaraṁ puruṣottama

O Parama Ishvara 'greatest among all controllers', since You have described Your nature as the Atmana 'ultimate Atma', and you are also Purusha Uttama 'the greatest Person who is beyond the reach of matter', I wish to see Your aishvara rupa 'magnificent universal form' by which you pervade and support everything within this universe.

418
Ch.11 v.4

manyase yadi tac chakyaṁ mayā draṣṭum iti prabho
yogeśvara tato me tvaṁ darśayātmānam avyayam

O Prabhu 'my beloved Master', if You think I am eligible to see this, O Yoga Ishvara 'greatest of yogis', please show me how your imperishable Self pervades the entire universe.

419
Ch.11 v.5

śrībhagavān uvāca
paśya me pārtha rūpāṇi śataśo 'tha sahasraśaḥ
nānāvidhāni divyāni nānāvarṇākṛtīni ca

SHRI BHAGAVAN then said:
O Arjuna, just see My many forms, hundreds and thousands of divine images, and each of various colours and shapes.

420
Ch.11 v.6

paśyādityān vasūn rudrān aśvinau marutas tathā
bahūny adṛṣṭapūrvāṇi paśyāścaryāṇi bhārata

Now you may see the Adityas, the Vasus, the Rudras, the Ashvins, the Maruts, and other divine beings who are also there. O Arjuna, behold the many marvels never seen before.

421
Ch.11 v.7

ihaikasthaṁ jagat kṛtsnaṁ paśyādya sacarācaram
mama dehe guḍākeśa yac cānyad draṣṭum icchasi

O Arjuna, just see how everything in the entire jagat, both the moving and unmoving, is standing together within my universal body as one grand being. Anything you wish to see is present here.

422
Ch.11 v.8

na tu māṁ śakyase draṣṭum anenaiva svacakṣuṣā
divyaṁ dadāmi te cakṣuḥ paśya me yogam aiśvaram

But you cannot see this form with your physical eyes, so I am giving you divine eyes. Behold, as I now reveal My universal and splendid qualities through My yoga aishvarya 'unlimited yogic powers'.

423
Ch.11 v.9

saṁjaya uvāca
evam uktvā tato rājan mahāyogeśvaro hariḥ
darśayām āsa pārthāya paramaṁ rūpam aiśvaram

Then, SANJAYA said to Dhritarashtra:
O King, after speaking in this way, Shri Krishna, the Maha Yoga Ishvara Hari 'the greatest master of yoga who removes all inauspicious things from one's heart' revealed to Arjuna his Parama Rupa Aishvara 'supreme and attractive universal form'.

424
Ch.11 v.10

anekavaktranayanam anekādbhutadarśanam
anekadivyābharaṇaṁ divyānekodyatāyudham

SANJAYA continued to speak:
Suddenly Arjuna saw countless mouths and eyes, unlimited marvelous visions extending everywherc. He saw divine ornaments of immeasurable splendour and endless mystic weapons upraised everywhere.

425
Ch.11 v.11

divyamālyāmbaradharaṁ divyagandhānulepanam
sarvāścaryamayaṁ devam anantaṁ viśvatomukham

SANJAYA continued:
Decorated with divine garments, garlanded with celestial flowers, fragrant with intoxicating perfumes, and exhibiting magical marvels of every description, Deva Ananta Vishvata Mukha 'the Supreme Deva whose uncountable faces look in every direction' appeared before Arjuna.

426 divi sūryasahasrasya bhaved yugapad utthitā
Ch.11 v.12 yadi bhāḥ sadṛśī sā syād bhāsas tasya mahātmanaḥ

Sanjaya said:
Divi surya sahasrasya 'if a thousand suns' rose up in the sky all at once, their brilliance would not equal the effulgence of the form that Arjuna now saw.

427 tatraikasthaṁ jagat kṛtsnaṁ pravibhaktam anekadhā
Ch.11 v.13 apaśyad devadevasya śarīre pāṇḍavas tadā

Sanjaya continued:
There, Arjuna saw the entire jagat as the grand cosmic body of Shri Krishna, who is Deva Devasya 'the Ultimate deva among them all'. Within that cosmic form, divided into the many species and classes of living entities, all individual beings live their lives.

428 tataḥ sa vismayāviṣṭo hṛṣṭaromā dhanaṁjayaḥ
Ch.11 v.14 praṇamya śirasā devaṁ kṛtāñjalir abhāṣata

Immediately, Arjuna was overwhelmed by the amazing sights he saw. With his hair standing on end, he bowed down to Shri Krishna. Holding out his hands in the anjali mudra, as if offering flowers, he began to speak.

arjuna uvāca
paśyāmi devāṁs tava deva dehe; sarvāṁs tathā
429 bhūtaviśeṣasaṁghān
Ch.11 v.15 brahmāṇam īśaṁ kamalāsanastham; ṛṣīṁś ca sarvān
uragāṁś ca divyān

ARJUNA said:
O greatest Deva, I see all the other devas there within Your cosmic body. Indeed, I see every kind of being assembled there. In addition, I see the creator of all, Brahma, who is the greatest of all material ishas, sitting upon his kamala asana 'lotus flower seat'. I also see the divya rishis 'the enlightened seers' and the mighty Nagas.

anekabāhūdaravaktranetraṁ; paśyāmi tvā sarvato
430 'nantarūpam
Ch.11 v.16 nāntaṁ na madhyaṁ na punas tavādiṁ; paśyāmi
viśveśvara viśvarūpa

I see Your infinite rupa 'form' extending in every direction. I see endless arms, bodies, faces, and eyes. There is no beginning, no middle, and no end to Your endless manifestations. O Shri Krishna, O Vishva Ishvara Vishvarupa, Your 'unlimited form is this entire universe'.

kirīṭinaṁ gadinaṁ cakriṇaṁ ca; tejorāśiṁ sarvato
431 dīptimantam
Ch.11 v.17 paśyāmi tvāṁ durnirīkṣyaṁ samantād;
dīptānalārkadyutim aprameyam

Now I see You. Your many heads are wearing crowns and You are armed with divine weapons like the club and the disk. Your immense splendour is shining brilliantly in every direction, but You are exceedingly difficult to see because of Your blazing, fiery, and immeasurable sun-like radiance.

Suddenly Arjuna saw countless mouths and eyes, unlimited marvelous visions extending everywhere. He saw divine ornaments of immeasurable splendour and endless mystic weapons upraised everywhere.

Decorated with divine garments, garlanded with celestial flowers, fragrant with intoxicating perfumes, and exhibiting magical marvels of every description, Deva Ananta Vishvata Mukha 'the Supreme Deva whose uncountable faces look in every direction' appeared before Arjuna.

Divi surya sahasrasya 'if a thousand suns' rose up in the sky all at once, their brilliance would not equal the effulgence of the form that Arjuna now saw.–424-426

432 tvam akṣaraṁ paramaṁ veditavyaṁ; tvam asya viśvasya paraṁ nidhānam
Ch.11 v.18 tvam avyayaḥ śāśvatadharmagoptā; sanātanas tvaṁ puruṣo mato me

You are the Supreme and unchanging reality. You are the ultimate vision to be seen. You are the resting place of all that exists. You are the immortal protector of dharma 'all that is true'. And I am certain that You are the original and Ultimate Person.

433 anādimadhyāntam anantavīryam; anantabāhuṁ śaśisūryanetram
Ch.11 v.19 paśyāmi tvāṁ dīptahutāśavaktraṁ; svatejasā viśvam idaṁ tapantam

Your infinite powers are without beginning, middle, or end. Your unlimited arms are reaching in every direction; the Sun and Moon are your eyes. Your mouth is a sacred fire into which all beings are being placed as an offering that you are continuously eating. In this way, the entire cosmos is being consumed by Your all-encompassing radiance.

434 dyāvāpṛthivyor idam antaraṁ hi; vyāptaṁ tvayaikena diśaś ca sarvāḥ
Ch.11 v.20 dṛṣṭvādbhutaṁ rūpam ugram tavedam; lokatrayaṁ pravyathitaṁ mahatman

From Earth to the limits of the starry firmament, it is only You who fills the ten directions. Seeing Your wondrous and yet terrifying cosmic rupa 'form', all the worlds tremble at the overwhelming sight of Your mighty being.

435 amī hi tvā surasaṁghā viśanti; ke cid bhītāḥ prāñjalayo gṛṇanti
Ch.11 v.21 svastīty uktvā maharṣisiddhasaṁghāḥ; stuvanti tvāṁ stutibhiḥ puṣkalābhiḥ

A great host of devas, some frightened and others trembling in awe, are entering into You, bowing and praising You with mantras. Throngs of great rishis, sages, and seers are also chanting and crying out songs of praise to You.

436 rudrādityā vasavo ye ca sādhyā; viśve 'śvinau marutaś coṣmapāś ca
Ch.11 v.22 gandharvayakṣāsurasiddhasaṁghā; vīkṣante tvā vismitāś caiva sarve

The Rudras, Adityas, Vasus, Sadhyas, Vishva Devas, the twin Ashvins, Maruts, Ushmapas, Gandharvas, Yakshas, Asuras, and Siddhas all behold You, amazed, astonished, and overcome with awe.

437 rūpaṁ mahat te bahuvaktranetraṁ; mahābāho bahubāhūrupādam
Ch.11 v.23 bahūdaraṁ bahudaṁṣṭrākarālaṁ; dṛṣṭvā lokāḥ pravyathitās tathāham

They see Your bahu bahu rupa pada 'massive cosmic form, with your endless arms, legs, and feet moving everywhere'. This form has eyes looking everywhere, mouths speaking endlessly, with hungry bellies and dangerous tusks all around. O mighty-armed Bhagavan, all the lokas are shaking with fear, and so am I.

438
Ch.11 v.24

nabhaḥspṛśaṁ dīptam anekavarṇaṁ; vyāttānanaṁ dīptaviśālanetram
dṛṣṭvā hi tvāṁ pravyathitāntarātmā; dhṛtiṁ na vindāmi śamaṁ ca viṣṇo

Seeing Your terrible virata rupa 'cosmic form blazing in all directions in every colour' and seeing Your massive face with a gaping, hungry mouth and Your fearsome blazing eyes, I am shaking with terror to the very core of my heart. O Vishnu, protector of all, I have lost all my courage and peace of mind!

439
Ch.11 v.25

daṁṣṭrākarālāni ca te mukhāni; dṛṣṭvaiva kālānalasaṁnibhāni
diśo na jāne na labhe ca śarma; prasīda deveśa jagannivāsa

After seeing Your fearsome mouths filled with razor-sharp teeth and feeling the blazing fires of time, unquenchable and burning everywhere, I have lost my way and cannot find comfort anywhere. Prasida 'have mercy', O Deva Isha Jagat Nivasa 'Supreme among the devas and residence of all beings!'

440
Ch.11 v.26

amī ca tvāṁ dhṛtarāṣṭrasya putrāḥ; sarve sahaivāvanipālasaṁghaiḥ
bhīṣmo droṇaḥ sūtaputras tathāsau; sahāsmadīyair api yodhamukhyaiḥ

I see the hundred sons of Dhritarashtra. I see throngs of beings. I see Bhishma, Drona, Karna, and all our greatest warriors.

441
Ch.11 v.27

vaktrāṇi te tvaramāṇā viśanti; daṁṣṭrākarālāni bhayānakāni
ke cid vilagnā daśanāntareṣu; saṁdṛśyante cūrṇitair uttamāṅgaiḥ

I see them racing madly into Your terrible mouths, gaping and horrific, with razor sharp teeth, some of them with crushed heads and some are trapped between Your teeth.

442
Ch.11 v.28
yathā nadīnāṁ bahavo 'mbuvegāḥ; samudram evābhimukhā dravanti
tathā tavāmī naralokavīrā; viśanti vaktrāṇy abhivijvalanti

Just as the many streams of a flooding river rush and swell with turbulence into the ocean, so those many warriors, those heroes among men, race to their destruction and enter Your flaming mouths.

443
Ch.11 v.29
yathā pradīptaṁ jvalanaṁ pataṁgā; viśanti nāśāya samṛddhavegāḥ
tathaiva nāśāya viśanti lokās; tavāpi vaktrāṇi samṛddhavegāḥ

Just as moths fly at great speed to certain annihilation in the flames of a blazing fire, so these many beings rush from this loka to another, racing to their destruction in Your fiery mouths.

444
Ch.11 v.30
lelihyase grasamānaḥ samantāl; lokān samagrān vadanair jvaladbhiḥ
tejobhir āpūrya jagat samagraṁ; bhāsas tavogrāḥ pratapanti viṣṇo

O great Vishnu, You are licking the lips of Your flaming mouths and swallowing everyone on all sides. Filling the lokas with intense radiation, Your terrible blazing rays are burning everywhere.

445
Ch.11 v.31
ākhyāhi me ko bhavān ugrarūpo; namo 'stu te devavara prasīda
vijñātum icchāmi bhavantam ādyaṁ; na hi prajānāmi tava pravṛttim

O Supreme Being among the devas, I bow before You. Prasida 'please be kind and merciful' unto me! Your terrible cosmic form is very painful to look at and appears to be destructive. Please tell me who You are, O Bhavantam Adyam 'greatest primal being'. Please explain your purpose.

śrībhagavān uvāca
446 kālo 'smi lokakṣayakṛt pravṛddho; lokān samāhartum iha pravṛttaḥ
Ch.11 v.32 ṛte 'pi tvā na bhaviṣyanti sarve; ye 'vasthitāḥ pratyanīkeṣu yodhāḥ

Shri Bhagavan said:
Kala asmi loka kshaya krit pravriddha 'I am time, the destroyer of all material worlds'. Even without your actions, I am going to annihilate all the warriors standing across from each other on this battlefield except for you and your brothers.

447 tasmāt tvam uttiṣṭha yaśo labhasva; jitvā śatrūn bhuṅkṣva rājyaṁ samṛddham
Ch.11 v.33 mayaivaite nihatāḥ pūrvam eva; nimittamātraṁ bhava savyasācin

Therefore, Arjuna, uttishta 'stand up' and achieve fame and honour for performing your dharma as a warrior. After defeating your opponents, you will rule over a noble and prosperous realm. As the Supreme Being, I have already decided the outcome of this conflict, and you are merely My instrument.

448 droṇaṁ ca bhīṣmaṁ ca jayadrathaṁ ca; karṇaṁ tathānyān api yodhavīrān
Ch.11 v.34 mayā hatāṁs tvaṁ jahi mā vyathiṣṭhā; yudhyasva jetāsi raṇe sapatnān

By My decree, Drona, Bhishma, Jayadratha, and all the other heroes and warriors are already destined to perish. So, do not tremble or hesitate. Go forward in this battle, fight with your adversaries, and you will triumph over them.

449 saṁjaya uvāca
etac chrutvā vacanaṁ keśavasya; kṛtāñjalir vepamānaḥ kirīṭī
namaskṛtvā bhūya evāha kṛṣṇaṁ; sagadgadaṁ bhītabhītaḥ praṇamya

Ch.11 v.35

At this point, SANJAYA spoke to Dhritarashtra:
After hearing the words spoken by Shri Krishna, Arjuna held out his hands in the anjali mudra of reverent offering. Bowing with palms joined, Arjuna, trembling and very frightened, began to speak to Shri Bhagavan in a plaintive and stammering voice.

450 arjuna uvāca
sthāne hṛṣīkeśa tava prakīrtyā; jagat prahṛṣyaty anurajyate ca
rakṣāṁsi bhītāni diśo dravanti; sarve namasyanti ca siddhasaṁghāḥ

Ch.11 v.36

ARJUNA said:
The entire Universe delights in seeing You and sings Your praises, while the asuras and rakshas are frightened and run in all directions. Meanwhile, the gatherings of siddhas and other perfected beings bow before You again and again.

451 kasmāc ca te na nameran mahātman; garīyase brahmaṇo 'py ādikartre
ananta deveśa jagannivāsa; tvam akṣaraṁ sadasat tatparaṁ yat

Ch.11 v.37

Why should they not bow to You? You are

1. Mahatma—the greatest of all atmas
2. Gariyase Brahmano—even greater than the creator Brahma
3. Adi Kartre—the unborn creator of all
4. Ananta Devesha—the greatest deva, full of infinite potential

5. Jagannivasa—the ultimate resting place of the universe
6. Akshara—the brilliant and imperishable source of everything
7. Sat asat tatparam yat—beyond the immortal and the temporary.

452
Ch.11 v.38

tvam ādidevaḥ puruṣaḥ purāṇas; tvam asya viśvasya paraṁ nidhānam
vettāsi vedyaṁ ca paraṁ ca dhāma; tvayā tataṁ viśvam anantarūpa

You are

8. Adideva—the unborn and original Deva
9. Purusha Purana—the most ancient and original person
10. Vishvasya Param Nidhanam—the supreme and ultimate resting place in this universe
11. Vettasi Vedyam—the knower and that which is to be known
12. Param Dhama—the highest dwelling place
13. Anantarupa—there is no end to Your unlimited forms.

453
Ch.11 v.39

vāyur yamo 'gnir varuṇaḥ śaśāṅkaḥ; prajāpatis tvaṁ prapitāmahaś ca
namo namas te 'stu sahasrakṛtvaḥ; punaś ca bhūyo 'pi namo namas te

You are

14. Vayu—the deva of the wind
15. Yama—the deva of justice and samsara
16. Agni—the deva of fire
17. Varuna—the deva of water
18. Shashanka—the deva of the Moon who controls the waters
19. Prajapatis—those who oversee the development of all beings
20. Prapitamaha—the original great grandfather of all beings.

I offer my obeisances and bow before You, and a thousand times more, and a thousand times again.

454
Ch.11 v.40

namaḥ purastād atha pṛṣṭhatas te; namo 'stu te sarvata eva sarva
anantavīryāmitavikramas tvaṁ; sarvaṁ samāpnoṣi tato 'si sarvaḥ

Again, I bow to You from the front and from behind and then again from all sides. Your strength has no limits. You are all-pervading and everything is You.

455
Ch.11 v.41

sakheti matvā prasabhaṁ yad uktaṁ; he kṛṣṇa he yādava he sakheti
ajānatā mahimānaṁ tavedaṁ; mayā pramādāt praṇayena vāpi

O Bhagavan, out of ignorance of Your all-powerful nature, I have in the past spoken to You as if You were my dear cousin and friend. Sometimes I did this out of excessive familiarity or the affection of friendship.

456
Ch.11 v.42

yac cāvahāsārtham asatkṛto 'si; vihāraśayyāsanabhojaneṣu
eko 'tha vāpy acyuta tatsamakṣaṁ; tat kṣāmaye tvām aham aprameyam

If to be humorous at play or while seated, while resting or eating together, alone or in the presence of others, I have been disrespectful to You, O Aprameya 'immeasurable and boundless Being', please forgive me.

457
Ch.11 v.43

pitāsi lokasya carācarasya; tvam asya pūjyaś ca gurur garīyān
na tvatsamo 'sty abhyadhikaḥ kuto 'nyo; lokatraye 'py apratimaprabhāva

You are the father of all the moving and non-moving beings in all the lokas. You are worthy of more honour than the most glorious guru. There is nothing like You or greater than You in all of existence. How could anyone be equal to You in all the three lokas, O Being of incomparable greatness?

458
Ch.11 v.44

tasmāt praṇamya praṇidhāya kāyaṁ; prasādaye tvām aham īśam īḍyam
piteva putrasya sakheva sakhyuḥ; priyaḥ priyāyārhasi deva soḍhum

Therefore, bowing before you flat on the ground, I ask You to please forgive my disrespect toward You, O great controller of all. Just as a father cares for his child, as one friend trusts another, or as a lover adores their beloved, please be kind and merciful to me.

459
Ch.11 v.45

adṛṣṭapūrvaṁ hṛṣito 'smi dṛṣṭvā; bhayena ca pravyathitaṁ mano me
tad eva me darśaya deva rūpaṁ; prasīda deveśa jagannivāsa

Now that I have seen what has never been seen before, I am delighted beyond all measure, yet still my manas is shaken and trembles with fear. So, please give me the vision of Your divine rupa as Vishnu, the sustainer of all life. O prasida 'have mercy upon me', Deva Isha Jagat Nivasa 'O great ruler of the universe'.

460
Ch.11 v.46

kirīṭinaṁ gadinaṁ cakrahastam; icchāmi tvāṁ draṣṭum ahaṁ tathaiva
tenaiva rūpeṇa caturbhujena; sahasrabāho bhava viśvamūrte

I wish to see You again in Your rupa wearing a crown, carrying a club, and bearing the sudarshana chakra. I want to see Your four-armed Vishnu form, O Sahasrabahu 'thousand-armed One', O Vishvamurti 'source of all the other forms in the Universe'.

śrībhagavān uvāca
461 mayā prasannena tavārjunedaṁ; rūpaṁ paraṁ darśitam ātmayogāt
Ch.11 v.47 tejomayaṁ viśvam anantam ādyaṁ; yan me tvad anyena na dṛṣṭapūrvam

Shri Bhagavan spoke:
As a kindness to you, Arjuna, I have revealed My param rupa 'Supreme form', manifesting it entirely through the yoga maya of My unlimited Atma. This brilliant, unborn, original, and universal form of Mine has never been revealed so completely to anyone before you.

462 na vedayajñādhyayanair na dānair; na ca kriyābhir na tapobhir ugraiḥ
Ch.11 v.48 evaṁrūpaḥ śakya' ahaṁ nṛloke; draṣṭuṁ tvad anyena kurupravīra

This cosmic form of Mine cannot be seen by reciting the vedic mantras, by offering large donations, or by performing the agnihotra yajna. Neither is it revealed to those who perform elaborate rituals nor to those who undertake harsh and demanding tapasya. On this human loka, Arjuna, you are the only person to whom this form has been so fully revealed.

463 mā te vyathā mā ca vimūḍhabhāvo; dṛṣṭvā rūpaṁ ghoram īdṛṅ mamedam
Ch.11 v.49 vyapetabhīḥ prītamanāḥ punas tvaṁ; tad eva me rūpam idaṁ prapaśya

So, do not tremble or remain in a state of bewilderment because you have seen My ghora rupa 'ghastly universal form'. Be free of all fears and feel love and joy in your heart as you now behold My original rupa, my all-attractive two-armed transcendental form as Shri Bhagavan.

464
Ch.11 v.50

saṁjaya uvāca
ity Arjunaṁ vāsudevas tathoktvā; svakaṁ rūpaṁ darśayām āsa bhūyaḥ
āśvāsayām āsa ca bhītam enaṁ; bhūtvā punaḥ saumyavapur mahātmā

SANJAYA said to Dhritarashtra:
After speaking these words of reassurance to Arjuna, Shri Krishna assumed His svaka rupa 'original and true form'. Having returned to His saumya vapu 'beautiful and all-attractive body', He calmed and consoled Arjuna, who was still fearful and disturbed.

465
Ch.11 v.51

arjuna uvāca
dṛṣṭvedaṁ mānuṣaṁ rūpaṁ tava saumyaṁ janārdana
idānīm asmi saṁvṛttaḥ sacetāḥ prakṛtiṁ gataḥ

ARJUNA then spoke:
O Janardana 'O cause of the many births of all beings', seeing Your gentle and pleasing human-like rupa once again, I have regained my true nature and my heart is full of delight.

466
Ch.11 v.52

śrībhagavān uvāca
sudurdarśam idaṁ rūpaṁ dṛṣṭavān asi yan mama
devā apy asya rūpasya nityaṁ darśanakāṅkṣiṇaḥ

SHRI BHAGAVAN said:
This vishva rupa of mine, which I have just revealed to you, is extremely difficult to see. Even the devas are constantly wishing to see that form.

467
Ch.11 v.53

nāhaṁ vedair na tapasā na dānena na cejyayā
śakya evaṁvidho draṣṭuṁ dṛṣṭavān asi māṁ yathā

But it is not through dana, yajna, tapasya, or the study of vedic knowledge that I can be seen in My universal form as you have seen Me.

468 bhaktyā tv ananyayā śakya aham evaṁvidho 'rjuna
Ch.11 v.54 jñātuṁ draṣṭuṁ ca tattvena praveṣṭuṁ ca paraṁtapa

Only by pure and unwavering bhakti yoga can I be seen, known, and understood in My most essential, true, and ultimate nature. O Arjuna, only in that way can you reach, attain, and fully enter into the mysteries of My many divine forms.

469 matkarmakṛn matparamo madbhaktaḥ saṅgavarjitaḥ
Ch.11 v.55 nirvairaḥ sarvabhūteṣu yaḥ sa mām eti pāṇḍava

O Arjuna, one who is mad bhakta 'lovingly dedicates all they do to Me', constantly thinking only of Me as the Ultimate Supreme Being and most loving friend, who has no attachments to matter, who is free of enmity with all living beings, and who is always devoted to Me is certain to come to Me.

Chapter 12

The Yoga of Love and the Secrets of Divine Seva

470
Ch.12 v.1

arjuna uvāca
evaṁ satatayuktā ye bhaktās tvāṁ paryupāsate
ye cāpy akṣaram avyaktaṁ teṣāṁ ke yogavittamāḥ

ARJUNA enquired:
Between those who are constantly engaged in acts of seva 'service and adoration' to You through bhakti yoga and those who seek to merge their atma entirely into Your imperishable and formless Brahman effulgence, which do You consider has achieved the most perfect knowledge of yoga?

471
Ch.12 v.2

śrībhagavān uvāca
mayy āveśya mano ye māṁ nityayuktā upāsate
śraddhayā parayopetās te me yuktatamā matāḥ

SHRI BHAGAVAN replied:
I regard those who perpetually focus their manas upon Me in the yoga of loving seva 'devoted service' to be established in the most perfect practice of yoga.

472
Ch.12 v.3

ye tv akṣaram anirdeśyam avyaktaṁ paryupāsate
sarvatragam acintyaṁ ca kūṭastham acalaṁ dhruvam

But those who are constantly focused upon the Brahman reality as

1. akshara—imperishable
2. anirdeshya—undefinable
3. avyakta—materially unmanifest
4. sarvatraga—all-pervading
5. achintya—inconceivable
6. kutastha—unchanging
7. achala—unmoving
8. dhruva—constant...

473 saṁniyamyendriyagrāmaṁ sarvatra samabuddhayaḥ
Ch.12 v.4 te prāpnuvanti mām eva sarvabhūtahite ratāḥ

...and those who have completely subdued their indriyas 'bodily senses', who are even minded and indifferent in all of life's situations, and who rejoice in the well-being of all living entities—they also attain Me.

474 kleśo 'dhikataras teṣām avyaktāsaktacetasām
Ch.12 v.5 avyaktā hi gatir duḥkhaṁ dehavadbhir avāpyate

Those whose yoga is focused upon My inconceivable, unmanifest, and imperceptible nature follow the most difficult yogic path. For those who are embodied, the pursuit of My quality-less, undifferentiated Brahman nature is the most difficult and troublesome way to approach Me.

475 ye tu sarvāṇi karmāṇi mayi saṁnyasya matparāḥ
Ch.12 v.6 ananyenaiva yogena māṁ dhyāyanta upāsate

But those who surrender all their actions to Me, who adore Me and are intent upon My association, dedicating everything to Me in undisturbed bhakti yoga...

476 teṣām ahaṁ samuddhartā mṛtyusaṁsārasāgarāt
Ch.12 v.7 bhavāmi nacirāt pārtha mayy āveśitacetasām

...those who approach Me in this way, O Arjuna, I quickly deliver them from the ocean of samsara 'repeated birth and death'.

477 mayy eva mana ādhatsva mayi buddhiṁ niveśaya
Ch.12 v.8 nivasiṣyasi mayy eva ata ūrdhvaṁ na saṁśayaḥ

Therefore, just focus your manas and buddhi upon Me in every way and under all circumstances, and you will dwell in Me always and forever. There is no doubt about this bhakti yoga practice.

478
Ch.12 v.9

atha cittaṁ samādhātuṁ na śaknoṣi mayi sthiram
abhyāsayogena tato mām icchāptuṁ dhanaṁjaya

But if you cannot hold the steady focus of your chit faculty upon Me, O Arjuna, then practice abhyasa yoga 'one-pointed concentration' in order to attain Me.

479
Ch.12 v.10

abhyāse 'py asamartho 'si matkarmaparamo bhava
madartham api karmāṇi kurvan siddhim avāpsyasi

Or, if you are unable to remain steady in abhyasa, then perform every action as karma yoga, as if you are working only for Me. In this way, you will also achieve perfection.

480
Ch.12 v.11

athaitad apy aśakto 'si kartuṁ madyogam āśritaḥ
sarvakarmaphalatyāgaṁ tataḥ kuru yatātmavān

If it is beyond your ability to take refuge in Me as your yoga, then give up all attachment to the karma phala 'results of your actions' while keeping your senses under control and seeing yourself as the atma.

481
Ch.12 v.12

śreyo hi jñānam abhyāsāj jñānād dhyānaṁ viśiṣyate
dhyānāt karmaphalatyāgas tyāgāc chāntir anantaram

Jnana yoga 'the cultivation of transcendental knowledge' is better than the mechanical practice of yoga asana. Yogic meditation upon me as the Supreme Being is even better than jnana yoga. Still better than meditation is complete detachment from the phala 'fruits of action' because it establishes one in shanti 'true and lasting contentment'.

482 adveṣṭā sarvabhūtānāṁ maitraḥ karuṇa eva ca
Ch.12 v.13 nirmamo nirahaṁkāraḥ samaduḥkhasukhaḥ kṣamī

One who does not hate any being, who is friendly and compassionate to all living beings, who realizes that they own nothing within matter, who does not identify their self with matter, who is not unbalanced by pleasure or pain, who is always patient...

483 saṁtuṣṭaḥ satataṁ yogī yatātmā dṛḍhaniścayaḥ
Ch.12 v.14 mayy arpitamanobuddhir yo madbhaktaḥ sa me priyaḥ

...one who is always contented, who acts as the atma under all circumstances, whose manas and buddhi are permanently fixed upon Me, and who is mad bhakta 'forever devoted to Me', such a person is most priya 'beloved' to Me.

484 yasmān nodvijate loko lokān nodvijate ca yaḥ
Ch.12 v.15 harṣāmarṣabhayodvegair mukto yaḥ sa ca me priyaḥ

One who is kind to the entire world, who is unafraid in the world, who is not addicted to material enjoyments, who is not envious of others, and who is not disabled by the effects of material distress is priya 'very dear' to Me.

485 anapekṣaḥ śucir dakṣa udāsīno gatavyathaḥ
Ch.12 v.16 sarvārambhaparityāgī yo madbhaktaḥ sa me priyaḥ

One who is free from all material desires, who is shuchi 'clean and pure', who is skilful and dexterous, who is detached from all material objects, who is free of anxiety, and who is unattached to the result of all action, is mad bhakta and priya 'deeply devoted and very dear to Me'. I adore such beings.

486 yo na hṛṣyati na dveṣṭi na śocati na kāṅkṣati
Ch.12 v.17 śubhāśubhaparityāgī bhaktimān yaḥ sa me priyaḥ

One who is not bound by attraction or repulsion to matter, who does not imagine the future nor dwell in the past, who is neither attached to nor repulsed by circumstances, who is beyond the duality of material opposites, and who is loyal and bhaktiman 'deeply devoted to serving Me'—I feel priya 'a deep loving connection' with such a person.

487 samaḥ śatrau ca mitre ca tathā mānāvamānayoḥ
Ch.12 v.18 śītoṣṇasukhaduḥkheṣu samaḥ saṅgavivarjitaḥ

One who treats friends and enemies the same, who is equipoised in both honour and disgrace, who is impervious to heat or cold, pleasure or pain, and who is not bound by material attachments...

488 tulyanindāstutir maunī saṁtuṣṭo yena kena cit
Ch.12 v.19 aniketaḥ sthiramatir bhaktimān me priyo naraḥ

...one who is indifferent to praise or blame, who is comfortable in silence, who is content with whatever comes of its own accord, who is not attached to any residence, whose manas is steady, and who is bhaktiman 'deeply devoted to serving Me', that person is always priya to Me.

489 ye tu dharmyāmṛtam idaṁ yathoktaṁ paryupāsate
Ch.12 v.20 śraddadhānā matparamā bhaktās te 'tīva me priyāḥ

One who always follows this sanatana dharma path which grants the amrita of immortal bliss, who is completely dedicated to these immortal truths, whose vision of Me never wavers, and whose bhakti 'loving intention' is to be with Me as the mat param 'ultimate destination', such a person is priya 'exceedingly dear and attractive' to Me.

Chapter 13

Discernment of the Quantum Field and Its Knower

490
Ch.13 v.1

arjuna uvāca
prakṛitiṁ puruṣhaṁ chaiva kṣhetraṁ kṣhetra-jñam eva cha
etad veditum ichchhāmi jñānaṁ jñeyaṁ cha keśhava

ARJUNA spoke:
O Shri Krishna, I wish to understand

1. prakriti—material nature
2. purusha—the transcendental person who is the source of matter
3. kshetra—the energetic field of matter
4. kshetrajna—the conscious beings who are the knowers of that field
5. jnana—the knowledge itself, and
6. jneya—the purpose of that knowledge.

491
Ch.13 v.2

śrībhagavān uvāca
idaṁ śarīraṁ kaunteya kṣetram ity abhidhīyate
etad yo vetti taṁ prāhuḥ kṣetrajña iti tadvidaḥ

SHRI BHAGAVAN said:
Those who truly understand proclaim that the five-element body is known as kshetra 'the field of activity', and the conscious perceiver within the body is called kshetrajna 'the knower of that field of action'.

492
Ch.13 v.3

kṣetrajñaṁ cāpi māṁ viddhi sarvakṣetreṣu bhārata
kṣetrakṣetrajñayor jñānaṁ yat taj jñānaṁ mataṁ mama

O Arjuna, I am the Supreme knower of the fields, which are all bodies. In my opinion, knowing this is true and complete knowledge.

493 tat kṣetraṁ yac ca yādṛk ca yadvikāri yataś ca yat
Ch.13 v.4 sa ca yo yatprabhāvaś ca tat samāsena me śṛṇu

And now Arjuna, listen to Me as I describe a brief summary of that kshetra 'field', what its variations are, what impels those transformations, who Prabhava 'the ultimate knower' is, and what is the extent and nature of the powers of that Being.

494 ṛṣibhir bahudhā gītaṁ chandobhir vividhaiḥ pṛthak
Ch.13 v.5 brahmasūtrapadaiś caiva hetumadbhir viniścitaiḥ

In the vedic texts, many great rishis have sung of these truths regarding the characteristics of Brahman and prakriti. They are also explained in the Brahma Sutras with profound reasoning and precise logical inquiry.

495 mahābhūtāny ahaṁkāro buddhir avyaktam eva ca
Ch.13 v.6 indriyāṇi daśaikaṁ ca pañca cendriyagocarāḥ

The field and its various modifications consist of

1. pancha mahabhutas—the five great elements
2. ahamkara—the faculty that identifies the atma with matter
3. buddhi—the ability to discern what is prakriti and what is not
4. avyakta—the great unmanifest reality
5. dasha indriyas—the ten senses (five perceptive and five active)
6. manas—the faculty that performs the tasks of thinking, feeling, willing, and memory
7. indriya gocharas—the objects of the ten senses

496 icchā dveṣaḥ sukhaṁ duḥkhaṁ saṁghātaś cetanā dhṛtiḥ
Ch.13 v.7 etat kṣetraṁ samāsena savikāram udāhṛtam

8. iccha—desire, hunger, and inclination for material pleasure
9. dvesha—aversion, repulsion, and disinterest in matter
10. sukha—pleasure, enjoyment, and happiness within matter
11. dukha—pain, unhappiness, and repulsion to matter
12. samghata—the entire holistic material manifestation of the body/mind complex
13. chetana—the life force and awareness that pervade that body
14. dhriti—the steady manifestation of that body as a complex arrangement of matter functioning according to its gunas and doshas.

All these are the knowledge of the field and its various modifications.

497 amānitvam adambhitvam ahiṁsā kṣāntir ārjavam
Ch.13 v.8 ācāryopāsanaṁ śaucaṁ sthairyam ātmavinigrahaḥ

[Shri Krishna next describes the virtues, habits, behaviours, and attitudes that purify one's life and illuminate it with the light of true knowledge.]

1. amanitva—humility, the absence of pride and arrogance or seeking for honour
2. adambhitva—straightforward, unpretentious, and without duplicity
3. ahimsa—causing the least amount of violence or harm while still adhering to one's dharma
4. kshanti—patience, tolerance, forbearance, and forgiveness of offenses given by another
5. arjava—simplicity, lack of guile, and honesty

6. acharya upasana—serving and honouring a guru whose life and actions embody the vedic ideals
7. shaucha—living a sattvic lifestyle while paying careful attention to cleansing and purifying all aspects of one's being
8. sthairya—staying steady, firm, and unwavering in one's practices and lifestyle
9. atma vinigraha—acting as the atma by controlling the manas and indriyas

498 indriyārtheṣu vairāgyam anahaṁkāra eva ca
Ch.13 v.9 janmamṛtyujarāvyādhiduḥkhadoṣānudarśanam

10. indriya arteshu vairagya—not being addicted to material pleasures or compelled by material desires that arise while engaging in life's activities
11. anahamkara—freedom from misidentification of one's atma with the various energetic states and actions of matter
12. dukha dosha anudarshana—remaining aware of problems caused by janma 'birth', mrityu 'death', jara 'the aging process', and vyadhi 'disease'

499 asaktir anabhiṣvaṅgaḥ putradāragṛhādiṣu
Ch.13 v.10 nityaṁ ca samacittatvam iṣṭāniṣṭopapattiṣu

13. asakti—a lack of attachment to all possessions and material objects
14. anabishvanga—not attached or bound by putra 'children', dara 'life partner', griha 'house', and anything else material
15. sama chittatva—balance and equanimity in the face of desirable and undesirable circumstances or events

500 mayi cānanyayogena bhaktir avyabhicāriṇī
Ch.13 v.11 viviktadeśasevitvam aratir janasaṁsadi

16. unswerving connection with Me in the joyful bond of bhakti yoga
17. dedication to Me that never fluctuates
18. avoidance of the masses of chaotic and unevolved human beings
19. residing in a sacred and secluded place

501 adhyātmajñānanityatvaṁ tattvajñānārthadarśanam
Ch.13 v.12 etaj jñānam iti proktam ajñānaṁ yad ato 'nyathā

20. realizing the knowledge of the Supreme and Ultimate Atma
21. realizing that this knowledge is immortal and always true.

And I declare that all this knowledge is truth, and anything other than this is ignorance.

502 jñeyaṁ yat tat pravakṣyāmi yaj jñātvāmṛtam aśnute
Ch.13 v.13 anādimat paraṁ brahma na sat tan nāsad ucyate

I will now explain to you that knowledge which, by knowing, you will be re-established in your immortal nature. The para Brahman is My supreme and ultimate energy which has no beginning or end, unlike the realm of prakriti where everything is temporary.

503 sarvataḥpāṇipādaṁ tat sarvatokṣiśiromukham
Ch.13 v.14 sarvataḥśrutimal loke sarvam āvṛtya tiṣṭhati

The para Brahman is My supreme and all-pervasive Being whose hands and feet reach everywhere, whose face, head, and eyes see in all directions, and whose ears hear all sounds everywhere throughout the countless lokas. It is forever standing with, surrounding, and pervading all that exists.

504 sarvendriyaguṇābhāsaṁ sarvendriyavivarjitam
Ch.13 v.15 asaktaṁ sarvabhṛc caiva nirguṇaṁ guṇabhoktṛ ca

That great Being is the one who shares the sensory experiences of all beings, and yet is not bound by them in any way. Completely detached and yet maintaining all beings at the same time, that all-pervading Brahman Being experiences all the actions within the three gunas, and yet is nirguna 'entirely beyond the influence of those gunas'.

505 bahir antaś ca bhūtānām acaraṁ caram eva ca
Ch.13 v.16 sūkṣmatvāt tad avijñeyaṁ dūrasthaṁ cāntike ca tat

That great Brahman Being is simultaneously inside and outside of all beings. It always appears to be moving, while in fact it is not moving at all. It is so subtle that it is all-pervading, and yet it is incomprehensible. It is always the most near, and yet at the same time, it is also the very farthest away.

506 avibhaktaṁ ca bhūteṣu vibhaktam iva ca sthitam
Ch.13 v.17 bhūtabhartṛ ca taj jñeyaṁ grasiṣṇu prabhaviṣṇu ca

That great Brahman Being is a singular and undivided reality, even though it appears to be divided and standing inside of all beings. This Being is also known as the sustainer and support of all beings, as well as the Creator and the One who devours all.

507 jyotiṣām api taj jyotis tamasaḥ param ucyate
Ch.13 v.18 jñānaṁ jñeyaṁ jñānagamyaṁ hṛdi sarvasya viṣṭhitam

This sustainer, the jyotisha api taj jyotish 'ultimate light of all lights', is the source of the stars and is always shining beyond the darkness of tamas. It is knowledge, the object that is to be known, the ultimate destination toward which knowledge is leading, as well as the being who is seated within the hearts of all living beings.

508 iti kṣetraṁ tathā jñānaṁ jñeyaṁ coktaṁ samāsataḥ
Ch.13 v.19 madbhakta etad vijñāya madbhāvāyopapadyate

Thus, I have briefly explained kshetra 'the field of experience', jnana 'the knowledge of all categories', and jneya 'that which is ultimately to be known'. Therefore, one who hears this becomes mad bhakta 'deeply and fully devoted to Me' and achieves madbhavaya upapadyate 'the state of realized understanding'. In this way, one who is devoted to Me achieves a direct understanding of My true divine nature.

509 prakṛtiṁ puruṣaṁ caiva viddhy anādī ubhāv api
Ch.13 v.20 vikārāṁś ca guṇāṁś caiva viddhi prakṛtisaṁbhavān

You should also know that both prakriti and the individual atmas have no beginning and no end. In addition, the three gunas 'transformations of matter' and their qualities and modifications arise only from matter.

510 kāryakāraṇakartṛtve hetuḥ prakṛtir ucyate
Ch.13 v.21 puruṣaḥ sukhaduḥkhānāṁ bhoktṛtve hetur ucyate

It is said that prakriti defines the causal principles behind action, the kind of actions needed to be done, the necessary instruments by which they are accomplished, and the kind of doer needed to conduct the actions, but only the jiva atma or purusha is the cause of the pleasure or pain that results from their actions.

511 puruṣaḥ prakṛtistho hi bhuṅkte prakṛtijān guṇān
Ch.13 v.22 kāraṇaṁ guṇasaṅgo 'sya sadasadyonijanmasu

All experiences within prakriti arise from combinations of the three gunas. At the death of the body, a person's attachment to a specific combination of the gunas determines which kind of womb they will enter in their next incarnation. This determines whether they will be born in a sattvic, rajasic, or tamasic body.

512 upadraṣṭānumantā ca bhartā bhoktā maheśvaraḥ
Ch.13 v.23 paramātmeti cāpy ukto dehe 'smin puruṣaḥ paraḥ

Within that deha 'body made of prakriti' I also reside as

1. Upadrashta—the ultimate seer and witness
2. Anumanta—the one who permits all to happen
3. Bharata—the support and resting place of all
4. Bhokta—the one who experiences all pleasure
5. Maha Ishvara—the greatest controller
6. Paramatma—the atma who pervades all atmas, and
7. Parama Purusha—the Supreme Person among all persons.

513 ya evaṁ vetti puruṣaṁ prakṛtiṁ ca guṇaiḥ saha
Ch.13 v.24 sarvathā vartamāno 'pi na sa bhūyo 'bhijāyate

When the jiva atma finally sees their self as the purusha 'controller' of their own deha 'material body'; when they also know that they and their body are pervaded by the Parama Purusha 'Supreme controller in all bodies'; and when they understand prakriti 'material nature' and how it is controlled by the three gunas; then such an awakened atma is never forced to take birth again.

514 dhyānenātmani paśyanti ke cid ātmānam ātmanā
Ch.13 v.25 anye sāṁkhyena yogena karmayogena cāpare

Some yogis see the atma and Paramatma through deep states of dhyana in ashtanga yoga meditation. Others use their atma as the instrument to enable them to look directly at their own atma and also to see Paramatma. Still others practice the science of sankhya or jnana yoga to discern the atma and Paramatma from the various categories of prakriti. And finally, some serve Paramatma directly through karma yoga, and in the process, see their own atma.

515 anye tv evam ajānantaḥ śrutvānyebhya upāsate
Ch.13 v.26 te 'pi cātitaranty eva mṛtyuṁ śrutiparāyaṇāḥ

However, there are others who are not very skillful in learning vedic knowledge. But even if they simply and sincerely hear from a guru and follow their instructions to focus upon and adore the Parama Ishvara, they too can go beyond samsara 'the cycle of repeated birth and death'.

516 yāvat saṁjāyate kiṁ cit sattvaṁ sthāvarajaṅgamam
Ch.13 v.27 kṣetrakṣetrajñasaṁyogāt tad viddhi bharatarṣabha

Then know, Arjuna, that any being, stationary or moving, arises from the union of the field of matter with the knowers of that field.

517 samaṁ sarveṣu bhūteṣu tiṣṭhantaṁ parameśvaram
Ch.13 v.28 vinaśyatsv avinaśyantaṁ yaḥ paśyati sa paśyati

One who sees the Supreme controller as the imperishable reality standing within all embodied beings sees things as they truly are.

However, there are others
who are not very skilful in
learning vedic knowledge.
But even if they simply
and sincerely hear from
a guru and follow their
instructions to focus upon
and adore the Parama
Ishvara, they too can go
beyond samsara 'the
cycle of repeated birth
and death'.–515

518 samaṁ paśyan hi sarvatra samavasthitam īśvaram
Ch.13 v.29 na hinasty ātmanātmānaṁ tato yāti parāṁ gatim

Once the atma is permanently established in seeing the Parama Ishvara 'Supreme ruler and director of all that exists' as existing in the same way everywhere and at all times, then that individual atma does not degrade their consciousness by allowing their attention to wander. In this way, they achieve the ultimate destination and highest state of divine being.

519 prakṛtyaiva ca karmāṇi kriyamāṇāni sarvaśaḥ
Ch.13 v.30 yaḥ paśyati tathātmānam akartāraṁ sa paśyati

One who finally realizes that the cause and effect happening within prakriti is being carried out entirely by reciprocal actions and reactions within matter finally sees that the atma has no permanent connection with matter and realizes themself to be akartara 'not the material doer within prakriti'.

520 yadā bhūtapṛthagbhāvam ekastham anupaśyati
Ch.13 v.31 tata eva ca vistāraṁ brahma saṁpadyate tadā

When the individual atma perceives that all states of being within prakriti are actually resting upon the platform of Brahman, then they are again restored to their original Brahman nature.

521 anāditvān nirguṇatvāt paramātmāyam avyayaḥ
Ch.13 v.32 śarīrastho 'pi kaunteya na karoti na lipyate

In addition, O Arjuna, even though Paramatma is abiding within each body, that Supreme maintainer of all is

1. anaditva—with no beginning
2. nirgunatva—never affected by the gunas

3. avyaya—imperishable
4. sharira stha—situated within each body
5. na karoti—not acting within the grasp of cause and effect
6. na lipyate—untouched by the results of any karma or action.

522 yathā sarvagataṁ saukṣmyād ākāśaṁ nopalipyate
Ch.13 v.33 sarvatrāvasthito dehe tathātmā nopalipyate

Just as vayu 'air' and akasha 'space' appear to be mixed together but do not really blend, so the deha 'physical body' and the dehi 'atma' also never blend, even though the atma is seated within the body.

523 yathā prakāśayaty ekaḥ kṛtsnaṁ lokam imaṁ raviḥ
Ch.13 v.34 kṣetraṁ kṣetrī tathā kṛtsnaṁ prakāśayati bhārata

Just as Ravi 'the Sun' lights up our entire planet, so the atma illuminates the body it occupies, while Paramatma is Kshetra Kshetri Kritsna 'the One who pervades and illuminates the entire universe'.

524 kṣetrakṣetrajñayor evam antaraṁ jñānacakṣuṣā
Ch.13 v.35 bhūtaprakṛtimokṣaṁ ca ye vidur yānti te param

Thus, the ability to distinguish between kshetra 'the field' and kshetrajna 'the knower of the field' within prakriti, and between the two purushas—the atma and Paramatma—causes the jnana chakshusha 'third eye of enlightened discernment' to open. The yogi then becomes permanently liberated from prakriti's control over their definition of self. In that fully awakened state, they return to the transcendental realm of Brahman, never to experience material bondage again.

Chapter 14

The Gunas: The Three Dynamic States of Matter

śrībhagavān uvāca

525
Ch.14 v.1

paraṁ bhūyaḥ pravakṣyāmi jñānānāṁ jñānam uttamam
yaj jñātvā munayaḥ sarve parāṁ siddhim ito gatāḥ

SHRI BHAGAVAN said:
Now I will again reveal to you the highest transcendental knowledge by which great munis in the past have gone beyond their limitations, achieved perfection, and attained the supreme and ultimate destination.

526
Ch.14 v.2

idaṁ jñānam upāśritya mama sādharmyam āgatāḥ
sarge 'pi nopajāyante pralaye na vyathanti ca

When the jiva atma embraces this jnana, they achieve a state of being very much like My own. The long-term effect of that knowing is that when this world is again created, they are not reincarnated, and when the world is finally destroyed, they have nothing to fear.

527
Ch.14 v.3

mama yonir mahad brahma tasmin garbhaṁ dadhāmy aham
saṁbhavaḥ sarvabhūtānāṁ tato bhavati bhārata

O Arjuna, just as two persons produce a child, so the transcendental realm of Brahman acts as a kind of cosmic yoni 'womb' into which I implant the garbhas 'seedling forms' of the countless atmas who are then born within prakriti as living beings.

528
Ch.14 v.4

sarvayoniṣu kaunteya mūrtayaḥ saṁbhavanti yāḥ
tāsāṁ brahma mahad yonir ahaṁ bījapradaḥ pitā

Listen Arjuna, among all the material wombs in which the many forms of material life emerge, know that the great womb of Brahman is their actual source and that I am the seed-giving father of all embodied life.

529 sattvaṁ rajas tama iti guṇāḥ prakṛtisaṁbhavāḥ
Ch.14 v.5 nibadhnanti mahābāho dehe dehinam avyayam

The three gunas—sattva, rajas, and tamas—are the three dynamic states of prakriti which, like ropes or strings, bind the dehi 'atma' to the deha 'five-element body within matter'.

530 tatra sattvaṁ nirmalatvāt prakāśakam anāmayam
Ch.14 v.6 sukhasaṅgena badhnāti jñānasaṅgena cānagha

O Arjuna, of the three gunas, the qualities of sattva are the most transparent, illuminating, and healthy. Like knotted ropes, each guna binds us to matter through our attraction to specific material experiences. Sattva binds us to matter through our attraction to knowledge, beauty, and happiness.

531 rajo rāgātmakaṁ viddhi tṛṣṇāsaṅgasamudbhavam
Ch.14 v.7 tan nibadhnāti kaunteya karmasaṅgena dehinam

Next, O Arjuna, rajas uses the promise of unlimited pleasure to create extreme attachment to matter by generating unlimited desires that ensnare our atma in various material entanglements. Rajas binds us to matter through our insatiable hungers for material pleasure.

532 tamas tv ajñānajaṁ viddhi mohanaṁ sarvadehinām
Ch.14 v.8 pramādālasyanidrābhis tan nibadhnāti bhārata

And finally, Arjuna, tamas causes delusion and bewilderment that destroy wisdom and cause addiction, destructive behaviours, and excessive sleep. This causes the inclination to violate the laws of nature on a regular basis. Just as sattva is enlightening, tamas is endarkening. Tamas binds us to matter through ignorance and acts of destruction.

533 sattvaṁ sukhe sañjayati rajaḥ karmaṇi bhārata
Ch.14 v.9 jñānam āvṛtya tu tamaḥ pramāde sañjayaty uta

Sattva is balanced action with correct knowledge, causing well-being and abundant happiness. Rajas creates with partial knowledge, dominated by attachment and selfish desires which at first produce intense pleasure but end in pain. Tamas is the deluded state of being in which ignorance appears to be freedom but in fact leads to darkness, negligence, misery, and finally extreme bondage.

534 rajas tamaś cābhibhūya sattvaṁ bhavati bhārata
Ch.14 v.10 rajaḥ sattvaṁ tamaś caiva tamaḥ sattvaṁ rajas tathā

O Arjuna, from moment to moment, these three gunas are competing to control matter. Sometimes sattva suppresses rajas and tamas; sometimes rajas controls sattva and tamas; and at other times, tamas overwhelms both rajas and sattva.

535 sarvadvāreṣu dehe 'smin prakāśa upajāyate
Ch.14 v.11 jñānaṁ yadā tadā vidyād vivṛddhaṁ sattvam ity uta

When all nine gates of the physical body are illuminated and clean, and the life-force becomes healthy, fully functioning, balanced, and joyful, one can know for certain that sattva guna is prevailing.

536 lobhaḥ pravṛttir ārambhaḥ karmaṇām aśamaḥ spṛhā
Ch.14 v.12 rajasy etāni jāyante vivṛddhe bharatarṣabha

Whereas, O Arjuna, when greedy attachment, intense hunger, restlessness, compulsion to action, and an overwhelming desire for material pleasure arise, then raja guna has gained control of the faculties.

537 aprakāśo 'pravṛttiś ca pramādo moha eva ca
Ch.14 v.13 tamasy etāni jāyante vivṛddhe kurunandana

And finally, Arjuna, when consciousness becomes endarkened, and when actions are compromised by inertia and a lack of discernment leading toward madness, delusion, and destruction, then tama guna dominates.

538 yadā sattve pravṛddhe tu pralayaṁ yāti dehabhṛt
Ch.14 v.14 tadottamavidāṁ lokān amalān pratipadyate

When the embodied atma leaves their deha while it is under the influence of sattva guna, they ascend to their next birth in the pure material lokas which are the home of the devas and other enlightened beings.

539 rajasi pralayaṁ gatvā karmasaṅgiṣu jāyate
Ch.14 v.15 tathā pralīnas tamasi mūḍhayoniṣu jāyate

Those who leave their body when raja guna is in control take their next birth among humans like themselves who are hungry for pleasure and still attached to their material actions and possessions. Those who depart when tama guna is dominant either take birth among deluded and degraded humans or even return as an animal.

540 karmaṇaḥ sukṛtasyāhuḥ sāttvikaṁ nirmalaṁ phalam
Ch.14 v.16 rajasas tu phalaṁ duḥkham ajñānaṁ tamasaḥ phalam

The phala 'fruit of actions' in sattva guna is a state of happiness and well-being; the result of actions in raja guna is a mixture of pleasure and pain; and the result of actions in tama guna is to plunge deeper into ignorance culminating in destruction.

When the embodied atma
goes beyond the binding
influence of the three gunas,
they achieve moksha
'ultimate freedom' and go
beyond the influence
of misery, birth, death,
and old age and regain
their long-forgotten
immortal nature.–544

541 sattvāt saṁjāyate jñānaṁ rajaso lobha eva ca
Ch.14 v.17 pramādamohau tamaso bhavato 'jñānam eva ca

From sattva guna, higher knowledge is born; from raja guna, desires are born; and from tama guna, delusion is born.

542 ūrdhvaṁ gacchanti sattvasthā madhye tiṣṭhanti rājasāḥ
Ch.14 v.18 jaghanyaguṇavṛttasthā adho gacchanti tāmasāḥ

Those who are sattvic rise upward; those who are rajasic stay in the middle; and those who are tamasic devolve downward.

543 nānyaṁ guṇebhyaḥ kartāraṁ yadā draṣṭānupaśyati
Ch.14 v.19 guṇebhyaś ca paraṁ vetti madbhāvaṁ so 'dhigacchati

When a person acting within matter sees that only the three gunas are directing the outcome of all actions, they achieve a divine state of being just like my own and eventually come to Me.

544 guṇān etān atītya trīn dehī dehasamudbhavān
Ch.14 v.20 janmamṛtyujarāduḥkhair vimukto 'mṛtam aśnute

When the embodied atma goes beyond the binding influence of the three gunas, they achieve moksha 'ultimate freedom' and go beyond the influence of misery, birth, death, and old age and regain their long-forgotten immortal nature.

arjuna uvāca
545 kair liṅgais trīn guṇān etān atīto bhavati prabho
Ch.14 v.21 kimācāraḥ kathaṁ caitāṁs trīn guṇān ativartate

ARJUNA enquired:
How does one recognize that someone has gone beyond the gunas? How do they behave? And how did they attain that state?

546 śrībhagavān uvāca
Ch.14 v.22 prakāśaṁ ca pravṛttiṁ ca moham eva ca pāṇḍava
na dveṣṭi saṁpravṛttāni na nivṛttāni kāṅkṣati

SHRI BHAGAVAN then said to Arjuna:
One who neither hates nor desires the presence or absence of joyful illumination, material attachment, or delusion;

547 udāsīnavad āsīno guṇair yo na vicālyate
Ch.14 v.23 guṇā vartanta ity eva yo 'vatiṣṭhati neṅgate

One who remains steady and undisturbed by the constant changes and transformations of the gunas, and who simply says, "only the gunas are changing";

548 samaduḥkhasukhaḥ svasthaḥ samaloṣṭāśmakāñcanaḥ
Ch.14 v.24 tulyapriyāpriyo dhīras tulyanindātmasaṁstutiḥ

One who views pleasure and pain as the same, only focused upon their atma; who sees a piece of clay, a stone, or gold as of the same value; who treats friends and enemies with equal regard and respect; and who is steady in both blame and praise;

549 mānāvamānayos tulyas tulyo mitrāripakṣayoḥ
Ch.14 v.25 sarvārambhaparityāgī guṇātītaḥ sa ucyate

One who sees honour and dishonour as the same; who treats both friend and foe impartially; and who has released attachment to the outcome of any action—that person is said to have gone beyond the effects of the gunas.

550 māṁ ca yo 'vyabhicāreṇa bhaktiyogena sevate
Ch.14 v.26 sa guṇān samatītyaitān brahmabhūyāya kalpate

And one who serves Me with unwavering affection in bhakti yoga goes beyond the influence of the three gunas and is qualified to enter the realm of Brahman.

551 brahmaṇo hi pratiṣṭhāham amṛtasyāvyayasya ca
Ch.14 v.27 śāśvatasya ca dharmasya sukhasyaikāntikasya ca

For I am the resting place of Brahman; I am the unlimited source of the nectar of immortality; I am that which always exists and can never perish; I am the essence of all that is; I am never-ending joy and unlimited ecstasy; and I am the one unique being who encompasses all that exists.

Chapter 15

The Supreme Being and the Tree of Life

552
Ch.15 v.1

śrībhagavān uvāca
ūrdhvamūlam adhaḥśākham aśvatthaṁ prāhur avyayam
chandāṁsi yasya parṇāni yas taṁ veda sa vedavit

Shri Bhagavan spoke:
It is said that this Universe is like an immortal ashvattha 'peepul tree' that grows with its roots extending upward and its branches blossoming downward. The leaves of this cosmic tree are the truths contained in the vedic knowledge, and one who knows this tree is a wise seer of the vedic truths.

553
Ch.15 v.2

adhaś cordhvaṁ prasṛtās tasya śākhā; guṇapravṛddhā viṣayapravālāḥ
adhaś ca mūlāny anusaṁtatāni; karmānubandhīni manuṣyaloke

The branches of this tree reach both upward and downward, nourished by the three gunas, while its budding sprouts manifest as the desirable objects of the senses. The roots of this tree also extend downward, creating an entangling confusion of cause and effect that eventually leads one to karmic bondage within matter.

554
Ch.15 v.3

na rūpam asyeha tathopalabhyate; nānto na cādir na ca saṁpratiṣṭhā
aśvattham enaṁ suvirūḍhamūlam; asaṅgaśastreṇa dṛḍhena chittvā

The actual form of this ashvattha tree cannot be seen from any location, and neither can a beginning nor an end to its branches be found. Therefore, one should cut this tree off at its very root with the sharp axe of vedic knowledge. This will result in detachment from all material actions.

555 tataḥ padaṁ tatparimārgitavyaṁ; yasmin gatā na nivartanti bhūyaḥ
Ch.15 v.4 tam eva cādyaṁ puruṣaṁ prapadye; yataḥ pravṛttiḥ prasṛtā purāṇī

Then saying, "I take refuge in the Supreme and Ultimate Being," one should seek to enter directly into the transcendental abode of param dhama 'the place from which no one is ever forced to return'.

556 nirmānamohā jitasaṅgadoṣā; adhyātmanityā vinivṛttakāmāḥ
Ch.15 v.5 dvaṁdvair vimuktāḥ sukhaduḥkhasaṁjñair; gacchanty amūḍhāḥ padam avyayaṁ tat

Then, without arrogance or delusion, having conquered all harmful attachments, finally freed from all material desires and without bondage to pleasure and pain, they should come directly to Me and enter my pada avyaya 'the final and ultimate destination'.

557 na tad bhāsayate sūryo na śaśāṅko na pāvakaḥ
Ch.15 v.6 yad gatvā na nivartante tad dhāma paramaṁ mama

My param dhama 'supreme immortal abode' is always brilliant, joyful, and self-luminous; the Sun, Moon, and fire are not needed there. One who enters that effulgent place never returns to the dark and temporary realms of matter.

558 mamaivāṁśo jīvaloke jīvabhūtaḥ sanātanaḥ
Ch.15 v.7 manaḥṣaṣṭhānīndriyāṇi prakṛtisthāni karṣati

The immortal atmas are all amshas 'individual and distinctive facets' of Me. Once they enter the realm of matter, they are called jiva atmas. They attract the inert particles of matter to themselves with their Brahman nature, and with that substance they construct the bodily senses and the sixth sense, manas, in order to manifest within the realm of prakriti.

559 śarīraṁ yad avāpnoti yac cāpy utkrāmatīśvaraḥ
Ch.15 v.8 gṛhītvaitāni saṁyāti vāyur gandhān ivāśayāt

When those jiva atmas take birth in a new body, the remaining material desires from their previous life still cling to them like a fragrance that is carried on a breeze.

560 śrotraṁ cakṣuḥ sparśanaṁ ca rasanaṁ ghrāṇam eva ca
Ch.15 v.9 adhiṣṭhāya manaś cāyaṁ viṣayān upasevate

Acting as the controller of the body, the atma rules over hearing, sight, touch, taste, smell, and the manas faculty. In this way, the atma within matter enjoys the pleasures of the vishayas 'material objects of the senses'.

561 utkrāmantaṁ sthitaṁ vāpi bhuñjānaṁ vā guṇānvitam
Ch.15 v.10 vimūḍhā nānupaśyanti paśyanti jñānacakṣuṣaḥ

Those who have developed yogic knowledge and have opened the jnana chakshusha 'the third eye of transcendental discernment' can see the atma enjoying the body under the control of the gunas and can observe the atma when it leaves at the death of the body. But those without such yogic vision do not see the atma at all.

562 yatanto yoginaś cainaṁ paśyanty ātmany avasthitam
Ch.15 v.11 yatanto 'py akṛtātmāno nainaṁ paśyanty acetasaḥ

Those who diligently practice yoga gain the ability to see the atma, while those who lack this discernment and have not perfected themselves in yoga look but cannot see.

563 yad ādityagataṁ tejo jagad bhāsayate 'khilam
Ch.15 v.12 yac candramasi yac cāgnau tat tejo viddhi māmakam

The splendour of the Sun that constantly illuminates the universe with its rays, which is also present in the Moon and in the fire—that brilliance is my effulgence and comes directly from Me.

564 gām āviśya ca bhūtāni dhārayāmy aham ojasā
Ch.15 v.13 puṣṇāmi cauṣadhīḥ sarvāḥ somo bhūtvā rasātmakaḥ

Pervading the Earth, I maintain all human beings by becoming the ojas 'life force' that nourishes all plants through soma 'the divine nectar' created by the Moon. That celestial juice nourishes all who live with the rasas 'flavours of food' which sustain the life of all beings.

565 ahaṁ vaiśvānaro bhūtvā prāṇināṁ deham āśritaḥ
Ch.15 v.14 prāṇāpānasamāyuktaḥ pacāmy annaṁ caturvidham

I am vaishvanara 'the digestive fire' of all beings. I reside unseen within the body, joining the prana with the apana 'incoming and outgoing breath' in order to promote digestion of the four kinds of food.

566 sarvasya cāhaṁ hṛdi saṁniviṣṭo; mattaḥ smṛtir jñānam apohanaṁ ca
Ch.15 v.15 vedaiś ca sarvair aham eva vedyo; vedāntakṛd vedavid eva cāham

I reside in the heart of all beings, and from Me come knowledge, remembrance, and forgetfulness. I am that which is known from the vedas, I am the author of the Vedanta Sutras, and I am also the knower of the vedas.

567 dvāv imau puruṣau loke kṣaraś cākṣara eva ca
Ch.15 v.16 kṣaraḥ sarvāṇi bhūtāni kūṭastho 'kṣara ucyate

In all the lokas, there are only dvi 'two' kinds of beings: those who are aware of their own immortal nature as the atma, and those who are lost within matter and still do not understand their true nature.

568 uttamaḥ puruṣas tv anyaḥ paramātmety udāhṛtaḥ
Ch.15 v.17 yo lokatrayam āviśya bibharty avyaya īśvaraḥ

Beyond these two kinds of atmas is the Uttama Purusha, the Supreme Being pervading all matter who is also known as Paramatma. That extension of My Supreme Being is also known as Ishvara Avyaya 'the imperishable controller of all life'. In that form, I support and direct all the realms of material existence.

569 yasmāt kṣaram atīto 'ham akṣarād api cottamaḥ
Ch.15 v.18 ato 'smi loke vede ca prathitaḥ puruṣottamaḥ

Since I am beyond both the mortal and immortal beings residing in this universe, I am celebrated in the vedas and throughout the worlds as the Purusha Uttama 'Ultimate Person and Supreme Being who is beyond the reach of matter'.

570 yo mām evam asaṁmūḍho jānāti puruṣottamam
Ch.15 v.19 sa sarvavid bhajati māṁ sarvabhāvena bhārata

O Arjuna, one who has overcome all illusions knows Me as the Purusha Uttama. Knowing this, they adore Me with all their hearts and devote their lives completely to My divine service through bhakti yoga.

571 iti guhyatamaṁ śāstram idam uktaṁ mayānagha
Ch.15 v.20 etad buddhvā buddhimān syāt kṛtakṛtyaś ca bhārata

O Arjuna, I have now revealed to you the guhyatama shastra 'most secret teachings of the vedic library'. One who realizes this secret wisdom becomes a discerning, awakened, and enlightened being. All other obligations are fulfilled by the realization of this secret.

Chapter 16

Devas and Asuras: The Enlightened and Endarkened Beings

572
Ch.16 v.1

śrībhagavān uvāca
abhayaṁ sattvasaṁśuddhir jñānayogavyavasthitiḥ
dānaṁ damaś ca yajñaś ca svādhyāyas tapa ārjavam

Shri Bhagavan said: O Arjuna
[These are the qualities of devas:]

1. abhaya—They live free from fear.
2. sattva samshuddhi—They are sattvic, pure and clean.
3. jnana yoga vyavasthiti—They always persevere and stand in the discernment of jnana yoga.
4. dana—They know how to hold, circulate, and apportion wealth and material resources correctly.
5. dama—They always have control over their bodily senses.
6. yajna—They perform ritual actions that keep them in harmony with the laws of nature.
7. svadhyaya—They constantly discern the difference between their atma and its material coverings.
8. tapas—They perform the correct yogic practices which restore them to their true nature.
9. arjava—They live in right relationship with everyone and everything around them.

573
Ch.16 v.2

ahiṁsā satyam akrodhas tyāgaḥ śāntir apaiśunam
dayā bhūteṣv aloluptvaṁ mārdavaṁ hrīr acāpalam

10. ahimsa—They cause the least harm while remaining true to their own responsibilities.
11. satya—They speak the truth in a way that is beneficial for all.
12. akrodha—They have overcome anger.
13. tyaga—They are not addicted to matter in any form.
14. shanti—They are balanced, equipoised, and free from the stress of opposing forces.

15. apaishuna—They do not slander or gossip about others.
16. daya bhuteshu—They treat all living beings with kindness and compassion.
17. aloluptva—They are not controlled by material hungers or desires.
18. mardava—They express gentleness and kindness with all beings.
19. hri—They are modest, shy, and unassuming.
20. achapala—They are loyal, not fickle, and unwavering in their dedication.

574 tejaḥ kṣamā dhṛtiḥ śaucam adroho nātimānitā
Ch.16 v.3 bhavanti saṁpadaṁ daivīm abhijātasya bhārata

21. teja—They are endowed with vigor, vitality, and a steady and healthy internal fire.
22. kshama—They are patient and tolerant of others.
23. dhriti—They show consistent strength, courage, and determination.
24. shaucha—They are internally and externally pure and clean.
25. adroha—They are not hateful to any living being.
26. na atimanita—They are humble with no craving for being honoured.

My dear Arjuna, these are the qualities of those who were born with or have achieved a divine nature and who, although human, resemble the devas. They live as enlightened beings who work with the divine light of Brahman and cooperate with the laws of prakriti.

575 dambho darpo 'timānaś ca krodhaḥ pāruṣyam eva ca
Ch.16 v.4 ajñānaṁ cābhijātasya pārtha saṁpadam āsurīm

O Arjuna, these are the qualities of those who are born as or become asuras 'beings who are opposed to the divine light of Brahman':

1. dambha—fraudulent, hypocritical, and cheaters
2. darpa—arrogant, self-serving, and insolent
3. abhimana—conceited, haughty, and hostile
4. krodha—angry, wrathful, and vengeful
5. parushya—vile, harsh, and malicious, and
6. ajnana—they lack, disregard, and are opposed to knowledge of the laws of nature.

576 daivī saṁpad vimokṣāya nibandhāyāsurī matā
Ch.16 v.5 mā śucaḥ saṁpadaṁ daivīm abhijāto 'si pāṇḍava

The devic temperament leads to vimoksha 'freedom from bondage to the laws of matter', while the asuric temperament leads to nibandha 'bondage within the laws of matter'. But do not worry, O Arjuna, for you were born with the devic qualities.

577 dvau bhūtasargau loke 'smin daiva āsura eva ca
Ch.16 v.6 daivo vistaraśaḥ prokta āsuraṁ pārtha me śṛṇu

My dear Arjuna, there are two kinds of beings on Bhumi Loka 'Mother Earth'. One has or is developing the enlightened deva qualities, and the other is of the endarkened asura nature. I have previously described the deva qualities in considerable detail, so now hear more about the asuras.

578 pravṛttiṁ ca nivṛttiṁ ca janā na vidur āsurāḥ
Ch.16 v.7 na śaucaṁ nāpi cācāro na satyaṁ teṣu vidyate

Asuras are

7. pravritti and nivritti—They do not understand or care to know what appropriate or inappropriate actions are.
8. na shaucha—They are inherently unclean.
9. na achara—They are unable to act in an exemplary manner.
10. na satya—They are not inclined to tell the truth.

579 asatyam apratiṣṭhaṁ te jagad āhur anīśvaram
Ch.16 v.8 aparasparasaṁbhūtaṁ kim anyat kāmahaitukam

In addition, they are

11. asatya—purposely against the truth, and
12. apratishta—unreliable, since they stand for no ideals and therefore, only act selfishly.

Because of this, they say

13. "There is no higher being or beings who control the universe."
14. "The universe is not caused by an intelligent, purposeful and sequential process of cause and effect."
15. Instead they assert, "It is merely random and held together only by the force of sexual desire."

580 etāṁ dṛṣṭim avaṣṭabhya naṣṭātmāno 'lpabuddhayaḥ
Ch.16 v.9 prabhavanty ugrakarmāṇaḥ kṣayāya jagato 'hitāḥ

Because they stand for that point of view, they become

16. nashtatma—beings whose atma is lost
17. alpabuddhi—beings without the discernment of the buddhi and
18. ugrakarma—their actions are cruel and ugly.

Thus, they become enemies of this world, here to cause its destruction.

581 kāmam āśritya duṣpūraṁ dambhamānamadānvitāḥ
Ch.16 v.10 mohād gṛhītvāsadgrāhān pravartante 'śucivratāḥ

They are

19. kama ashritya dushpura—attached to insatiable and degrading desires

20. dambha—fraudulent and full of hypocrisy
21. mana—filled with arrogance and pride
22. mada—addicted to intoxicants of various types
23. moha—deluded and constantly spreading confusion
24. grihit asat graha—deluded by and attached to ideas which are untrue, and
25. ashuchi vrata—they take vows to accomplish actions that are unclean and degrading to all.

582
Ch.16 v.11

cintām aparimeyāṁ ca pralayāntām upāśritāḥ
kāmopabhogaparamā etāvad iti niścitāḥ

Those who are asuras are

26. chinta aparimeya—perpetually filled with endless fears and anxieties
27. pralayanta upashrita—they cling to matter and material thoughts right up until the moment of death
28. kama upabhoga parama—they hold the view that the gratification of material desires is the only aim of life
29. etavaditi nishchita—they are completely convinced there is nothing more to life than this.

583
Ch.16 v.12

āśāpāśaśatair baddhāḥ kāmakrodhaparāyaṇāḥ
īhante kāmabhogārtham anyāyenārthasaṁcayān

Asuras are

30. ashapasha shataih—bound by hundreds of vain hopes and futile wishes
31. kama krodha parayanta—filled with anger and selfish material desires as their highest aim
32. kama bhoga artha—filled with selfish and unwholesome desires which they arrange to satisfy by degrading means, and

33. anyayena artha samchaya—they will obtain money by any means, no matter how unscrupulous or harmful.

584 idam adya mayā labdham idaṁ prāpsye manoratham
Ch.16 v.13 idam astīdam api me bhaviṣyati punar dhanam

This is the way that asuras think:

34. "Today I have obtained the objects that I desired. Tomorrow I will get even more of the things I want. All of this should belong to me and in the future more and more wealth and power will someday be mine.

585 asau mayā hataḥ śatrur haniṣye cāparān api
Ch.16 v.14 īśvaro 'ham ahaṁ bhogī siddho 'haṁ balavān sukhī

35. "In the past, I have destroyed all my enemies and I will hate and kill whoever opposes me in the future. Aham ishvara 'I am the ruler and controller of all'. Aham bhogi 'I am greedy for endless enjoyment'. Aham siddhi 'I am perfect and the best in whatever I do'. And so, aham balavan sukhi 'I am powerful and will have whatever I desire for my pleasure'.

586 āḍhyo 'bhijanavān asmi ko 'nyo 'sti sadṛśo mayā
Ch.16 v.15 yakṣye dāsyāmi modiṣya ity ajñānavimohitāḥ

36. "I am wealthy and possessed of greatness because of my superior birth. No one else is my equal. I will make a public show of giving charity and pseudo-worship to show my greatness, and then I will always be happy."

In this way, asuras are deluded, bewildered and ajnana 'completely lost in the darkest ignorance'.

587
Ch.16 v.16

anekacittavibhrāntā mohajālasamāvṛtāḥ
prasaktāḥ kāmabhogeṣu patanti narake 'śucau

Those who are asuric are finally led astray by a myriad of vain and confused imaginings. Covered, enveloped, and trapped in a web of delusions, addicted to material desires to satisfy their bodily senses, they become degraded and descend deeper into despicable realms of addiction, pain, and darkness.

588
Ch.16 v.17

ātmasaṁbhāvitāḥ stabdhā dhanamānamadānvitāḥ
yajante nāmayajñais te dambhenāvidhipūrvakam

The asuras are

37. atma sambhavita—their atma has become completely lost in conceited and self-serving material causes
38. stabdha—they are obstinate and stubborn in their attitude
39. dhana mana mada anvita—they display the arrogance that so easily accompanies excessive wealth
40. yajante nama yajna—they pretend to perform vedic ceremonies under the pretext of helping others, but in fact, they are
41. dambhena avidhi purvaka—hypocrites who violate vedic dharma while acting only for their own selfish interests.

589
Ch.16 v.18

ahaṁkāraṁ balaṁ darpaṁ kāmaṁ krodhaṁ ca saṁśritāḥ
māṁ ātmaparadeheṣu pradviṣanto 'bhyasūyakāḥ

They are

42. ahamkara—clinging desperately to a temporary material conception of self
43. bala—violent and forceful
44. darpa—haughty and arrogant

45. kama—filled with endless material desires
46. krodha—angry and vengeful
47. atma para deheshu—hateful to the atma in all beings and even within their own heart, and
48. pradvishan abhyasuyaka—hateful and averse to Me as Paramatma.

590
Ch.16 v.19

tān ahaṁ dviṣataḥ krūrān saṁsāreṣu narādhamān
kṣipāmy ajasram aśubhān āsurīṣv eva yoniṣu

I continually throw these cruel-hearted and malevolent human beings back into the wombs of other asuras where they remain bound up in the cycles of repeated samsara.

591
Ch.16 v.20

āsurīṁ yonim āpannā mūḍhā janmani janmani
mām aprāpyaiva kaunteya tato yānty adhamāṁ gatim

Because they continuously enter the darkened wombs of asuric beings as a result of their own harmful actions, their delusion continues janmani janmani 'from birth to birth', leading them gradually toward the darkest destinations in existence.

592
Ch.16 v.21

trividhaṁ narakasyedaṁ dvāraṁ nāśanam ātmanaḥ
kāmaḥ krodhas tathā lobhas tasmād etat trayaṁ tyajet

Those dark destinations are called Naraka 'the most painful and degraded realms of material existence'. There are three dvaram 'doors or gateways' that lead the atma to the lower asuric realms. These doorways to degradation are kama 'unlimited material desires', krodha 'destructive anger', and lobha 'endless greed for material experience'. Therefore, one must abandon these three.

593 etair vimuktaḥ kaunteya tamodvārais tribhir naraḥ
Ch.16 v.22 ācaraty ātmanaḥ śreyas tato yāti paraṁ gatim

O Arjuna, if a human being avoids these three gates to tamas, they are gradually elevated by their personal actions until they finally ascend to Brahman, the param gati 'ultimate destination'.

594 yaḥ śāstravidhim utsṛjya vartate kāmakārataḥ
Ch.16 v.23 na sa siddhim avāpnoti na sukhaṁ na paraṁ gatim

But those who ignore the wisdom and conclusion of the vedic teachings and only follow the impulses of their own material hungers and desires cannot achieve siddhi 'perfection of their potential' or sukha 'lasting happiness'. They cannot go to the supreme destination of Brahman.

595 tasmāc chāstraṁ pramāṇaṁ te kāryākāryavyavasthitau
Ch.16 v.24 jñātvā śāstravidhānoktaṁ karma kartum ihārhasi

Therefore, let the vedic shastra instruct you on what should and should not be done. By following what is prescribed in the vedic shastra, you will perfect your actions in the world.

Chapter 17

How the Gunas Modify Our Most Essential Actions

Shraddha, Yajna, Tapasya, Dana

596
Ch.17 v.1

arjuna uvāca
ye śāstravidhim utsṛjya yajante śraddhayānvitāḥ
teṣāṁ niṣṭhā tu kā kṛṣṇa sattvam āho rajas tamaḥ

ARJUNA enquired:
O Krishna, when someone rejects the divine guidance given in the vedas, and yet continues to perform yajnas with shraddha 'a condition of the manas which creates certainty in the correctness of perception and confidence that a specific path of action will produce the desired result', are they acting in sattva, raja, or tama guna?

597
Ch.17 v.2

śrībhagavān uvāca
trividhā bhavati śraddhā dehināṁ sā svabhāvajā
sāttvikī rājasī caiva tāmasī ceti tāṁ śṛṇu

SHRI BHAGAVAN replied:
Because the gunas colour and define one's intrinsic nature, there are three kinds of shraddha. Now listen as I explain the characteristics and qualities of shraddha in the context of sattva, rajas, and tamas.

598
Ch.17 v.3

sattvānurūpā sarvasya śraddhā bhavati bhārata
śraddhāmayo 'yaṁ puruṣo yo yacchraddhaḥ sa eva saḥ

According to their previous life, who they associate with, and how they live, every person assumes the qualities of a specific combination of the gunas, which in turn determines how they behave. The shraddha of every being also reflects the guna in which they are living. O Arjuna, whatever you like, you become like.

599 yajante sāttvikā devān yakṣarakṣāṁsi rājasāḥ
Ch.17 v.4 pretān bhūtagaṇāṁś cānye yajante tāmasā janāḥ

Those who are sattvic dedicate themselves to the devas. Those who are rajasic try to become like the Yakshas 'servants of Kuvera, the deva of wealth' and the rakshas who only pursue power and whose nature is to dominate, exploit, and consume. Those who are tamasic seek empowerment by offering themselves to the pretas, bhutas, and ganas 'disembodied and ghostly beings who live in darkness and create chaos and confusion.'

600 aśāstravihitaṁ ghoraṁ tapyante ye tapo janāḥ
Ch.17 v.5 dambhāhaṁkārasaṁyuktāḥ kāmarāgabalānvitāḥ

Those persons who are opposed to the vedic conclusions undergo tapasya that is ghora 'violent and ghastly'. The ahamkara binds them to hypocrisy and selfishness. They are motivated by excessive desires, are intensely attached to matter, and easily resort to anger and violence.

601 karśayantaḥ śarīrasthaṁ bhūtagrāmam acetasaḥ
Ch.17 v.6 māṁ caivāntaḥśarīrasthaṁ tān viddhy āsuraniścayān

Without thoughtfulness or sensitivity, they abuse their bodies and disturb the balance of its elements. By doing this, they also indirectly torture me since I reside within their bodies as Paramatma. Those who do such things are asuric.

602 āhāras tv api sarvasya trividho bhavati priyaḥ
Ch.17 v.7 yajñas tapas tathā dānaṁ teṣāṁ bhedam imaṁ śṛṇu

The food desired by humans is also of three kinds, and so is their practice of yajna, tapasya, and dana. Now, listen as I explain the distinctions of each of them.

According to their previous
life, who they associate
with, and how they live,
every person assumes the
qualities of a specific
combination of the gunas,
which in turn determines
how they behave. The
shraddha of every being
also reflects the guna in
which they are living.
O Arjuna, whatever you like,
you become like.–598

603 āyuḥsattvabalārogyasukhaprītivivardhanāḥ
Ch.17 v.8 rasyāḥ snigdhāḥ sthirā hṛdyā āhārāḥ sāttvikapriyāḥ

Foods which promote longevity, power and strength; increase immunity; give happiness and true satisfaction; are full of delightful flavours and beneficial fats; steady and sustain life; and are hearty and satisfying are sattvic. Such foods create balance, steady all functions in the system, and are dear to those in sattva guna.

604 kaṭvamlalavaṇātyuṣṇatīkṣṇarūkṣavidāhinaḥ
Ch.17 v.9 āhārā rājasasyeṣṭā duḥkhaśokāmayapradāḥ

Foods that are too bitter, sour, salty, hot, pungent, or astringent are rajasic. These foods are liked by those who are rajasic in nature, though they eventually cause pain, misery, and disease.

605 yātayāmaṁ gatarasaṁ pūti paryuṣitaṁ ca yat
Ch.17 v.10 ucchiṣṭam api cāmedhyaṁ bhojanaṁ tāmasapriyam

Foods that are stale, tasteless, putrid, and rotting, with no remaining nutrition, are tamasic. They are not fit to offer to anyone, yet they are dear to those who are tamasic in nature.

606 aphalākāṅkṣibhir yajño vidhidṛṣṭo ya ijyate
Ch.17 v.11 yaṣṭavyam eveti manaḥ samādhāya sa sāttvikaḥ

The gunas apply to yajna just as they do to food. Any yajna that is in alignment with vedic principles and is performed with no desire for a material outcome, with one's manas entirely focused upon the process of sacred offering, is sattvic in nature.

607 abhisaṁdhāya tu phalaṁ dambhārtham api caiva yat
Ch.17 v.12 ijyate bharataśreṣṭha taṁ yajñaṁ viddhi rājasam

O Arjuna, yajna that is performed only for a self-motivated material result and as an ostentatious public display to achieve prestige and admiration is rajasic in nature.

608 vidhihīnam asṛṣṭānnaṁ mantrahīnam adakṣiṇam
Ch.17 v.13 śraddhāvirahitaṁ yajñaṁ tāmasaṁ paricakṣate

And yajna which is contrary to the instructions of the vedic shastra—where sanctified food is not offered, without the appropriate mantras, without an appropriate offering to the one conducting the yajna, and performed without shraddha—is considered tamasic.

609 devadvijaguruprājñapūjanaṁ śaucam ārjavam
Ch.17 v.14 brahmacaryam ahiṁsā ca śārīraṁ tapa ucyate

Honouring and offering rituals of respect to the devas, brahmins, and gurus; maintaining external and internal cleanliness; behaving in an honourable and respectful manner; vowing not to engage in degrading sexual behaviours; and doing the least harm while adhering to one's svadharma—these actions are known as tapasya of the physical body.

610 anudvegakaraṁ vākyaṁ satyaṁ priyahitaṁ ca yat
Ch.17 v.15 svādhyāyābhyasanaṁ caiva vāṅmayaṁ tapa ucyate

Speaking words that are satya 'always true', in a manner that is gentle and refined, as if all beings are priya 'dear friends', and regularly reciting vedic vidya—these are vanmaya tapasya 'gradual perfection of one's self through speech'.

611 manaḥprasādaḥ saumyatvaṁ maunam ātmavinigrahaḥ
Ch.17 v.16 bhāvasaṁśuddhir ity etat tapo mānasam ucyate

Using the thinking, feeling, willing, and memory faculties of manas in a calm and gentle manner; atma vinigraha 'exercising self-restraint through acting as the atma'; and creating states of well-being in others through pure and beneficial thoughts and emotions—these are spoken of as tapasya of the manas.

612 śraddhayā parayā taptaṁ tapas tat trividhaṁ naraiḥ
Ch.17 v.17 aphalākāṅkṣibhir yuktaiḥ sāttvikaṁ paricakṣate

When a person practices this tapasya pertaining to body, speech, and manas in a steady state of shraddha, without attachment to the phala, they are said to be acting in sattva guna.

613 satkāramānapūjārthaṁ tapo dambhena caiva yat
Ch.17 v.18 kriyate tad iha proktaṁ rājasaṁ calam adhruvam

When a person practices this tapasya simply to be honoured and respected by others, with an ulterior motive, and directed toward achieving selfish material objectives, they are said to be acting in raja guna.

614 mūḍhagrāheṇātmano yat pīḍayā kriyate tapaḥ
Ch.17 v.19 parasyotsādanārthaṁ vā tat tāmasam udāhṛtam

And finally, when a person practices this tapasya based upon a deluded understanding of the atma, abusively, and with the goal of causing harm to one's self or others, they are said to be acting in tama guna.

615 dātavyam iti yad dānaṁ dīyate 'nupakāriṇe
Ch.17 v.20 deśe kāle ca pātre ca tad dānaṁ sāttvikaṁ smṛtam

Dana which gives, grants, or bestows beneficial energies by circulating or distributing them throughout the social body, with no ulterior motive, at the right time and place, and to a worthy recipient—that dana is said to be in sattva guna.

616 yat tu pratyupakārārthaṁ phalam uddiśya vā punaḥ
Ch.17 v.21 dīyate ca parikliṣṭaṁ tad dānaṁ rājasaṁ smṛtam

Dana which gives, grants, or bestows, but is offered grudgingly or with misgivings, or with the motive of receiving a benefit in return—that dana is said to be in raja guna.

617 adeśakāle yad dānam apātrebhyaś ca dīyate
Ch.17 v.22 asatkṛtam avajñātaṁ tat tāmasam udāhṛtam

Dana which gives, grants, or bestows unhelpful gifts; is distributed at an inappropriate kala 'time' and desha 'place'; is given to the wrong patra 'person'; or is given in a manner that is ignorant, disrespectful, and contemptuous—that dana is said to be in tama guna.

618 oṁ tat sad iti nirdeśo brahmaṇas trividhaḥ smṛtaḥ
Ch.17 v.23 brāhmaṇās tena vedāś ca yajñāś ca vihitāḥ purā

The three words aum, tat, and sat have been described in vedic shastra as the vibratory emanation of the transcendental Brahman realm. In ancient times, the brahmins began performing yajna by repeating these mantras, and thus these mantras are still remembered to this day as the prerequisite to any vedic ritual.

619 tasmād om ity udāhṛtya yajñadānatapaḥkriyāḥ
Ch.17 v.24 pravartante vidhānoktāḥ satataṁ brahmavādinām

Therefore, the vibration of aum or omkara is always uttered aloud at the beginning of activities involving yajna, dana, and tapasya. This sacred precept is always performed by those who are brahmavadins 'expounders of the teachings of Brahman'.

620 tad ity anabhisaṁdhāya phalaṁ yajñatapaḥkriyāḥ
Ch.17 v.25 dānakriyāś ca vividhāḥ kriyante mokṣakāṅkṣibhiḥ

Thus, by uttering tat 'may it be so', without desiring the phala from any act of yajna, tapasya, or dana, those only seeking Brahman perform all their actions with the sole desire of achieving moksha from prakriti by entering the realm of Brahman.

621 sadbhāve sādhubhāve ca sad ity etat prayujyate
Ch.17 v.26 praśaste karmaṇi tathā sacchabdaḥ pārtha yujyate

The word sat means that which endures all change or transformation and is always true under any circumstance. It also describes the person who is sadhu 'the personification of ultimate Brahman reality whose words and actions cut away the bonds of material illusion'. Thus, the word sat is spoken while performing any action that is intended to be sat.

622 yajñe tapasi dāne ca sthitiḥ sad iti cocyate
Ch.17 v.27 karma caiva tadarthīyaṁ sad ity evābhidhīyate

When one is sthiti 'steady, balanced, and constant' in the sattvic performance of yajna, tapasya, and dana, those sacred activities are called sat, and all related actions are also considered to be sat.

623 aśraddhayā hutaṁ dattaṁ tapas taptaṁ kṛtaṁ ca yat
Ch.17 v.28 asad ity ucyate pārtha na ca tat pretya no iha

Therefore, O Arjuna, any yajna whose hutam 'sacred offering' is placed into the fire without sattvic shraddha, and any tapasya that is undertaken and practised without sattvic shraddha, are known as asat and are without satya 'future truth and beneficial outcome', in this life or the next.

Chapter 18

Secrets of Moksha and the Final Goal of Yoga

624
Ch.18 v.1

arjuna uvāca
saṁnyāsasya mahābāho tattvam icchāmi veditum
tyāgasya ca hṛṣīkeśa pṛthak keśiniṣūdana

ARJUNA spoke:
O Krishna, please explain to me the distinction between sannyasa and tyaga, the two processes of detaching the atma from its relationship with matter according to the vedas.

625
Ch.18 v.2

śrībhagavān uvāca
kāmyānāṁ karmaṇāṁ nyāsaṁ saṁnyāsaṁ kavayo viduḥ
sarvakarmaphalatyāgaṁ prāhus tyāgaṁ vicakṣaṇāḥ

SHRI BHAGAVAN said:
According to the vedic rishis, the sannyasa path is followed by someone who has taken formal vows of renunciation or entered a monastic lifestyle. Whereas those who follow the path of tyaga act in the world without attachment to the fruit of their actions.

626
Ch.18 v.3

tyājyaṁ doṣavad ity eke karma prāhur manīṣiṇaḥ
yajñadānatapaḥkarma na tyājyam iti cāpare

Some learned scholars say that all actions should be given up because they are filled with flaws that cause future karmic reactions. Other sages say that the sacred actions of yajna, dana, and tapasya should never be abandoned.

627
Ch.18 v.4

niścayaṁ śṛṇu me tatra tyāge bharatasattama
tyāgo hi puruṣavyāghra trividhaḥ saṁprakīrtitaḥ

O Arjuna, now listen as I explain tyaga. According to the vedic literature, Arjuna, detachment is either sattvic, rajasic, or tamasic.

628 yajñadānatapaḥkarma na tyājyaṁ kāryam eva tat
Ch.18 v.5 yajño dānaṁ tapaś caiva pāvanāni manīṣiṇām

The wise seers have determined that yajna, dana, and tapasya should never be given up in the name of tyaga because those actions cleanse and purify all who perform them.

629 etāny api tu karmāṇi saṅgaṁ tyaktvā phalāni ca
Ch.18 v.6 kartavyānīti me pārtha niścitaṁ matam uttamam

O Arjuna, it is My unwavering position that the three sacred actions of tapasya, yajna, and dana go beyond the gunas. Therefore, they must be performed with no attachment to the results.

630 niyatasya tu saṁnyāsaḥ karmaṇo nopapadyate
Ch.18 v.7 mohāt tasya parityāgas tāmasaḥ parikīrtitaḥ

Even the practice of sannyasa does not justify neglecting one's obligatory responsibilities of tapasya, yajna, and dana. Abandoning these is a form of moha 'delusion' that leads to tamas.

631 duḥkham ity eva yat karma kāyakleśabhayāt tyajet
Ch.18 v.8 sa kṛtvā rājasaṁ tyāgaṁ naiva tyāgaphalaṁ labhet

When tapasya, yajna, and dana are not performed because they seem painful or too difficult, that tyaga is said to be compromised and is in raja guna.

632 kāryam ity eva yat karma niyataṁ kriyate 'rjuna
Ch.18 v.9 saṅgaṁ tyaktvā phalaṁ caiva sa tyāgaḥ sāttviko mataḥ

But when tapasya, yajna, and dana are performed because they are the appropriate thing to do and with no attachment to the result, then that tyaga is sattvic.

633 na dveṣṭy akuśalaṁ karma kuśale nānuṣajjate
Ch.18 v.10 tyāgī sattvasamāviṣṭo medhāvī chinnasaṁśayaḥ

One whose tyaga is sattvic is not attached to pleasing actions nor repulsed by unpleasant work and is freed from all doubts about the results of their work.

634 na hi dehabhṛtā śakyaṁ tyaktuṁ karmāṇy aśeṣataḥ
Ch.18 v.11 yas tu karmaphalatyāgī sa tyāgīty abhidhīyate

Indeed, it is not possible for an embodied being to give up all work. Thus, only one who is entirely detached from the karma phala 'fruits of their action' can be called a tyagi.

635 aniṣṭam iṣṭaṁ miśraṁ ca trividhaṁ karmaṇaḥ phalam
Ch.18 v.12 bhavaty atyāgināṁ pretya na tu saṁnyāsināṁ kva cit

When those who are tyagi leave their body and receive the fruits of their past actions, what they receive is either anishta 'undesirable', ishta 'desirable', or mishra 'mixed' according to their guna when they performed the actions. But, because of the constancy of their sacred vows, those who are monks in the order of sannyasa only perform tapasya, yajna, and dana, and therefore receive no karmic reactions at all.

636 pañcaitāni mahābāho kāraṇāni nibodha me
Ch.18 v.13 sāṁkhye kṛtānte proktāni siddhaye sarvakarmaṇām

O Arjuna, now focus your buddhi faculty and listen to Me very carefully as I describe the five factors of accomplishing any action, as it is proclaimed in the vedic darshan of the sankhya teachings.

637 adhiṣṭhānaṁ tathā kartā karaṇaṁ ca pṛthagvidham
Ch.18 v.14 vividhāś ca pṛthakceṣṭā daivaṁ caivātra pañcamam

There are five separate factors in all actions performed by human beings:

1. adishtana—the platform or situation from which action is initiated
2. karta—the agent or doer of the action
3. karana—the instruments of the ten bodily senses
4. cheshta—the many methods used to accomplish any action
5. daiva—the unseen devas who also subtly influence all human actions.

638 śarīravāṅmanobhir yat karma prārabhate naraḥ
Ch.18 v.15 nyāyyaṁ vā viparītaṁ vā pañcaite tasya hetavaḥ

All actions performed by human beings as thought, speech, or bodily action, whether beneficial or unbeneficial, are manifested in the context of these five factors of action.

639 tatraivaṁ sati kartāram ātmānaṁ kevalaṁ tu yaḥ
Ch.18 v.16 paśyaty akṛtabuddhitvān na sa paśyati durmatiḥ

Thus, any human being who believes that their personal use of free will as an atma is the only factor producing the outcome of an action lacks the discernment that results from activating their buddhi faculty, and therefore is foolish and cannot see.

640 yasya nāhaṁkṛto bhāvo buddhir yasya na lipyate
Ch.18 v.17 hatvāpi sa imām̐ lokān na hanti na nibadhyate

If a person has overcome the influence of ahamkara and their buddhi is not distorted, then even though they are apparently killing others, in fact, they do not kill at all, and they are not bound in the future by the karmic results of their actions.

641
Ch.18 v.18

jñānaṁ jñeyaṁ parijñātā trividhā karmacodanā
karaṇaṁ karma karteti trividhaḥ karmasaṁgrahaḥ

The three factors that motivate action are knowledge, the objects of knowledge, and the knower. The three constituents of action are the senses, the work, and the doer.

642
Ch.18 v.19

jñānaṁ karma ca kartā ca tridhaiva guṇabhedataḥ
procyate guṇasaṁkhyāne yathāvac chṛṇu tāny api

Knowledge, action, and the doer of action are known to be of three kinds according to the three gunas in which they are established. Now, hear the subtleties of these distinctions.

643
Ch.18 v.20

sarvabhūteṣu yenaikaṁ bhāvam avyayam īkṣate
avibhaktaṁ vibhakteṣu taj jñānaṁ viddhi sāttvikam

The state of knowing by which one perceives all living beings to be both an immortal and indivisible individual as well as undivided and in essence the same as all other beings, all the while surrounded by the duality and divisiveness of matter—that knowing is said to be sattvic in nature.

644
Ch.18 v.21

pṛthaktvena tu yaj jñānaṁ nānābhāvān pṛthagvidhān
vetti sarveṣu bhūteṣu taj jñānaṁ viddhi rājasam

The state of knowing by which one sees all beings as not connected and entirely different from one another simply because of external expressions of material differentiation—that knowing is said to be rajasic in nature.

645 yat tu kṛtsnavad ekasmin kārye saktam ahaitukam
Ch.18 v.22 atattvārthavad alpaṁ ca tat tāmasam udāhṛtam

The state of knowing by which one performs actions without a clear purpose, believing that whatever they do is right, and considering trivial material details to be of great importance—that knowing is said to be tamasic in nature.

646 niyataṁ saṅgarahitam arāgadveṣataḥ kṛtam
Ch.18 v.23 aphalaprepsunā karma yat tat sāttvikam ucyate

When an obligatory action is performed as indicated in the vedic shastra, with neither raga 'attachment' nor dvesha 'aversion' to the outcome, and performed without expectation of the phala 'result'—that action is said to be sattvic in nature.

647 yat tu kāmepsunā karma sāhaṁkāreṇa vā punaḥ
Ch.18 v.24 kriyate bahulāyāsaṁ tad rājasam udāhṛtam

When an action is performed with a strong desire for personal pleasure and self-gratification, is deluded by ahamkara 'misidentification of the atma with matter' and is enacted with extreme effort and exertion—that action is said to be rajasic in nature.

648 anubandhaṁ kṣayaṁ hiṁsām anapekṣya ca pauruṣam
Ch.18 v.25 mohād ārabhyate karma yat tat tāmasam ucyate

When an action is performed in a state of delusion, with no regard for the outcome, disregarding loss or injury, and without the necessary ability to succeed—that action is said to be tamasic in nature.

649 muktasaṅgo 'nahaṁvādī dhṛtyutsāhasamanvitaḥ
Ch.18 v.26 siddhyasiddhyor nirvikāraḥ kartā sāttvika ucyate

One whose activities are free from any attachments; who is without vanity and speaks modestly about themself; who is endowed with enthusiasm and determination; and who is unperturbed in both success and failure—that person is said to be in sattva guna.

650 rāgī karmaphalaprepsur lubdho hiṁsātmako 'śuciḥ
Ch.18 v.27 harṣaśokānvitaḥ kartā rājasaḥ parikīrtitaḥ

One who is extremely attached to the fruits of their actions; is filled with lobha 'intense desires and greed'; is inclined toward violence; is unclean; and fluctuates irrationally between elation and sadness—that person is said to be in raja guna.

651 ayuktaḥ prākṛtaḥ stabdhaḥ śaṭho naikṛtiko 'lasaḥ
Ch.18 v.28 viṣādī dīrghasūtrī ca kartā tāmasa ucyate

One who is undisciplined in all their actions; dull, gross, and vulgar in nature; stubborn and obstinate; deceitful and untrustworthy; hypercritical of others; lazy, inclined to depression, and always procrastinating—that person is said to be in tama guna.

652 buddher bhedaṁ dhṛteś caiva guṇatas trividhaṁ śṛṇu
Ch.18 v.29 procyamānam aśeṣeṇa pṛthaktvena dhanaṁjaya

Now, Arjuna, please listen carefully as I describe the distinctions between the three kinds of buddhi 'discernment' and the three kinds of dhritya 'determination and steadiness' as they manifest in each of the gunas.

653 pravṛttiṁ ca nivṛttiṁ ca kāryākārye bhayābhaye
Ch.18 v.30 bandhaṁ mokṣaṁ ca yā vetti buddhiḥ sā pārtha sāttvikī

O Arjuna, when one's buddhi knows when to act and when not to act, what is to be feared and what not to be feared, and which actions lead to bondage or freedom—that buddhi is sattvic.

654 yayā dharmam adharmaṁ ca kāryaṁ cākāryam eva ca
Ch.18 v.31 ayathāvat prajānāti buddhiḥ sā pārtha rājasī

When one's buddhi cannot discern dharma from adharma and cannot distinguish what should be done from what should not be done—that buddhi is rajasic.

655 adharmaṁ dharmam iti yā manyate tamasāvṛtā
Ch.18 v.32 sarvārthān viparītāṁś ca buddhiḥ sā pārtha tāmasī

O Arjuna, when one's buddhi is certain that dharma is adharma, when their manas is enveloped in darkness, and when they see all things and processes in a perverted and distorted way—that buddhi is tamasic.

656 dhṛtyā yayā dhārayate manaḥprāṇendriyakriyāḥ
Ch.18 v.33 yogenāvyabhicāriṇyā dhṛtiḥ sā pārtha sāttvikī

When the dhritya 'determination' of a person holds the manas, prana, and indriyas focused in an unwavering yogic discipline—that dhritya is said to be sattvic.

657 yayā tu dharmakāmārthān dhṛtyā dhārayate 'rjuna
Ch.18 v.34 prasaṅgena phalākāṅkṣī dhṛtiḥ sā pārtha rājasī

O Arjuna, when the dhritya of a person is attached to their work, to their hunger for pleasure, to the needs of their financial development, and with an intense desire to enjoy the results of their actions—that dhritya is said to be rajasic.

658 yayā svapnaṁ bhayaṁ śokaṁ viṣādaṁ madam eva ca
Ch.18 v.35 na vimuñcati durmedhā dhṛtiḥ sā pārtha tāmasī

When the dhritya of a person is confused by fantasies, filled with irrational fears, distorted by unresolved grief, and is depressed and deluded—that dhritya is said to be tamasic.

659 sukhaṁ tv idānīṁ trividhaṁ śṛṇu me bharatarṣabha
Ch.18 v.36 abhyāsād ramate yatra duḥkhāntaṁ ca nigacchati

Listen to me, Arjuna, as I describe the three approaches by which humans seek to achieve sukha 'pleasure' and to put an end to their dukha 'pain.'

660 yat tadagre viṣam iva pariṇāme 'mṛtopamam
Ch.18 v.37 tat. sukhaṁ sāttvikaṁ proktam ātmabuddhiprasādajam

Sukha which in the beginning tastes like visha 'poison' but in the end tastes like amrita 'nectar' and which is born from the buddhi faculty being focused upon one's own atma—that sukha is said to be sattvic.

661 viṣayendriyasaṁyogād yat tadagre 'mṛtopamam
Ch.18 v.38 pariṇāme viṣam iva tat sukhaṁ rājasaṁ smṛtam

Sukha that arises from the union of the senses with their objects of enjoyment, which at first tastes like amrita 'nectar' but in the end will be remembered as visha 'poison'—that sukha is said to be rajasic.

662 yad agre cānubandhe ca sukhaṁ mohanam ātmanaḥ
Ch.18 v.39 nidrālasyapramādotthaṁ tat tāmasam udāhṛtam

And finally, sukha which from the very beginning until the end causes delusion and bewilderment and is caused by sleep, negligence, and laziness—that sukha is said to be tamasic.

663 na tad asti pṛthivyāṁ vā divi deveṣu vā punaḥ
Ch.18 v.40 sattvaṁ prakṛtijair muktaṁ yad ebhiḥ syāt tribhir guṇaiḥ

There are no beings on Bhumi Loka 'Mother Earth' or on Svarga Loka 'home of the devas' who can exist without being controlled by the three gunas of prakriti.

664 brāhmaṇakṣatriyaviśāṁ śūdrāṇāṁ ca paraṁtapa
Ch.18 v.41 karmāṇi pravibhaktāni svabhāvaprabhavair guṇaiḥ

Listen, Arjuna, all humans are divided into four different occupational categories according to their inherent abilities and their guna. The four categories of workers are brahmins 'professors', kshatriyas 'protectors', vaishyas 'producers', and shudras 'providers'.

665
Ch.18 v.42

śamo damas tapaḥ śaucaṁ kṣāntir ārjavam eva ca
jñānaṁ vijñānam āstikyaṁ brahmakarma svabhāvajam

One's svadharma is to work as a brahmin if they are endowed with the following qualities:

1. shama—equilibrium
2. dama—restraint of the senses
3. tapas—daily correct practice of yogic activities
4. shaucha—internal and external cleanliness
5. kshanti—peacefulness under all circumstances
6. arjava—unbiased truth-telling
7. jnana—theoretical knowledge
8. vijnana—realized knowledge, and
9. astikya—a direct experience of the reality of Brahman.

666
Ch.18 v.43

śauryaṁ tejo dhṛtir dākṣyaṁ yuddhe cāpy apalāyanam
dānam īśvarabhāvaś ca kṣatrakarma svabhāvajam

One's svadharma is to work as a kshatriya if they are endowed with the following qualities:

1. shaurya—consistently courageous and protective
2. teja—filled with the power of an intense, unextinguishable fire
3. dhriti—determined and steadfast in all circumstances
4. dakshya yuddhe—skilful in battle, strategic, and a master of the martial arts
5. apalayana—fearless and determined in conflict
6. dana—generous and unattached to wealth, and
7. ishvara bhava—the ability to be a noble leader.

667 kṛṣigorakṣyavāṇijyaṁ vaiśyakarma svabhāvajam
Ch.18 v.44 paricaryātmakaṁ karma śūdrasyāpi svabhāvajam

One's svadharma is to work as a vaishya if they are endowed with the following qualities:

1. krishi—skilled in growing and bringing to market all the products of agriculture
2. gorakshya—skilled in animal husbandry, including raising and protection of cows
3. vanijya—entrepreneurial, can manage people, resources, and all forms of trade and commerce.

One's svadharma is to work as a shudra if they are endowed with the following qualities:

1. paricharya atmaka—trustworthy, confidential, and dedicated to performing the many tasks that perfect and enhance human life, and all forms of skilled labour and work through service, including musicians, artists, and labourers.

668 sve sve karmaṇy abhirataḥ saṁsiddhiṁ labhate naraḥ
Ch.18 v.45 svakarmanirataḥ siddhiṁ yathā vindati tac chṛṇu

One who takes pleasure in working according to their svadharma 'own inherent nature' attains perfection. Now hear how one achieves that siddhi 'perfection' in life.

669 yataḥ pravṛttir bhūtānāṁ yena sarvam idaṁ tatam
Ch.18 v.46 svakarmaṇā tam abhyarcya siddhiṁ vindati mānavaḥ

Humans can achieve perfection by performing the activities that arise naturally from their own intrinsic material nature and by performing them as an offering of devotion to Pravritti Bhutanam 'that Being from whom all beings have their origin and by whom everything is pervaded'.

670 śreyān svadharmo viguṇaḥ paradharmāt svanuṣṭhitāt
Ch.18 v.47 svabhāvaniyataṁ karma kurvan nāpnoti kilbiṣam

It is always better to perform the actions that arise from one's own svadharma, even if they appear imperfect, rather than performing another's svadharma perfectly. Working against one's own particular nature always leads to a negative outcome.

671 sahajaṁ karma kaunteya sadoṣam api na tyajet
Ch.18 v.48 sarvārambhā hi doṣeṇa dhūmenāgnir ivāvṛtāḥ

O Arjuna, just as fire is always accompanied by smoke, so all material actions are flawed and imperfect. Therefore, one should not abandon the responsibilities of their svadharma because of such defects.

672 asaktabuddhiḥ sarvatra jitātmā vigataspṛhaḥ
Ch.18 v.49 naiṣkarmyasiddhiṁ paramāṁ saṁnyāsenādhigacchati

When one's buddhi does not cling to the outcome of any action, when one's atma has entirely subdued the hungers of their material nature, and when one is free from all material desires, then they have achieved complete freedom from all the negative karmas that could result from any action.

673 siddhiṁ prāpto yathā brahma tathāpnoti nibodha me
Ch.18 v.50 samāsenaiva kaunteya niṣṭhā jñānasya yā parā

Now listen carefully, Arjuna, as I share a brief description of how to attain the realm of Brahman, the highest state and final goal of all knowledge.

674 buddhyā viśuddhayā yukto dhṛtyātmānaṁ niyamya ca
Ch.18 v.51 śabdādīn viṣayāṁs tyaktvā rāgadveṣau vyudasya ca

When one's buddhi is steady and all material distortions have been removed, when the atma is constantly controlling all sensory functions by the correct practice of yoga, when one is completely detached from all the objects of the senses, and when attraction and aversion no longer control consciousness or impel action...

675 viviktasevī laghvāśī yatavākkāyamānasaḥ
Ch.18 v.52 dhyānayogaparo nityaṁ vairāgyaṁ samupāśritaḥ

...when one dwells in a sacred and peaceful place, when one eats the right kind and amount of food, when one's speech is always appropriate and sattvic, when one is constantly absorbed in dhyana 'deep meditation', and when one is always detached from material circumstance...

676 ahaṁkāraṁ balaṁ darpaṁ kāmaṁ krodhaṁ parigraham
Ch.18 v.53 vimucya nirmamaḥ śānto brahmabhūyāya kalpate

...when one is completely free of ahamkara 'identification of self with matter', bala 'inappropriate use of force', darpa 'pride', kama 'material desires', krodha 'anger', parigraha vimuchya 'grasping anything material', nirmama 'not claiming to own any matter', and is shanti 'calm, tranquil and balanced in all circumstances', then they identify themselves as the same as Brahman and are therefore qualified to enter the realm of Brahman.

677 brahmabhūtaḥ prasannātmā na śocati na kāṅkṣati
Ch.18 v.54 samaḥ sarveṣu bhūteṣu madbhaktiṁ labhate parām

Once their identity is re-established as Brahman, they become calm and undisturbed in all circumstances. They neither hunger for nor lament the loss of anything. They are also impartial toward all beings. In that state of transcendental consciousness, their adoration of and devotion for Me is also reawakened.

678 bhaktyā mām abhijānāti yāvān yaś cāsmi tattvataḥ
Ch.18 v.55 tato māṁ tattvato jñātvā viśate tadanantaram

As this Divine reawakening continues to unfold, the atma's natural affection for Me is reawakened. As it continues to grow, they increasingly understand the truth of who I really am, and that increases their desire to love, adore, and serve Me. In this ecstatic mood, they finally come to be with Me.

679 sarvakarmāṇy api sadā kurvāṇo madvyapāśrayaḥ
Ch.18 v.56 matprasādād avāpnoti śāśvataṁ padam avyayam

When one performs all material actions completely surrendered to Me and trusting in Me, I enfold them in mat prasada 'My loving embrace', and then they enter shashvata pada avyaya 'My supreme and imperishable abode'.

680 cetasā sarvakarmāṇi mayi saṁnyasya matparaḥ
Ch.18 v.57 buddhiyogam upāśritya maccittaḥ satataṁ bhava

If you place all actions and their outcome into My hands, surrendering to Me as the Ultimate Being, using the discernment of buddhi yoga to be constantly connected with Me;

681 maccittaḥ sarvadurgāṇi matprasādāt tariṣyasi
Ch.18 v.58 atha cet tvam ahaṁkārān na śroṣyasi vinaṅkṣyasi

If you turn to Me when facing all difficulties, then under My protection, you will overcome all problems. But if instead you are bound by ahamkara 'defining yourself as matter' and do not listen to Me, then you will again lose your way.

682 yad ahaṁkāram āśritya na yotsya iti manyase
Ch.18 v.59 mithyaiṣa vyavasāyas te prakṛtis tvāṁ niyokṣyati

But even if you listen to the voice of ahamkara and try to avoid fighting in this conflict, you will fail because your irrepressible material nature will compel you to act all the same.

683 svabhāvajena kaunteya nibaddhaḥ svena karmaṇā
Ch.18 v.60 kartuṁ necchasi yan mohāt kariṣyasy avaśo 'pi tat

Bound by the unstoppable impulses that arise from the gunas and doshas of your material nature, you will invariably do that which, out of delusion, you are currently refusing to do.

684 īśvaraḥ sarvabhūtānāṁ hṛddeśe 'rjuna tiṣṭhati
Ch.18 v.61 bhrāmayan sarvabhūtāni yantrārūḍhāni māyayā

O Arjuna, I am that Supreme Being who is the ruler and director of all beings, and I live in their hearts just as they reside in a place. From there I cause all things and all beings to revolve, yantra arudhani mayaya 'just as if they were attached to a machine that turns them around and around'.

685 tam eva śaraṇaṁ gaccha sarvabhāvena bhārata
Ch.18 v.62 tatprasādāt parāṁ śāntiṁ sthānaṁ prāpsyasi śāśvatam

Therefore, O Arjuna, wholeheartedly take shelter in the divine refuge of My Being, receive the loving gift of blissful existence, and soon you will attain to My immortal realm.

686 iti te jñānam ākhyātaṁ guhyād guhyataraṁ mayā
Ch.18 v.63 vimṛśyaitad aśeṣeṇa yathecchasi tathā kuru

Now, I have revealed to you guhyad guhyatara 'that knowledge which is the secret of secrets.' This is the most secret understanding that I have shared with you thus far. After considering this very carefully, do as you wish.

687 sarvaguhyatamaṁ bhūyaḥ śṛṇu me paramaṁ vacaḥ
Ch.18 v.64 iṣṭo 'si me dṛḍham iti tato vakṣyāmi te hitam

Now, listen again, as I share with you what is sarva guhyatama 'the most secret and confidential teachings of all'. Please hear My supreme words, for you are most beloved to Me and I speak only for your benefit.

688 manmanā bhava madbhakto madyājī māṁ namaskuru
Ch.18 v.65 mām evaiṣyasi satyaṁ te pratijāne priyo 'si me

Focus your manas and discernment upon Me, ardently dedicate yourself to Me, offer everything you have to Me, bow to Me, and vow to adore Me, and in this way, you will surely come to Me. I promise you this because you are most dear to Me.

689 sarvadharmān parityajya mām ekaṁ śaraṇaṁ vraja
Ch.18 v.66 ahaṁ tvā sarvapāpebhyo mokṣayiṣyāmi mā śucaḥ

Just abandon all lesser dharmas and dedicate yourself entirely to Me. Take refuge in Me and I will protect you from all negative reactions. Do not be afraid, for I will free you from all forms of bondage.

690 Idaṁ te nātapaskāya nābhaktāya kadā cana
Ch.18 v.67 na cāśuśrūṣave vācyaṁ na ca māṁ yo 'bhyasūyati

O Arjuna, please do not share these intimate teachings with one who is not ready to hear them or with one who is not yet ready to devote themself to this deep yogic practice. If they do not want to hear these teachings or will speak badly of Me and still have animosity to this path of learning, please do not share this sacred wisdom with them.

691 ya idaṁ paramaṁ guhyaṁ madbhakteṣv abhidhāsyati
Ch.18 v.68 bhaktiṁ mayi parāṁ kṛtvā mām evaiṣyaty asaṁśayaḥ

But one who does share this parama guhya 'most sacred and secret wisdom' with those who sincerely wish to hear performs the very highest service to Me and without doubt will come to live with Me.

692 na ca tasmān manuṣyeṣu kaś cin me priyakṛttamaḥ
Ch.18 v.69 bhavitā na ca me tasmād anyaḥ priyataro bhuvi

Among all human beings, no one is more beloved and pleasing to Me. There is no one on Earth whose service is more intimately connected with Me.

693 adhyeṣyate ca ya imaṁ dharmyaṁ saṁvādam āvayoḥ
Ch.18 v.70 jñānayajñena tenāham iṣṭaḥ syām iti me matiḥ

And I declare that whoever chooses to hear this sacred dharmic conversation between you and Me performs the jnana yajna just by listening to Me with an open, discerning mind and a loving heart.

694 śraddhāvān anasūyaś ca śṛṇuyād api yo naraḥ
Ch.18 v.71 so 'pi muktaḥ śubhāṁl lokān prāpnuyāt puṇyakarmaṇām

Even if one hears this conversation with no understanding and merely trusts its message, they will achieve the complete freedom and liberation of moksha and then they will enter the realms of the immortal beings.

695 kaccid etac chrutaṁ pārtha tvayaikāgreṇa cetasā
Ch.18 v.72 kaccid ajñānasaṁmohaḥ pranaṣṭas te dhanaṁjaya

O Arjuna, have you heard this knowledge with a one-pointed, focused manas, and have your ignorance and delusion now been removed?

696 naṣṭo mohaḥ smṛtir labdhā tvatprasādān mayācyuta
Ch.18 v.73 sthito 'smi gatasaṁdehaḥ kariṣye vacanaṁ tava

Arjuna said:
My illusion has now been completely removed, and my memory and knowledge have been restored by Your words. I am now standing once again. My doubts have all been removed and I am ready to do as You request.

And I declare that whoever
chooses to hear this sacred
dharmic conversation
between you and Me
performs the jnana yajna
just by listening to Me with
an open, discerning mind
and a loving heart.
Even if one hears this
conversation with no
understanding and merely
trusts its message, they will
achieve the complete
freedom and liberation
of moksha and then they
will enter the realms of
immortal beings. –693-694

697
Ch.18 v.74

saṁjaya uvāca
ity ahaṁ vāsudevasya pārthasya ca mahātmanaḥ
saṁvādam imam aśrauṣam adbhutaṁ romaharṣaṇam

SANJAYA said:
Thus, I have now heard this wondrous conversation between these two great beings, the ultimate Supreme Being Shri Krishna, the illustrious son of Vasudeva, and the heroic Arjuna. After hearing this amazing conversation, my hair is standing on end.

698
Ch.18 v.75

vyāsaprasādāc chrutavān etad guhyam ahaṁ param
yogaṁ yogeśvarāt kṛṣṇāt sākṣāt kathayataḥ svayam

Through the grace of Vyasadeva, we have just heard the supreme secrets of yoga from the Yoga Ishvara 'the ultimate master of yoga' Shri Krishna, who just spoke it before our very eyes.

699
Ch.18 v.76

rājan saṁsmṛtya saṁsmṛtya saṁvādam imam adbhutam
keśavārjunayoḥ puṇyaṁ hṛṣyāmi ca muhur muhuḥ

O Maharaja Dhritarashtra, as I remember this remarkable conversation between the ultimate Supreme Person Bhagavan Shri Krishna and the great warrior Arjuna, I am thrilled and I celebrate over and over again.

700
Ch.18 v.77

tac ca saṁsmṛtya saṁsmṛtya rūpam atyadbhutaṁ hareḥ
vismayo me mahān rājan hṛṣyāmi ca punaḥ punaḥ

Remembering again and again the endlessly marvelous forms of Shri Krishna, my amazement continues to grow while I become more and more ecstatic from moment to moment...

701 yatra yogeśvaraḥ kṛṣṇo yatra pārtho dhanurdharaḥ
Ch.18 v.78 tatra śrīr vijayo bhūtir dhruvā nītir matir mama

And I am certain that wherever Yoga Ishvara Shri Krishna, the immortal source of all that is sacred and true, is present with Arjuna, the most courageous, enlightened and honourable warrior, there will also be Shri 'beauty, wealth, strength, fame, knowledge, and generosity', freedom, purest love, and endless joy for all beings.

Part II

All the World Is a Stage

All the world is a stage,
With you the directing sage,

So eventually your story
Becomes obligatory.

Be careful that the plot,
Is not that all is naught,

For the audience is here for thrills,
For heroes with hearts and wills,

For heroines sublime,
For good to overcome crime.

And as you build the narrative,
Make room for all to live.

Remember the title of your script,
Will be engraved upon your crypt.

What you do with effect or cause,
Comes back as booing or applause,

So your feedback from the aisles,
Will either be frowns or smiles.

Remember in every scene,
To convey the truth you mean,

Design each soliloquy,
To be heard for eternity.

Be clear and analytic,
To silence every critic;

Invoke a flood of tears;
Drive away petty fears,

Tie love in chains and locks,
Bind her with paradox,

Then give her wings of glory,
On the winds of oratory,

Until again all see,
Love lasts for perpetuity.

And do not forget to dance,
In the midst of circumstance.

Raise your voice and sing,
Until the rafters ring.

And as you draw the conclusion,
Remove all petty confusion.

Give to the poor in charity,
Free the cynic with clarity,

Give irony to the clown,
And before the curtain goes down,

Speak what cannot be forgotten,
Remind them of what they have gotten.

And when your play is all the rage,
Remember all the world is a stage.

Jeffrey Armstrong | Kavindra Rishi

About the Glossary

Sanskrit is a deep, precise, and philosophical language with descriptions and explanations of concepts and worldviews that cannot be translated directly into English, which is a far less precise or consistent language. In this translation of the Bhagavad Gita, we consciously left out biased, religious, misleading, and overly subjective English words from the text. Instead, we left in the Sanskrit words, to force the original meaning of the text to be protected, revealed, and ultimately shine through for the benefit of the reader. To maximize the effectiveness of the process, we have included this glossary of essential Sanskrit terms.

Why is the glossary so important?

In linguistics, there are 'skinny' words and 'fat' words. An example of a skinny word is 'cup'—an object used to hold or contain liquid. No matter how you translate cup, it still means cup and its meaning is clear. Conversely, a word like 'love' would be described as a 'fat' word because it contains many layers of meaning that leave the word open to multiple interpretations and misinterpretations. Complex Sanskrit words are 'fat' words and can have upwards of ten levels of meaning. Most of the words that appear in this glossary are 'fat' words.

Although this glossary will only have space for one or two levels of meaning, the definitions will be revealing, accurate, and clear, the result of a deep linguistic excavation and research process that I began decades ago. The passion behind the research was intensified by two revelations. One, I discovered that Sanskrit was the source language for nearly every other human language.

Two, with most translators ignoring the fact of Sanskrit primacy, English versions of the Bhagavad Gita could not help but suffer in their translations—whether accidentally or deliberately.

My intention with the glossary and this Gita is to provide for the reader the deepest and clearest possible meaning of the text. The process is not static. I will continue to refine the definitions of these crucial Sanskrit words, but my hope remains the same: that the richer truths and wisdom previously hidden in the Sanskrit words of the Vedas will now be revealed to the reader. In this way, anyone who wants to can imbibe the sweet divine medicine that Bhagavan Shri Krishna left behind for the benefit of all.

Glossary of Select Sanskrit Terms

Acharya: A person who knows and lives according to the *achara* 'Vedic rules of conduct' and is qualified to give initiation to one who is prepared to study Vedic knowledge. An *acharya* leads others on a path of wisdom toward their ultimate liberation both by precept and as a living example of what they teach. An *acharya* would usually be an accomplished person in a Vedic *sampradaya* 'lineage' to whom other teachers defer.

Achintya: See *chinta*

Achit: See *chit*

Adharma: See *dharma*

Agni: The element of fire or the *deva* associated with it. He is present in our belly when we eat, when we cook, or in the fireplace when we heat our home. *Agni* is the force of sunlight in its active forms as fuel on Earth. The Vedic culture explains that we can also use *agni* as a means to send our gratitude to all the divines in a ritual called the *agnihotra yajna*. The smoke rising skyward from a piece of food placed in the fire (the mouth of *Agni*) sends smoke upward into Nature, offering our love and appreciation skyward to thank the *devas* and the Supreme Being for the gifts we have received.

Ahamkara: The most subtle material energy. Its function is to cause the *atma* to erroneously define itself as matter. *Aham* 'I am' and *kara* 'matter'. Bewildered by *ahamkara*, the immortal *atma*, whose actual nature is Brahman, identifies with matter as self and will remain in that delusion forever until it once again asserts *aham brahmasmi* 'I am Brahman in nature' and behaves as if that is true. This is the process of all forms of yoga. *Ahamkara* is removed and replaced with the assertion of self as the immortal *atma*.

The Vedic knowledge and *sankhya yoga* explain that the dense human physical body, the *karana*, is made of earth, water, fire, air, and space, while the subtle body, the *antakarana*, is made of *manas, buddhi*, and *ahamkara*. That subtle body is the body we dream with; it is also the body with which the *atma* moves on to reincarnate at the death of the *karana*. Within that subtle body, *manas* is thinking, feeling, willing, and memory. *Buddhi* is the discernment of one thing from another and *ahamkara* is attachment to matter.

Ahimsa: See *himsa*

Akarma: See *karma*

Ajnana: See *jnana*

Amrita: See *mrityu*

Ananda: Transcendental joy or bliss. This word describes the highest state of ecstatic pleasure and enjoyment, far beyond the mundane pleasures available within matter. The root is *nand* 'to rejoice' plus the prefix *an* 'without end.' The Vedas say that the *atma* has three qualities called *tattva traya*. Those qualities are *sat* 'immortal', *chit* 'always conscious', and *ananda* 'ecstatically and permanently joyful' in nature.

Aryan: One who sees their as Brahman in nature, who sees all beings as *atmas,* and who wishes to live in harmony in every life situation. Its root is *ri* 'to rise upward by co-operation with the laws of Nature'. An *aryan* sees that everyone is on a gradual journey of divine evolution. They have respect for all, and they wish to progress in a balanced, respectful way. This word was distorted through its use by the Nazi movement. *Aryan* does not support caste or racism, nor does it claim superiority over others.

Asana: This is the third limb of *ashtanga yoga*. *Asanas* are yogic postures for correctly channeling the life force, healing, and bringing the body to a state of stillness and balance for the purpose of meditation. The physical body functions correctly when all the gateways and channels are opened and interconnected. *Asanas* unlock the blocked channels allowing the *prana* 'life force' to circulate and flow abundantly throughout the body. In the later stages of this style of yoga, the senses are withdrawn, and the body must sit without moving in deep meditation for long periods of time.

Asat: See *sat*

Asura: The negative prefix *a* 'not' and *sura* 'light.' The *asuras* are *atmas* who have aligned their identity with the dark, unconscious, and temporary nature of matter. They are against the light of divine will and wisdom. *Asuras* are opposed to the regulating influence of light and the laws of nature and become destabilizing agents of chaos and destruction. Chapter 16 has a comprehensive description of the qualities of *asuras*. The opposite is *sura*.

Atma: The invisible, indivisible individual. Though smaller in magnitude, the *atma* is the same in quality as Paramatma, the Supreme Being who pervades and sustains all matter. *Atma* is not a synonym for "soul". Soul is an Abrahamic term used to refer to a 'one-lifetime-then-consequences' paradigm. In contrast, the *atma* is immortal, with no beginning and no end. The *atma* is a facet of the Brahman reality and is described as *sat* 'immortal', *chit* 'conscious', and *ananda* 'joyful by nature'. By expressing the desire to experience the realm of matter, the *atma* begins its journey of *samsara* 'repeated births and deaths'. The *atma* can incarnate as any or all of the species of life. Like a student in a grand 'universe-ity', when the *atma* has perfected its yoga and is ready to graduate, they conclude *aham brahmasmi*—I am the same as Brahman. Only then is the *atma* eligible to return to Brahman and resume the long-forgotten relationship with Bhagavan. Another term for the incarnated *atma* is *jiva atma* 'air-breathing *atma*', which refers to the *atma* existing in material form. The term *jiva bhuta* refers to 'the countless *jiva atmas*'.

Aum: This sound vibration is described in the Vedas as the original vibration from which all material existence emanated. *Om*, spelled *aum*, is composed of the first, an intermediate, and the last letter in the Sanskrit alphabet. The idea is that the universe was spoken into existence by the Supreme Being. The Sanskrit alphabet is the pure and direct manifestation of Brahman as sound vibration. The phrase 'in the beginning was the word' comes directly from the Vedas. *Aum* is also the carrier signal for the immortal truths of Brahman to reach us.

Avatar: The roots of this word are *ava* 'to descend' and *tara* 'to heal and restore.' *Avatar* is the purposeful descent of a divine or of the Supreme Divine Being to the human plane of existence in order to restore balance and transmit wisdom, knowledge, or other necessary information to human beings for their enlightenment and evolutionary well-being. *Avatars* are either partial or full manifestations of either devas or a personal descent from the Brahman realm. Both Shri Ram and Bhagavan Shri Krishna are considered full and therefore ultimate *avatars*. Full *avatars* descend to Earth to restore the *dharma* of society and to reveal the beauty of the Brahman realm and invite the *atmas* to return.

Bhagavan: That person or being who possesses the six *bhagas* to an unlimited degree. The root *van* 'one who possesses' and *bhagas* 'the six most attractive and desirable qualities'. Only one who possesses all these qualities to an unlimited degree can be called Bhagavan. Therefore, "God" or any other name of a facet of the divine is *not* a synonym for Bhagavan and should not be used as such. The Vishnu Purana gives the precise definition of these six *bhagas* or ultimate qualities which Bhagavan possesses to an unlimited degree: *aishvaryasya*—beauty, elegance, and charisma; *dharmasya*—strength, uprightness, heroism, and valor; *yasya samagrasya*—fame, popularity, and recognition; *yasasas shriyah*—opulence, wealth, prosperity, and valuables; *jnana*—knowledge, awareness, and understanding; and *vairagyayas*—non-attachment, detachment, renunciation, and generosity.

Bhakti: From the root *bhaj* 'to honour, serve, and adore'. The path of yogic connection characterized by intense emotion, complete devotion, loving service, and surrender to the Supreme Persons. Someone who practices *bhakti yoga* is known as a *bhakta*.

Brahman: The unlimited, unified, and ever-expanding field of transcendental existence. Brahman is from the root *bri*—the always shining and conscious energy and realm of existence upon which everything rests and from which everything has emerged. According to the Rig Veda, the dark realm of *prakriti* is one-quarter of existence and the unseen realm of Brahman from which all beings originally emanated is the other three-quarters. The ultimate *guru* of Vedic civilization is named Brihaspati 'the spout of Brahman'. All the Vedas affirm the truth, so all perfected yogis in a single voice say '*aham brahmasmi*—I am Brahman'.

Brahmin: The first level of meaning is one who knows, lives, and can transmit the knowledge of Brahman. The secondary meaning of a *brahmin* is one who serves society by using their intellect, as a professor of some subject. As it turns out, not all *brahmins* are teachers of Brahman. In the original Vedic culture, almost all *brahmins* would have known Sanskrit, but as a *varna, brahmins* are skilled as teachers and behave with the values appropriate to that profession. See *varna*

Buddhi: The primary meaning of *buddhi* is discernment, the ability to distinguish one thing from another. It is the basis of science. The Vedas describe all humans as having a five-element body and an *antakarana* or subtle body composed of *manas, buddhi,* and *ahamkara*. The depiction of a third eye in the forehead of the enlightened represents the full awakening of their discernment. In *sankhya yoga*, that discernment of *buddhi* studies the categories of matter to excel in science. It identifies what the *atma* is or is not. The enlightened final conclusion of *buddhi* is 'none of this matter is me or mine'.

Chinta/achintya: *Chinta* means 'the thinking faculty of *manas* applied to enquiry, thought, discussion, and understanding of principles within matter'. *Chinta* is 'cognition of that which is knowable within matter'. Its opposite *achintya* is defined by words like unthinkable, inconceivable, etc. This word is most often used to refer to concepts that defy the laws of Nature within *prakriti*. Brahman, the *atma*, Bhagavan, and all such non-material realities are considered *achintya*—beyond material law, logic, and experience.

Chit/achit: Permanently conscious. The *atma* has three essential qualities—*sat* 'immortal', *ananda* 'always joyful', and *chit* 'permanently conscious'. The essence of yoga is actions that retrieve the *chit* faculty of awareness from its misidentification with matter. That consciousness is distributed throughout the body via the thinking, feeling, willing, and memory faculties of *manas*. The opposite is *achit* 'unconscious'.

Dana: To give, grant, bestow, offer, yield, impart, circulate, or distribute resources into the social body of human beings. Words like *dana* are actions which are inevitably modified by the *guna* of the person distributing the resources. *Sattvic dana* is the appropriate circulation of resources to where they are needed in such a way that the result is sustainable, healthy, dignified, integrated, and harmonious with no ulterior motive. *Rajasic dana* is given with selfish motives, with a desire to be recognized and is distorted by personal desires. *Tamasic dana* is given to the wrong recipients, in a harmful way, and produces a negative or harmful outcome. *Dana* is also the last stage of the *agnihotra yajna*.

Darshan: The root of *darshan* is *drishti* 'to see or be seen' in a progression of seeing and knowing that leads the *atma* out of the darkness caused by association with matter and into an enlightened state of awareness where all that was lost, hidden, or obscured is finally visible. This seeing is not with the two eyes of everyday living. It results from hearing the truths of the Sanskrit Vedic *vidya*, the wisdom passed down by Vedic *rishis*, which opens the 'third eye'. One may give *darshan* by speaking Vedic wisdom to those in darkness, or one may receive *darshan* by listening to the words of an *acharya* or *guru* who has seen the ultimate realities and can pass that vision on. Sanskrit *mantras* from the lips of one who can see the Supreme reality is also *darshan*. It penetrates through the ears and awakens the sleeping *atma* with divine visions. *Darshan* of Vedic *mantras* also opens the third eye of the listener.

Darshan also refers to a perspective or way of looking at the body of Vedic knowledge. The six *darshans* are: *sankhya*—the analytical study of the categories of matter; *nyaya*—the rules of logical thinking; *vaisheshika*—pattern recognition and nuclear physics; *yoga*—removing the misconceptions that cover our awareness of who we are; *purva mimamsa*—understanding our relationship with the devas and the laws of Nature; and *uttara mimamsa* or *vedanta*—understanding the ultimate truths of who we are, where we come from, and where we are going.

Deva: Divine intelligences who sustain matter and conduct the laws of Nature on behalf of Vishnu and Lakshmi. They are *atmas* just like we humans, but they have attained posts in the cosmic administration. They can range from the fairies and sprites in our gardens to the highest management positions in the cosmos. *Deva* gives us the English word 'divine' because they live in a bright realm. Enlightened humans may become *devas* in their next life. To become a *deva* one must temporarily give up their free will to serve as the laws of Nature. After having the *deva* experience, they return to Earth as humans born into a good family and become yogis. They resume their yoga and exercise free will to attain final *moksha*. It is *not* correct to call them "gods" nor are they in competition with the Supreme Being. These misunderstandings arose during the colonial period and are incorrect.

Dharma/adharma: From the root *dhri*—the essential nature of anything, which, if you take it away, that thing is no longer itself. For example, the *dharma* of water is to be liquid. *Dharma* is the basis of the English 'truth'. *Dharma* also means to stand for what is true. Once someone knows their *dharma,* their duty is to live that truth.

The next level of dharma is called one's *svadharma,* which is the correct use of the talents, abilities, and structure of one's body/mind complex. This culminates in an occupation and working within the rules associated with it. Another form of *dharma* is *kula dharma,* the family responsibilities that arise from birth in a clan or extended family.

The widest use of dharma is *sanatana dharma,* truths that

are always true under any circumstance. These form the structure of the *Vedic sanatana dharma culture* or civilization, the culture that tries to cooperate with all the laws of Nature as its guiding principle. I propose that the correct definition of Vedic civilization is that it actually is a *dharmocracy,* where everyone first learns the truths of their 'self' and then does their best to optimize their lives and those around them based on their best qualities.

Dharma Kshetra: This word has several levels of meaning, just as the conflict that precipitated Bhagavan speaking the Bhagavad Gita is a metaphor for human life in general. It is the alternative name for the location Kurukshetra, where the battle took place between the Pandavas and the Kauravas. On the cosmic level, it represents the unified field of matter on which all humans determine their future by the use of free will in the realm of *prakriti* where all actions are governed by the laws of Nature. In that sense, Dharma Kshetra is the place of struggle where the *atmas* are continually being tested on their grasp of *dharma*, or what is always true.

Dosha: The conversational use of *dosha* is 'faults, defects, or imperfections'. The wider use of *dosha* is within Ayurvedic medicine. The five elements that constitute organic life, and especially human bodies, combine together into three *doshas* known as *vata* (air and space), *pitta* (fire), and *kapha* (water and earth). All bodies are made of some kind of balance of the three *doshas*, and because the *doshas* in bodies can be destabilized, they are also called faulty.

Guna, trigunas: In the Vedas, two realms of existence are described—the luminous realm of Brahman, and the dark, unconscious realm of *prakriti.* We, the many *atmas,* are from Brahman and we are here visiting matter to experience this realm. Matter is called the *gu*, a dark, inert, and unconscious substance which passes through three dynamic states of manifestation known as the *trigunas*. The first is *rajas*, the creative stage where energy is infused into matter, giving it a temporary form. The second stage is *sattva*, the maintaining and sustaining stage where something exists for a certain period of time. The third is *tamas*, the deconstructive stage where objects are destroyed or recycled. As humans we experience this as beginning, growth, duration, producing by-products, withering, and dying. All matter and beings within matter are influenced by the *gunas* at all times—invisible realities are filtered by our *guna*. Each *guna* comes with a diet, lifestyle, and very specific behaviours. The goal for yogis is to go from *tamas* to *rajas* and then to live in *sattva guna* as much as possible, avoiding *tamasic* destructive behaviour, *rajasic* selfish behaviours, and practicing universally beneficial *sattvic* behaviours.

This ancient Vedic scientific explanation of the transformative stages of matter was articulated by modern science as the two laws of thermodynamics: (1) Matter is neither created nor destroyed—it merely changes form, and (2) All manifest matter is infused with energy and is gradually moving from a higher state of energy to a lower state, and in the process gives off heat and waste. That process of deconstruction and decomposition is called entropy.

Guru: Literally means 'heavy'. The implication is that one who is filled with knowledge of the supreme eternal truth becomes heavy. The students are *laghu* 'less weighty objects'. A *guru* is one who removes the mistaken notion that consciousness arises from matter and guides the student to remember their immortal nature as the *atma*. Therefore, the Vedic *guru* is a *gu* 'matter' *ru* 'remover', one who helps the student remove their material illusions. *Gurus* are honoured not only because they are carriers of the truths of Brahman and Bhagavan, but because they are exemplars in the way they live their lives.

Himsa/ahimsa: *Ahimsa* is usually translated as 'non-violence' or doing no harm at all, however *ahimsa* means 'the appropriate use of violence according to the *dharma* of the actor and the situation'. A policeman protecting the innocent by use of violence is still *ahimsa*, since it is their *svadharma*—their occupational responsibility—to use appropriate force. The general rule of *ahimsa* followed by all Vedic yogis is governed by a simple rule: Create the least amount of harm while performing one's *svadharma* and one's *sanatana dharma*. There is not just one rule of *ahimsa*, but the principle is to always do the least harm while doing what one must do. The opposite is *himsa* 'causing harm'.

Indriyas: The bodily senses. The human body is constructed out of the *gu* of matter by various combinations of the five elements—earth, water, fire, air, and space. Each of these elements is connected to the five *jnana indriyas* 'perceptive senses': smelling (earth), tasting (water), seeing (fire), touching (air), and hearing (space). There are also five *karma indriyas* 'active senses': evacuating (earth), sex (water), locomotion (fire), grasping (air), and speaking (space). Together, these are called the *dasha indriyas* 'ten bodily senses'. If our body is a vehicle, then the ten senses are its equipment or its structural characteristics. All of this knowledge of matter is called *jnana* 'knowing' and it is part of *sankhya yoga*—the analytical study of what we are and are not. We are not the body, but by studying it carefully we become detached from it and realize that we are the *atma*.

Isha, ishta, ishvara: An *isha* or *ishvara* is a being acting as controller over some department of Nature. Just as a government has functionaries in charge of departments, so the Vedas explain that the realm of matter has departments supervised by purposeful beings. Those *ishas* (also known as *devas* and *devis*) are controllers of particular material domains. Though all of them work for the *Parama Ishvara*, the Supreme controller, they still have departmental control over certain areas of Nature and the humans who live there. In a similar way—as above, so below—each atma is the *isha* of their own body and so are called *purushas*, from which we derive the English word 'person'. See *deva*

Jagat: Usually defined as 'material universe'. The English word universe means 'one turning', and the Sanskrit *jagat* is even more specific. *Ja* means *janma* 'repeated birth and death', and *gat* 'to move and go forward'. The Vedic principle is that we are immortal *atmas* visiting matter, thus it is *samsara* 'reincarnation' that turns the wheel of repeated birth and death. That is *the* cycle that creates all other cycles, and this turning creates all the circular and cyclical forces that govern existence within matter. The entire universe is called *Jagat Purusha* 'the material body of Paramatma'. Just as each human body is animated by an *atma* dwelling within, so each one of the countless *jagats* have a Paramatma dwelling within it. All of the *atmas* and Paramatmas are extensions of Bhagavan.

Jati: Part of the *varna* system of organizing the functions of society. At the beginning of their Vedic education, children are observed to identify their natural abilities and qualifications for certain occupations. Eventually they are divided into four *varnas* or groups for advanced training: *brahmin* 'professor', *kshatriya* 'protector', *vaishya* 'producer', and *shudra* 'provider'.

Within these four groups, there are many professional sub groups that are specialists in a particular skill or subject. These are the *jatis*. Each *jati* has a self-regulating hierarchy of skill and experience which is called the *shreni* 'career ladder'. This Vedic social system was not based on birth or influence; it was based on ability.

Jati is not to be confused with the word 'caste' which is the Portuguese word *casta*. The colonizers of India purposely used that word to discredit and disparage the Vedic social system. Caste or a caste system is not Vedic, but is globally present wherever property, wealth, or power is passed on to children just because they are family but with no regard for their qualification.

Jnana/ajnana: The cultivation of knowledge, culminating in the ability to distinguish between matter and the conscious self. The root of this word is *jna* 'to know'. The essence of *jnana* is to become a 'diagnostician', meaning to analyze every subject and object. Before European culture even existed, what to speak of modern science, the method of meticulously studying every detail of the realm of *prakriti* was called *sankhya* or *jnana yoga*, the analytical study of the categories of matter. The opposite is *ajnana* 'ignorance or lack of knowing'.

Kala: Modern scientists use the term 'space/time continuum' to discuss our world. That same paradox is explained in Chapter 11 of the Bhagavad Gita, where Arjuna asks Bhagavan to demonstrate how He pervades the universe. This, again, is the space/time question from another perspective. Krishna gives Arjuna special vision to see the entire universe. Terrified, Arjuna watches all beings rush into a massive mouth that is eating everyone. Trembling with fear, Arjuna asks, "Who are You and what is Your purpose?" To this, Krishna replies, "*Kalo asmi*...I am time, here to destroy everything; but you, Arjuna, will not be consumed."

Time, then, will consume anything made of parts, everything made of matter. The message of the Gita is that time cannot eat the *atma*, our immortal self, but will eat everything else. The space/time continuum will be eaten, but the *atma*, personified by Arjuna, is immortal and will return to the realm of Brahman, where time and space do not exist.

Kama: Often translated as desires for and pursuit of pleasure. It is one of the four *purusharthas* (*kama, artha, dharma, moksha*) or the four universal activities of human life. All four of these pursuits are conducted from a *guna*, either *sattvic*, *rajasic*, or *tamasic*. *Sattvic kama* would manifest as artistic, tasteful, and harmonious pleasures. *Rajasic kama* would be focused on selfish pleasures, sexually oriented, and more likely to be disruptive or cause harm. *Tamasic kama* would be dark, destructive, painful, dangerous, or degrading. All forms of *kama* are driven by pleasure-seeking activities, and it is fair to say that *rajasic* and *tamasic kama* are most common. Yogis restrict themselves to *sattvic kama* and avoid the rest.

Karma/akarma: Derived from *kri* 'to do'. *Karma* is actions of any kind and the reactions generated by the *atma's* use of free will. The consequence of action is residual cause and effect from life to life. Within matter, every action has an equal and opposite reaction. In the Vedic system of reincarnation, immortal *atmas* keep reincarnating on the wheel of *samsara* 'repeated birth and death' according to their actions in previous lives, until they cease to accrue *karma*. The Bhagavad Gita explains all the methods for doing this, and it is one of the main subjects of *sankhya yoga*. Both Ayurvedic medicine and Jyotish study *karma* intensively. *Karma* is summarized in Ch. 18 v. 61 #684. The opposite is *akarma* 'inaction'.

Krishna: Bhagavan Shri Krishna is known in the Vedic culture to have appeared on Earth a little over 7000 years ago as the ninth *avatur* of Shri Vishnu, the maintainers of all beings. Krishna's descent was the most personable and intimate of any of the divine manifestations who preceded him. Krishna means 'that being who attracts all beings by displaying the most irresistible qualities toward which all are helplessly drawn'. As Bhagavan Shri

Krishna, he performed a myriad of *lilas,* ways of loving, playful intimacy in order to draw all beings toward his realm within Brahman. Although the Supreme Being, He entered this world as an *avatar* of Vishnu. He acted for *dharma* in the dilemma of the Pandavas. With the *gopis* of Vrindavan and all his *lila* friends, He left behind the most delicious and beautiful theological legacy in history, and He left the Bhagavad Gita as the summary of all the wisdom we *jiva atmas* need to return to His immortal abode.

Kshatriya: 'To hurt and protect'; those who serve and protect with their strength, as well as those who lead and administer society. This is one of the groups in the four *varna* classification system. Some characteristics of a *kshatriya* are fearlessness in the face of confrontation, a sense of fair play, and an ability to withstand pain. This *kshatriya* temperament is visible in the more aggressive careers such as sports, police, military, fire, and ambulance. As with all the *varnas,* they are not occupations inherited by birth but are tendencies inherent to them that were trained and perfected. *Kshatriya* is a *svadharma.* There are benefits as well as constraints, and well-defined responsibilities that are expected of each *varna.* See *varna*

Kshetra: The field of activity within nature. Also used to refer to the material body as our 'field of activities' in which the seeds of *karma* 'cause and effect' are planted through our actions.

Kula: One's extended family group or a special interest group with which one has important principles in common. The Sanskrit *kula* became English 'clan', 'cult', and it is easy to hear the English word 'school' as a direct derivative. In agricultural communities, people often spend more time together and have a deeper sense of kinship. Krishna spent his childhood living in a cow-herding community called *go* (cow) *kula.* Finally, the English word 'cultivate' is from the same source.

Loka: English 'location' is from the Sanskrit *loka*. In Vedic cosmology, a *loka* is one of the 14 levels of existence or dimensions within a *jagat* 'material universe'. Humans live on level 8—Bhumi Loka; devas live on level 10—Svarga Loka; and the creators Brahma and Saraswati live on Satya Loka—level 14. Our *antakarana* 'dream body' can interact with the higher or lower *lokas*. The devas on the higher *lokas* can see us, but they are invisible to us. Some advanced yogis are able to visit the higher *lokas* in their subtle body and have conscious interactions with higher beings. Some artists and monastics experience this as a source of divine inspiration.

Maharaja: Great ruler or king. The female equivalent is *Maharani*. Since the *guna* of *rajas* is predominant in the *kshatriya varna*, such warriors would also be called *rajas*. If they were in the upper echelon of the warrior groups, they would be called *maharajas* or *maharanis*. These honourific terms are used for rulers, kings, and even high-ranking military officers.

Manas, manushya: *Manas* is often mistranslated as only 'mind'; however, it is much more. *Manas* is the uniquely human faculties of thinking, feeling, willing, and memory. Because of *manas*, we are called *manushya* or 'mind-kind'. In English, it has been incorrectly translated as mankind (meaning male). However, both human males and females are *manushya* 'mind-kind'. Wherever we focus our *manas* at the moment of the death of the body will take us either to Brahman or to our next birth. Thus, yogis say that *manas* is the best friend or the worst enemy.

Mantra: *Mantras* are like thunder. They are divine sound vibrations that attune us to the divine reality of greater beings, Brahman, and the Supreme Being. *Mantras* are a specific arrangement of Sanskrit letters and words which, when vibrated while holding the correct image and intention, form a link or connection with an invisible divine reality. When chanting a *mantra,* one attains specific states of direct perception and realization which impart knowledge and lead to the perfection of the self in predictable ways.

Maya: That which appears to be whole but is made of parts; appears permanent but is temporary. From the root *ma,* 'to create an appearance using separate parts' and *miti* 'to measure'. The root *ma* gives us the English words *mathematics, magic* 'the art of illusion', and *mage* 'one who sees beyond illusion'. Modern science is based upon the premise that the study of matter is the ultimate knowledge, whereas, in the Vedas, matter is studied because it is real, but it is also seen to be a temporary manifestation and a reflection of a higher transcendental reality. Like a mirage, an object is not what or where it appears to be. Because we are immortal beings, the temporary aspect of *maya* keeps us in bondage to matter.

Moksha, mukta, mukti: The Sanskrit word *moksha,* also called *mukti,* means liberation, ultimate freedom, release, going beyond all material limitations. The final goal of all yoga practice is the release of the *atma,* who is originally Brahman in nature, from the bondage of repeated birth and death, to return to Brahman and Bhagavan.

Mrityu/amrita: *Mrityu m*eans death and mortality; its opposite, *amrita,* means immortal and undying. *Amrita* 'the nectar of immortality' was fed to the *devas* so they could perform their various jobs of maintaining the universe. *Amrita* also refers to anything that counteracts the influence of death or disease due to violating the laws of material Nature. It is also used metaphorically to describe a teacher or speaker pouring the nectar of truth, *amrita,* into someone's ears. Because we are all immortal *atmas,* we need the nectar of immortality. It is also said to be the food of the *devas* as they protect and nourish the world.

Nirvana, Brahman nirvana: *Nir* 'without' and *van* 'ownership' simply means 'none of this matter is mine'. Defined differently by the Buddhists, they say it means *nir* 'not' *van* 'air' or 'to extinguish the self (*atma*) like blowing out a candle'. Since yoga does not wish to remove the *atma,* the Bhagavad Gita uses *Brahman nirvana* as a paired term meaning the positive assertion 'I am Brahman by nature, so none of this matter is mine'. Since this word has been used to represent the conclusion of Buddhist teaching as extinction of the self, its Sanskrit meaning has sometimes been overlooked.

Papa, punya: *Punya* creates future merit; *papa* creates future demerits. All *karmas* 'actions within matter' create a response that will at some future time return to the performer of the action. Actions aligned with the *ritam* 'laws of Nature' create *punya.* Actions opposed to the laws of Nature create *papa.* You could say that all humans are collecting green or red marbles, which at some future date will be redeemed as pleasure or pain. This is the result of human free will which inevitably creates a future of some kind or another. *Papa* and *punya* are merely the score card in the game of life within matter.

Prakriti: This important Sanskrit word has three roots: *pra*—to move forward or produce; *kri*—by applying cause and effect; and *iti*—to do the same thing over and over again. *Prakriti* is Mother Nature. It is the dark realm of unconscious matter. Its opposite is Brahman where everything is self luminous and immortal. All *atmas* are originally from Brahman and are only visiting *prakriti.* Once the *atma* is within *prakriti,* it is covered with earth, water, fire, air, and space and lives in a body subject to birth, death, old age, and disease. When a yogi leaves *prakriti* and returns to Brahman—that is called *moksha.*

Punya: See *papa*

Purusha: The word *purusha* has two roots—*pura* 'city' and *isha* 'ruler, leader, or controller'. The metaphor here is that our body is like a metropolis, and our immortal *atma* is the mayor, the ruler of the body. The Sanskrit *purusha* gave us the English word 'person'. We as the *atma* are the person in charge of our body. According to this view, our entire universe is also a *pura,* and Paramatma is the Supreme Person in charge of the universe. Our *atma* is a *purusha* and Paramatma is also a *purusha.* One is the person controlling the body, and the other is the person controlling the universe. Both, though, are *purushas,* divine persons. Yoga is reconnecting the *atma* with Paramatma in a loving relationship, living person-to-person with the Supreme Being.

Raja: See *Maharaja*

Raja guna: The creative *guna,* the active state of the material energy of *prakriti,* the symptom of which is intense desire or passion. Also *rajas, rajasic.* See *guna*

Rishi: A *rishi* is a perfected yogi who has developed or been granted the ability to see realities that are usually invisible. Throughout history, *rishis* have been the means by which divine wisdom is downloaded to the human plane of existence. A *rishi* has opened the third eye of seeing beyond matter. The Sanskrit language has made it possible for sacred *mantras* and knowledge to be clearly received and passed down over long periods of history. This special seeing is called *drishti* and it enables the *rishi* to be a seer of what is sacred and always true. *Rishi* also means 'they heard the mantras', referring to the ancient sages who revealed the divine Vedic wisdom, first by perceiving it in deep states of yogic meditation and then through passing it on as an oral tradition that was eventually written down.

Ritam: The underlying patterns or laws of Nature, the regulating structural and moral principles that underlie and sustain the universe. The words *rita, ritam, rishi,* and *drishti* all share the root *ri* 'to rise upward through correct action'. The *rita* is the foundational structural relationship and truth which acts as the substratum of reality. The *ritam* is all the laws of Nature that govern *prakriti.* A *rishi* is a human being who has evolved to the point that they have attained *drishti* 'direct sight' of all these principles of the *ritam* and are therefore known as seers. In its next stage of manifestation, the *rita* creates the *dhri,* the root of *dharma* 'the correct use of everything based upon its essential nature'. The *kri* then emerges into *karma* 'the strings of cause and effect that unite everything'. And finally, the *ritus* 'seasons', in which everything has an appropriate time, forms the basis for the rituals that create a sacred life.

Rupa/arupa: 'Form/formless'. These words are necessary vocabulary for describing two aspects of ultimate reality. Because we live within the temporarily manifest forms of matter, it is easy for us to conclude that all forms are material. It is equally the case that the Veda discusses many formless realities. Some Vedantic lineages promote an *arupa* 'formless' state as the final goal, while others use Vedic evidence to show that there are invisible and immortal forms that are not material and never decay. Some schools of thought reconcile both perspectives as mutually and inconceivably true. What is certain is that both views are true and Vedic. Formless Brahman is a fact, just as the form of Bhagavan is timeless and not made of matter. Try to understand both before jumping to a conclusion. Also *svarupa:* the original form of one's *atma* or true identity.

Samadhi: A state of complete absorption in the object of one's meditation, especially on the transcendental reality. The roots are *sam* 'together' and *dha* 'to focus or to hold'. *Samadhi* is the eighth step in the eight-limbed *ashtanga yoga* system of Patanjali. It is preceded by some kind of meditation on a specific *isha* 'divine being'. That focused meditation is called *dharana*. In any deep meditation, the goal is to connect so completely with the object of focus that one achieves *samadhi* and becomes 'the same as'. If we meditate upon an object, we grasp its essence. If we meditate upon Brahman, our original nature as Brahman is restored. If we meditate on Bhagavan, in the mood of *bhakti*, instead of just becoming the same as, we also develop a loving relationship with the Source of all—which is the ultimate stage of *samadhi*. All of these are forms of *samadhi*.

Sankhya: The yoga of discernment. *Sankhya* is an empirical and mathematically based tool for investigating matter, its use, and its functions. In the Vedic library of ultimate truths, there are six different schools or ways of looking at ultimate reality. They are called *shad darshan*, six ways of seeing. *Sankhya* is the origin of what we now call 'science'. Beyond its empirical basis, *sankhya* is a negative process of finding the *atma* by eliminating what we are not from the conversation of who we are. *Sankhya's* method is *neti neti*—I am not this, I am not that; because they are categories of matter. As a yoga practice, at the end of eliminating what we are not, we could realize *aham brahmasmi*—I am not matter or from matter. I am *Brahman* and I am from *Brahman*.

Sanatana: Always true and everlasting. See *dharma*

Sannyasa, sannyasi: The three roots of this word are *sam*—complete; *ni*—down; and *as*—to throw. The Vedic culture divides human life into four *ashrams* 'stages of involvement in life'. They are *brahmacharya*—celibate student; *grihastha*—married with family; *vanaprastha*—retired couple living in a country environment; and *sannyasa*—one who has thrown down all material actions and lives as a celibate monk in an ashram. Mostly popular with men, sannyasa was strictly monastic, living as a monk or *guru* with no material interests or activities. This *ashram* was usually entered from 75 years of age to end of life. Some persons become *sannyasa* at a young age, but it is the exception, not the rule.

Sat/asat: Eternal. One of the characteristics of the *atma*. The opposite is *asat* 'temporary'.

Sattva guna: The harmonizing and maintaining energetic state within the material nature. Also *sattva, sattvic.* See *guna*

Shastra: Knowledge originally revealed through the descent of sound vibration from the transcendental realm. The root of this word is *shas*—to teach, give rules, and to instruct by referring to a particular part of the Vedic library of knowledge, all of which is called *shastra.* Each branch of Vedic learning has a name and contains specific texts, all written primarily in Sanskrit. One branch of this curriculum is *shruti* 'that which was heard'. Another is called *smriti* 'that which was remembered'. There are two epics, the Ramayana and the Mahabharata, known as *itihasa* 'remembered history'. There are 18 Puranas 'old but always fresh in meaning'. There are 108 Upanishads, which are intensely philosophical in nature. There are many more departments of Veda, and a proper *guru* knows how, when, and to whom to teach each branch of *shastra.* See *veda*

Shraddha: The insight or degree of inner sight that is the result of previous lifetimes of experience. This creates a sense of certainty in our perception. Thus, *shraddha* is the trust, confidence, belief, or intention that a person invests or gives to a particular state of reality. *Shraddha* is trust in what one is seeing within.

The three *gunas* act as a filter, colouring *shraddha* and causing the person to see what is visible in their own heart according to their stage of awakening and evolution. The degree of enlightenment governing *shraddha* depends upon the *guna* of the perceiver and the extent of their listening to the Vedic *shastras*. In this way, the experience of *shraddha* creates a sense of certainty which is either blatantly wrong (*tamasic*), tinged with self-motivated desires (*rajasic*), or enlightened direct perception (*sattvic*). *Shraddha* is not 'faith', as that implies belief without reason or blind faith.

Shri and Vishnu: The source of radiance, grace, splendour, beauty, wealth, affluence, and prosperity—Shri Lakshmi. Vishnu and his exquisite and sublime female counterpart, Lakshmi Devi or Shri, are the resting place of all existence. They are health and well-being personified. They reveal in their natures profound patience and unlimited caring for every living being. Among the luminous *devas,* they are the ultimate regents, the mother and father of all. All races, species, and persuasions are loved by them and rescued, revived, and restored by their unlimited love and abundant grace. From them all the great *avatars* descend into *prakriti* to lead the lost and darkened *atmas* back to their joyful and loving original nature. *Jai Shri Vishnu.*

Shudra: *Shudras* are the most numerous workers in the Vedic *varna* system. Just as in any enterprise, there are a few thought leaders, a group of protectors, a team of business specialists, and a large group of skilled workers, the *shudras*. *Shudras* are the 'providers' of all the skills necessary to make any enterprise successful. They include the working and labouring class; those who serve and support others; artisans, musicians, and craftsmen. This *varna* system is based on the organization of workers by their ability and chosen profession. It is *not* a caste system. All these workers enjoy their jobs because they use the skills they have chosen to cultivate. See *varna*

Tama guna: The deconstructive stage of material matter where objects are destroyed or recycled. Also *tamas, tamasic*. See *guna*

Tapas, tapasya: In *ashtanga yoga*, *asanas*—postures; *pranayama*—control of the breath; *yama* and *niyama*—internal and external lifestyle; *dhyana*—meditation; and *mantra* practice are all *tapasyas* that eventually lead to self-perfection. Just as athletes say, 'practice makes perfect,' so in the science of reawakening our *atma*, we must consistently repeat *tapasyas* to burn off our material illusions.

Vaishya: The entrepreneurs of society. Imagine you own a large business providing healthy foods to the world. As the owner and director of your enterprise, you would need to know agriculture, money management, and all the rest of the skills that go with such a position. In the Vedic culture, your *varna* would be *vaishya* 'producer'. Your parents or birth would not matter at all, just your skills in business. See *varna*

Varna: The word *varna* means a cover or covering. The word varnish 'a covering on the outside' is from *varna*. Our *varna* is our covering and skill set, but an enlightened yogi sees all beings as the *atma* on the inside.

A person's *varna* is also called their *svabhava*—state of embodiment. The other term is *svadharma*—the function within society that a person is best suited to perform. The primary occupational categories are: *brahmin*—professor or scholar; *kshatriya*—protector or warrior; *vaishya*—producer or farmer/merchant; and *shudra*—provider or skilled worker. These are neither class nor caste; they are not from birth or by appointment. One has inherent ability in one of these *varnas*, then is trained, tested, and qualified. *Varna* means the role one plays in the social body. Scholars are the head, warriors the arms, producers the belly, and providers the legs. These are the real *brahmana, kshatriya, vaishya,* and *shudra*. See *brahmin, kshatriya, vaishya,* and *shudra*

Veda, vedic: The Vedas are an ancient library of knowledge which was transmitted orally in Sanskrit for thousands of years. During the time Shri Krishna was on the planet, the Vedas were written down to secure their future existence. Those many texts provide scientific knowledge for working with matter and a complete knowledge of our ultimate nature as *atmas,* our final destination in Brahman, and our personal relationship with the Source of all.

The primary Vedic texts include the Rig, Sama, Yajur, and Atharva Vedas; 108 Upanishads; 18 Puranas; and the two *itihasas*—the Ramayana and the Mahabharata which contains the Bhagavad Gita. The Vedic texts also include the Vedanta Sutras of Vyasadeva and hundreds of other texts on a wide variety of scientific subjects. See *shastra*

Vedanta, Vedanta Sutras: The word *sutra* means 'thread of meaning', and the text called the Vedanta Sutras or the Brahma Sutras literally stitches together the various strands of Vedic meaning into a single, logical, and self-consistent text. Those *sutras,* being very terse, are often interpreted with the aid of various commentaries written and handed down by the main schools of Vedantic thought. The author of the Bhagavad Gita was Vyasadeva, also known as Badarayana.

There are six *darshans* 'ways of seeing Vedic philosophy'; Vedanta is the sixth and is considered the most advanced. 'Vedanta' is a compound of *veda* 'the knowledge in the Vedic library' and *anta* 'the end or conclusion'. Thus, the Vedantic *darshan* is concerned with the ultimate conclusion and aim of the Vedas and discusses in detail the precise nature of the final transcendental goal.

Vidya: That which gives the recipient the ability to see what was otherwise obscure. Root vid—to reason upon, to know, to acquire understanding. The various forms of knowledge, practices, and the entire ancient legacy of wisdom in the Vedic library are all known as *vidya.* The word 'video', which allows one to see, is taken directly from the Sanskrit.

Ultimate and absolute truth does not lose value over time. *Vidya* is timeless truths that were divinely given or seen by great *rishi* seers over many thousands of years. The Vedic *vidya* is a legacy of immortal wisdom and enlightenment, carried forward by the perfected and unvarying Sanskrit language carried through time by ancient lineages of seers who held themselves accountable to preserve the Vedic *vidya* for the benefit of all beings. The human condition is blinded by the darkness of matter, and Vedic *vidya* is the carrier for the timeless light and truth of Brahman, Bhagavan, and all that is true.

Vritti: The twists in matter; specifically, the twisted and confusing results of *karmas.* Just as our double-helix DNA suggests, everything within matter is orbiting, cyclic, and twisted together. Our immortal *atma*, however, is from the realm of Brahman, where nothing is temporary, opposite, or twisted.

The second verse of Patanjali's Yoga Sutras tells us the purpose of yoga: *yogas chit vritti nirodha.* Yoga is removing the twisted *vrittis* from the consciousness of the *atma.* The Bhagavad Gita is also a yoga manual teaching us the methods of extracting our *atma* from matter and returning to Brahman and our relationship with Bhagavan.

Yajna: A process of reciprocation between humans with free will and *devas* who personify the laws of Nature. They provide the substances we need to live well, and *yajna* is a ceremony reminding us to show gratitude and to recycle. Metaphorically, the fire eats our offerings, carrying our appreciation to the divines as the smoke. After the *yajna,* the mineral rich ashes are mixed with the soil in the garden as fertilizer for the next planting cycle. Though it appears that the *yajna* is thanking only the *devas,* it is well known in Vedic culture that the *devas* work for the Supreme Being, Bhagavan.

Yoga, yogi, yogic: The root of yoga is *yuj* 'to connect, unite, join with', and yoga is all processes that facilitate forming a union between an *atma* and some form of the Supreme and Ultimate Being. The Yoga Sutras of Patanjali, pada II verse 1, says: the three activities of yoga are *tapasya*—correct practices; *svadhyaya*—self-examination and realization of our true nature as the *atma*; and *ishvara pranidhana*—meditation upon all *ishas* (divine beings) until the Supreme and Ultimate *Isha* is attained. These three principles of *ashtanga yoga* apply to all styles and methods of yoga. What they all have in common is that they are all methods of reconnecting lost and deluded humans with their own *atma,* with the *devas,* with Brahman, and with Bhagavan Shri Krishna, the Parameshvara (Parama Ishvara), the ultimate destination and source of all, and uniting in an ecstatic and devoted immortal relationship. Some methods of yoga are *ashtanga, bhakti, buddhi, jnana, karma* and *sankhya yoga.*

Yuga: Most cultures on Earth conceive of historical time in thousands of years, whereas ancient India is the home of a scientific theory called *yugas* that describes the age of our planet and solar system in billions of years, which now has the agreement of modern science.

Vedic culture says that like our annual seasons, planetary seasons are called *yugas,* in which a cosmic year is 4,320,000 Earth years. The four *yugas* are *Satya*—1,728,000 years; *Treta*—1,296,000 years; *Dvapara*—864,000 years; and *Kali*—432,000 years; just like spring, summer, fall, and winter for planetary systems. Shri Krishna's historical appearance just before the beginning of *Kali Yuga* and the speaking of the Bhagavad Gita are considered a divine tonic to keep us safe in the winter age of *Kali Yuga*.

If you have linguistic suggestions or insights for this glossary, we would love to hear them. We will be making ongoing updates at www.GitaComesAlive.com.

Appendix 1

Names of Shri Krishna

In the Bhagavad Gita, Arjuna addresses Shri Krishna by various descriptive names and titles in Sanskrit, which we have removed in the translation for ease of reading. Some of these names are:

- Achyuta—The unchanging one
- Anantarupa—The one having infinite forms
- Arisudana—Destroyer of the foe
- Bhagavan—The person who possesses the six bhagas unlimitedly
- Bhuta Bhavana—One who creates well-being for all
- Bhutesha—Ruler of all beings
- Devavarah—Greatest among the devas
- Devadeva—The deva who is beyond all the devas
- Govinda—Protector of the land, cows, and senses
- Hari—One who removes all inauspicious things
- Hrishikesha—Master of the senses of all beings
- Jagatpati—The master of the universe
- Jagannivasa—The residence of the whole world
- Janardana—Master of the arduous human journey of rebirth
- Kamalapatraksha—One whose eyes are like lotus blossoms
- Keshinisudana—The slayer of the asura named Keshi
- Keshava—The one with the most beautiful hair
- Krishna—That supreme being who is the attractor of all
- Purusha Uttama—The ultimate person

- Madhusudana—That being who is sweeter than anything else
- Mahabahu—Whose arms are stronger than any other being
- Madhava—The descendent of Madhu in the Yadava dynasty
- Yadava—Most illustrious descendent of the Yadhu dynasty
- Yogavittama—The yogi who is beyond tamas
- Vasudeva—That being who contains all other beings
- Varshneya—Illustrious descendent of the Vrishni dynasty
- Vishnu—The maintainer and support of all within matter

Appendix 2

Names of Arjuna

The word Arjuna means 'white, clear or silver'. Arjuna is called by many other names in the Bhagavad Gita. Again, we have removed these for ease of reading. Some of Arjuna's other names are:

- Vijaya—Always victorious, invincible, or undefeatable
- Dhananjaya—One who wins prosperity and wealth
- Savyasachin—Ambidextrous in archery
- Shvethavahana—One with milky white horses mounted to his pure white chariot
- Parantapa—One who chastises the enemy
- Gandivadhanvan—One who possessed the mighty bow named Gandiva which was created by the creator Brahma
- Gudakesa—One who has control over sleep; one with curly hair
- Bibhatsu—One who always fights fairly in battle
- Kapidhvajah—One who has the flag of Kapi (Hanuman) waving above his chariot
- Kiriti—One who wears the celestial diadem, Kirita, that was presented to him by the deva Indra
- Jishnu—One who is always triumphant
- Partha—Son of Pritha (Kunti)
- Phalguna—Born with the stars of Uttara Phalguni nakshatra rising in the East
- Madhya Pandava—The middle child of the Pandavas, younger than Yudhishthira and Bhima, older than Nakula and Sahadeva

Selected Bibliography

Adidevananda, Swami. *Sri Ramanuja Gita Bhasya.* Chennai: Sri Ramakrishna Math, n.d.

Arnold, Sir Edwin. *Bhagavad Gita: The Song Celestial.* New York: Heritage Press, 1965.

_____. *The Bhagavadgita: India's Great Epic*. Delhi: Vijay Goel, 2009.

Basu, Major B. D., ed. *The Sacred Books of the Hindus, Vol. 5: The Vedanta-Sutras of Badarayana with the Commentary of Baladeva.* New York: AMS Press, 1974.

Bon, Tridandi Swami B.H. *The Geeta: As A Chaitanyite Reads It.* Bombay: Popular Book Depot, 1938.

Chidbhavananda, Srimath Swami. *The Bhagavad Gita.* Tirupparaithurai: Sri Ramakrishna Tapovanam, 2005.

Desikachar, T. K. V. *The Heart of Yoga: Developing a Personal Practice.* Revised ed. Rochester, VT: Inner Traditions International, 1999

Duneja, Prabha. *The Legacy of Yoga in Bhagwad Geeta.* Delhi: Govindram Hasanand, 1998.

Eco, Umberto. *Mouse or Rat? Translation as Negotiation.* London: Phoenix, 2003.

Gambhirananda, Swami. *Madhusudana Sarasvati Bhagavad-Gita with the Annotation Gudhartha Dipika.* Calcutta: Advaita Ashrama, 1998.

Ganguli, Kisari Mohan. *The Mahabharata.* 12 vols. New Delhi: Munshiram Manoharlal Publishers, 2013.

Goswami, Srila Bhakti Raksaka Sridhara Deva. *Srimad Bhagavad-Gita: The Hidden Treasure of the Sweet Absolute.* Trans., Tridandi Bhiksu Sripad Aksayananda Swami Maharaja. Nabadwip Dham: Sri Chaitanya Saraswat Math, 1985.

Goyandaka, Jayadayal. *Srimad Bhagavad Gita: Tattva Vivecani (English*

Commentary). Gorakhpur: Gita Press, 1995 and 2003 eds.

Grimes, John. *A Concise Dictionary of Indian Philosophy: Sanskrit Terms Defined in English.* New & Revised ed. Varanasi: Indica Books, 2009.

Iyer, Raghavan. *The Bhagavad Gita with the Uttara Gita.* London: Concord Grove Press, 1987.

Jnanadeva, Sri. *Bhavartha-Dipika Jnaneshwari.* Pondicherry: Samata Books, 1989.

Kriyananda, Swami. *The Essence of the Bhagavad Gita, Explained by Paramhansa Yogananda.* Nevada City, CA: Crystal Clarity Publishers, 2007.

Macdonell, Arthur Anthony. *A Practical Sanskrit Dictionary.* Delhi: Motilal Banarsidass, 2007.

Maharaja, Sri Srimad Bhaktivedanta Narayana. *Sri Brahma-samhita, Fifth Chapter.* Vrndavana: Gaudiya Vedanta Publications, 2003.

Maharaja, Narayana. *Srimad Bhagavad-Gita.* Vrindavana: Gaudiya Vedanta Samiti, 1998.

Mani, Vettam. *Puranic Encyclopaedia.* Delhi: Motilal Banarsidass, 1998.

Monier-Williams, Sir Monier. *A Sanskrit-English Dictionary.* New ed. Delhi: Motilal Banarsidass, 2011.

Oak, Nilesh Nilkanth. *When Did the Mahabharata War Happen? The Mystery of Arundhati.* Vishweshwar Nagar: Subbu Books, 2011.

Oak, P. N. *World Vedic Heritage: A History of Histories.* 2 vols. 3rd ed. New Delhi: Hindi Sahitya Sadan, 2003.

Onions, C. T., ed. *The Oxford Dictionary of English Etymology.* Oxford: Clarendon Press, 1983.

Partridge, Eric. *Origins: A Short Etymological Dictionary of Modern English.* New York: Macmillan, 1958.

Prabhupada, A.C. Bhaktivedanta Swami. *Bhagavad Gita As It Is.* Los Angeles: Bhaktivedanta Book Trust, 1972 and 1983 editions.

_____. *Krsna, The Supreme Personality of Godhead: A Summary Study of Srila Vyasadeva's Srimad-Bhagavatam, Tenth Canto.* Los Angeles: Bhaktivedanta Book Trust, 2003.

_____. *Srimad Bhagavatam.* 30 vols. Los Angeles: Bhaktivedanta Book Trust, 1981.

Ramsukhdas, Swami. *Srimad Bhagavadgita: Sadhaka-Sanjivani.* 2 vols. Trans., S. C. Vaishya. Gorakhpur: Gita Press, 2009.

Rendich, Franco. *The Origin of Indo-European Languages: Structure and Genesis of the Mother Tongue of Sanskrit, Greek and Latin.* 3rd ed. Translated by Gordon Davis. Charleston, SC: CreateSpace Independent Publishing, n.d.

_____. *Comparative Etymological Dictionary of Classical Indo-European Languages: Sanskrit, Greek, Latin.* 3rd ed. Translated by Gordon Davis. Charleston, SC: CreateSpace Independent Publishing, 2016.

Sadhus of BAPS Swaminarayan Sanstha. *The Vachanamrut: Spiritual Discourses of Bhagwan Swaminarayan (An English Translation).* Amdavad: Swaminarayan Aksharpith, 2006.

Sanyal, Nisikanta. *Sree Krishna Chaitanya.* Vol 1. Madras: Tridandi Swami Bhakti Hridaya Bon, 1933.

Saraswati, Pujyasri Chandrasekharendra. *The Guru Tradition.* Bombay: Bharatiya Vidya Bhavan, 1991.

_____. *The Vedas.* 6th ed. Mumbai: Bharatiya Vidya Bhavan, 2005.

_____. *Hindu Dharma: The Universal Way of Life.* Mumbai: Bharatiya Vidya Bhavan, 2008.

Saraswati, Siddhanta. *Shri Chaitanya's Teachings.* Madras: Shri Nandadulal Brahmachari Bhaktivaibhava, 1967.

Sargeant, Winthrop. *The Bhagavad Gita.* Albany: State University of New York Press, 1994.

Sarup, Lakshman, *The Nighantu and the Nirukta of Sri Yaskacarya: The Oldest Indian Treatise on Etymology, Philology and Semantics.* Delhi: Motilal Banarsidass, 2015. (First Edition, 1920)

Sharma, Rama Nath. *The Astadhyayi of Panini.* 6 vols. New Delhi: Munshiram Manoharlal Publishers, 2002.

Shipley, Joseph T. Dictionary of Word Origins. New York: Philosophical Library, 1945.

Shorter Oxford English Dictionary. 6th ed. 2 vols. Oxford: Oxford University Press, 2007.

Sivananda, Sri Swami. *The Bhagavad Gita*. Tehri-Garhwal: The Divine Life Society, 2003 and 2010 eds.

Swami, Devamrita. *Searching for Vedic India*. Los Angeles: Bhaktivedanta Book Trust, 2002.

Tripurari, Swami. *The Bhagavad Gita: Its Feeling and Philosophy*. San Rafael, CA: Mandala Publishers, 2002.

Tyberg, Judith M. *The Language of the Gods: Sanskrit Keys to India's Wisdom*. 2nd ed. Los Angeles: East-West Cultural Centre, 1976.

Venkatesananda, Swami. *The Song of God*. Elgin, South Africa: The Chiltern Yoga Trust, 1972.

Woodham, Carl. *Bhagavad Gita: The Song Divine*. Badger, CA: Torchlight Publishing, 2004.

Yogananda, Paramahansa. *The Bhagavad Gita: God Talks with Arjuna. Royal Science of God-Realization*. 2 vols. 2nd ed. Los Angeles: Self-Realization Fellowship, 2005.

Gratitude

In the early years of this translation, we received help with typing and proofreading from Richelle Jarrell, Larry Ogrodnick, Paul Tootalian, Beryle Chambers, and Sue Chambers—thank you for doing the initial and tedious typing. While most of this preliminary work did not end up in the final edition, it did alert the author and lead him to solve the two translation issues. It definitely laid the groundwork for this version.

At about year three, when we realized the scope of the English colonization of the Sanskrit and the mischief it played with the text, we pretty much had to start the project over. For zny years, it was mainly Jeffrey who did the tedious etymological study. It was not until the last three years of the project that he was ready to bring in the next round of typists, editors, and assistants.

During the last five years, there were many VASA financial supporters and students who contributed according to their means. We are very grateful for everyone's timely contribution—it all added up to the completion of this dharmic project. Thank you to Alice Zhou, Antonina Ananda, Anthony Kuschak, Arjenn Penndari, Siddharthas Choudhary, Adrian Armstrong, Amy Armstrong, Chuck Hunner, Dave Fogarty, Robin and Paul Noll, Sarala Thompson, Umanji, VASA students, as well as the 'anonymous' and the 'mysterious' donors—thank you!

We are especially grateful to Andrea Goldsmith, Paul Hansen, and Pete McCormack, without whose help it may have taken us another ten years!

May this Vedic vidya bless you always,

Jeffrey Armstrong | Kavindra Rishi
Sandi Graham | Shyamasundari
VASA Vedic Academy of Sciences and Arts

Other Books By

Jeffrey Armstrong | Kavindra Rishi

The Spiritual Teachings of the Avatar
Karma: The Ancient Science of Cause and Effect
The Vedic Astrology Learning Deck
God/Goddess the Astrologer: Soul, Karma & Reincarnation
The Night We First Met
The Binary Bible of St. Silicon
Dreaming the Countless Worlds
Swept Away – Volume 1
The Secret of Delight – Volume 2
Sandhya the Twilight of Love – Volume 3
Swan of Endless Love
Lotus Eyes Lotus Feet
This Way Never Lies
Smile When You've Had Enough
The Mountain Climbed Me Up
Black Light of the Goddess
Visions from the Fire
Heart of the Night
75 Light Bulb Jokes

Musical Collaborations

Change of Heart, with Michael Cassidy
Trust, with Thomas Barquee
There Is Only One Love, with Patrick Bernard

Upcoming Books

The UltiMate™ Relationship
Love Letters from a Yogi Series (6)

We Are Especially Grateful to Our Sponsors

Sewa International
The Palan Foundation
Nitin and Kamu Palan
Shrinarayan and Asha Chandak
Maryada Foundation
Vijay Pallod
Ramesh Bhutada

With special thanks to
Dr. Vimal and Kusum Patel, Indianapolis
Dr. Dwarka and Seema Rathi, New York
Mr. Vasant and Prabha Rathi, California
Mr. Hemant and Sakshi Kale, Texas